Stumbling THROUGH THE Tulips

....

AN AMERICAN FAMILY IN HOLLAND

DANIEL PAUL MARTIN

Copyright © 2011 Daniel Paul Martin
All Rights Reserved.

ISBN-10: 146113174X
ISBN-13: 9781461131748

Library of Congress Control Number: 2011906692
CreateSpace, North Charleston, SC

*For The Martin Family
Mitra, Darius, Melika*

*And, of course,
Nazy*

ABOUT THE AUTHOR

Born in Massachusetts, Dan Martin grew up in Georgia and New Jersey before entering Georgia Tech. Unaware that his job would activate adventure genes in his offspring and wife, Dan spent a large portion of his professional life commuting—not between the suburbs and the city, but between one country and another. For three years he flew between Zürich and Amsterdam every single week. He became so well-known that on one flight the cabin crew, afraid that he might have forgotten his wedding anniversary, gave him a bottle of champagne "Just in case, Dan." (For the record, he did not, had not, and would not forget his anniversary.)

Dan was also (somewhat) popular with KLM corporate management: they appreciated his regular flights, but were not impressed by the parsimoniousness of his employer's corporate travel division. To express appreciation for the number of flights, they named a seat in his honor. However, disappointed by the skillfully negotiated (low) fare, they chose Seat 26B: a middle seat in the last row next to the lavatory.

Dan's wandering lifestyle began shortly after being awarded a Ph.D. by Georgia Tech where he met his wife Nazy. Following graduation, Dan and Nazy visited her impressive family in their native country of Iran. Nazy's Mother founded and ran her own school for girls and was one of the first 12 women to graduate from Teheran University. Her dad, retired, had been a full admiral. (Correction: 'Had been' is a misnomer: once you're an admiral, you're *always* an "Admiral". Dan called him "The Admiral.") Dan and Nazy subsequently moved to Memphis so he could take up his calling and become a university professor. The arrival of a baby girl (Mitra) accelerated acceptance of financial reality and Dan made a transition into the business world. Believing he was on a smooth road to prominence as a corporate executive, Dan and Nazy had two additional children, Darius and Melika.

Dan discovered the dangers of business when "his" department was sold to a Vancouver start-up that collapsed as soon as the family relocated. Because Immigration Canada wasn't amused, the family had to move again. Relocation to Houston and the solid, stable and secure oil business, followed shortly thereafter. In less than a year, oil prices crashed and another move—this time to idyllic Hanover, New Hampshire— followed. By now, The Martin Family had spent four consecutive Christmas seasons in four different cities, they settled. (For a while.) Hanover was beautiful, but the international gene mandated a change. Somehow Dan was able to convince the family to accept a transfer to The Netherlands. (The Berlin Wall fell a few weeks after The Martin Family arrived in The Netherlands. Coincidence? Unlikely!) This book chronicles their adventures there.

Working in The Netherlands was unique (for Dan) because he lived there too. The Martin Family used the opportunity to see Europe while Dan polished his corporate negotiation skills in Lagos, Kuala Lumpur, Melbourne, Hong Kong, Tokyo, Seoul, Manila, San Juan, Singapore, Bangkok, and Houston. As he completed his project, Dutch taxation authorities that had been warbling in the background began an assault on the family pocketbook; repatriation quickly followed.

When the kids entered college, it became clear that a cosmic-sized family planning error had occurred. Darius and Melika would be at university simultaneously. Family solvency mandated a return to Europe. The kids were now in college, so Dan and Nazy moved to Zürich by themselves. Now experienced in the ways of business, Dan also moved from a corporate overhead job into a revenue-generating position.

In spite of their frequent moves, Nazy and Dan built a supportive, creative, and fun existence for their children, nurturing family spirit no matter where they lived. As a result, Mitra, Darius and Melika developed principles of independence and tolerance. Although they now live in different parts of the world (in fact, the sun never sets on The Martin Family), they get together at least once a year.

After hobbing and nobbing at high corporate levels and buckling his swash all over the globe, Dan left the corporate world to work with international organizations and write about his travels and his family. Visit his website at www.seat26b.com. He lives with Nazy in Zurich, Switzerland.

WHO IS THE MARTIN FAMILY?

This story chronicles our family coping with the challenge, thrill, excitement, and frustration of setting up a home in The Hague (*Den Haag*). It follows the Martins through the joys and pitfalls of relocation to a foreign country. We were ready for the new assignment. It turned out that Europe was ready for us.

We discovered different approaches to everyday tasks, such as calendars that depict the weeks vertically. We learned a new language and were bewildered by a government that uses forms and created in the Middle Ages. (We suspect that procedures that the buearcracy uses to process the forms were created in the Jurassic *Age*. We came to that conclusion after spotting fossilization in several ministries.) We observed European queue courtesy and Dutch swimming attire. We mastered the trains, trams, buses, and taxies.

Mostly, however, we learned about ourselves—and how we cope with transition. Since this is the family story, you should know about The Martin Family members. Before the move, I asked each of my children for three self-descriptive adjectives. They all came up with essentially the same words: brilliant, pretty, and capable. (My son substituted "handsome" for "pretty.") I shouldn't make light of the result; I filled out the same form myself. I cheated and used their words, but added "modest."

Melika: Our youngest daughter. Smart, pretty, and capable. Also feisty, dependable, meticulous, and ingenious. She feels responsible for her older brother; he complains that "Melika acts like she's older than me." Melika was the champion letter writer while I was in Holland and the rest of the family was in New England. (And, Melika? I love you soooo much, too.)

Darius: The middle child and our only son. Smart, handsome, and clever. An expert in anything complex. (Want to know the capitol of Morocco in the tenth century? How about how to use fat laser bits on the Macintosh computer? Or the family tree of all 5,230,123 Greek gods? Darius knows.) Simple things are more of a problem (Are both socks the same color?). He's adept at making friends—*everybody* knows Darius.

Mitra: Our first child and the big sister. Brilliant, pretty, and capable. Mitra is always happy—living in Europe is *so* exciting. Sailing on a canal is *so* wonderful. Seeing Dutch windmills is such a thrill. Taking out the garbage—well, there are limits to her joy. Mitra delights in outrageously dazzling colors. She can do anything, with the possible exception of long-distance running and edible cooking. She's a great student, a helpful sibling, and exceptionally skilled at housework avoidance.

Nazy: My wife and the mother of our kids. Smart, pretty, capable, friendly, and compassionate. We moved many times, and each time Nazy coordinated the relocation and kept family spirits high. She instantly makes friends, which quickly converts a new house into a home. She's health conscious (other children may get peanut butter and Coca-Cola for lunch—ours get yogurt, fruit, carrots, nuts, and an "I love you" note). The consummate shopper, Nazy knows where to get anything.

Dan: That's me. Smart, handsome, capable (and modest). Why argue with the collective family wisdom?

The Martin Family in The Hague, The Netherlands

STUMBLING THROUGH THE TULIPS

CHAPTER 1
GETTING READY

We are a normal American family. Well, we are a wandering American family. After completing graduate school at Georgia Tech, Nazy and I moved to Memphis, where I fulfilled a lifelong ambition by becoming a college professor. Soon, however, economic reality, in the form of baby Mitra, mandated entry into the "real world." Turning down a job offer at FedEx (overnight package delivery didn't seem viable to me), I joined the "more stable" commodity brokerage business. Two children (Darius and Melika) later, a corporate sale dictated a move to Vancouver. We missed the Memphis barbecue, but we loved the great Northwest. Events beyond our control (company bankruptcy and Immigration Canada) forced yet another relocation. Shunning nearby Microsoft (I thought Bill Gates was a nerd), we chose the stability of the oil industry in Texas. My mother, aware of my track record, immediately sold all oil shares just before the market crashed. The children had accepted the move to Vancouver with excitement. The move to Houston was somewhat more problematic. Melika, four years old at the time, summed up the situation on Christmas Eve. It was about eighty degrees and I was outside raking leaves.

"*Daddy?*"

"*Yes, Melika.*"

"*It's Christmas Eve.*"

"*I know.*"

"When's it going to snow?"
"It's never going to snow in Houston, Melika."
"Well…who decided to move here?"
"I'm working on it, Melika."

So, after a short stay in Houston, I found a job at a small software development firm in Hanover, New Hampshire. We were enamored with the beauty of New England. We learned to ski, we visited Montreal, and we made friends. After spending four successive Christmases in four different cities, we finally put down roots. To settle the matter, we even embarked on a major kitchen renovation project.

For the traditional American family, it was the traditional harbinger of doom. It tested the bonds of matrimony and the ability to live in harmony while surrounded by rubble. At the same time, it stretched our budget and shortened our tempers. (But we got granite countertops!) It is through events like this that the indomitable American spirit is borne. The calm, confidence, and unflappability exhibited by the astronauts is forged in the chaotic caldron of home renovation.

The project was over budget and late. It also activated my world adventure gene. It was time for a family meeting.

BUT I LIKE IT HERE!

We had been living in Hanover, New Hampshire, home of Dartmouth College, for three years. I was working at DTSS, a small software development company that was a Dartmouth spinoff. I didn't miss international corporate life; I liked working where I could really make a difference. I would have liked it a lot more if the company was making money. Aware of the (lack) of cash flow, I secured a job offer from Shell International Petroleum in The Hague. It was the end of summer, 1989, and it seemed like a good time to break the news to the family.

We were in the midst of a major home renovation. The kitchen was in a shambles, with a twelve-foot hole exposed to the elements and a layer of dust growing by the day. We couldn't find the refrigerator, but carpenter ants, unearthed in the demolition phase, had found us. To top it all off, it had been the hottest and most humid summer on record in northern New England. The builder told us it would be done in "two weeks." He had been saying "two weeks" since the project began in April. Tempers were short and everyone was frustrated. I seized my chance and called a family meeting.

The first item on the agenda was the renovation. We wondered whether it would ever be finished. Nazy and I were stunned at the children's cheerful attitude, which didn't make the next agenda point—relocation—easier. Melika made things even more complicated.

"You know, Daddy," she said, "I'm sooo glad we're fixing up the house."

"Why is that, Melika?"

"Because we've finally found a place to stay and live. Nobody would do all this work and then move. That would be really stupid, wouldn't it?"

"Why do you want to stay in Hanover?"

"I like Hanover. I have friends in Hanover. And I'm tired of moving."

"What about living in an exciting new place? Would you like that?"

"Exciting? You're the one who said Houston would be exciting."

"Anyone can make a mistake, dear. What would you think of Holland?"

"Holland? Wooden shoes? Yuck!"

And so the idea was introduced. The family didn't know much about Holland, but Darius knew it was in Europe. Darius knew that Amsterdam was 3,542 miles away. He knew about the Dutch capitol confusion between Amsterdam and The Hague. He could provide its latitude and longitude. He knew it used to have windmills. He also knew it didn't have ski slopes—and that was his way to quash the idea.

"We can't move there, Dad. No hills. We'd have to do cross-country skiing. It's out of the question."

"I think they have a few mountains in Europe, Darius."

"That's right, but they're all in other countries. Holland is unthinkable. They even speak Dutch."

"Dutch?"

"Yes, Dutch. We'd have to learn Dutch. Nobody speaks Dutch."

"They speak Dutch in the Netherlands."

"They also speak it in Suriname, but who cares? Pick someplace like France or Switzerland. Holland? Impossible."

"Unfortunately, the job offer is in Holland."

"Job offer?"

"Precisely. Job offer!"

Mitra, who had been quietly gluing glitter to her sneakers, looked up. "We're moving to Europe? Wow! What a neat idea. That's great. When do we go?"

"Thank you, Mitra," I thought silently as I looked to Nazy for help.

"Your Dad and I think living in Europe would be exciting for the whole family. Besides, it's a really good job opportunity for Daddy. It will be exciting."

Melika was unimpressed. "Exciting? Huh? It's exciting living here. It's exciting looking for the refrigerator. The kitchen isn't even finished. What are we going to do? Stay here until everything is finished and *then* move? Boy, is that dumb!"

Unfortunately, Melika had a point. If we'd known we were going to move, we wouldn't have started the renovation. On the other hand, the renovation was over budget and behind schedule. If it had been on schedule, it would have already been completed, and if it was within budget, the financial glories of the job with Shell wouldn't have seemed so important.

"We're not going to sell the house," I told the children. "We'll rent it. We plan to come back to Hanover in two or three years."

Melika was disgusted and silent.

Darius dashed off to the computer to compose a contract under which his parents would pledge, promise, commit, vow, guarantee, agree, attest, affirm, vouch, and warrant that the family would return in two years. (I am convinced that he used the built-in thesaurus.)

Mitra, the only family member with European experience—she had spent three weeks in Geneva—was ecstatic. (Although she hadn't listened to Darius's geography proclamation and thought Holland's topography was just like the Swiss Alps.)

The preparatory weeks passed quickly. Melika and Darius continued a rear-guard action. They liked Hanover. Perhaps we could just visit Europe. Did we really want to go?

Meanwhile, Nazy and I equitably divided the moving tasks. I agreed to forward the mail. Nazy negotiated with the movers and potential tenants. We all struggled through the sophisticated, comprehensive medical examinations required by Shell International Petroleum Maatschappij, BV, my new employer. (Melika's hope that the medical exam would detect rocks in my head was dashed.)

Our feelings were decidedly mixed as moving day approached. Typically, I had to leave before anyone else. I *had* to establish a beachhead in The Hague. I was supposed to find a place to live, locate adequate schools, open a bank account, and make a good impression at work.

Nazy, ever cheerful, stayed to push the contractors to completion and deal with the international movers. The children, somewhat less cheerful but by now resigned, stayed with her.

"When will we come to Holland, Daddy?" Melika asked as I was leaving.

"About two weeks."

"Yeah, right."

The adventure was about to begin.

Looking back, Melika's logic had been spot on. Our "lifelong" commitment to Hanover had ended after only three years. We were moving. Again! We left friends and family in America and a house with a renter who'd had to sign (in blood) a pledge to "enjoy the kitchen." The move itself took place over a few months. We had dawdled so long with the offer that school had started before we left.

My final days in Hanover were marked by a series of parties and farewell visits with friends. My sisters drove up from Boston and took me to Logan Airport. Except for the job situation, Hanover had really been wonderful. Now, however, I was off to fend for myself in Europe. Shell had arranged temporary quarters at the Pullman Centraal Hotel in The Hague.

"This can't be too difficult," I thought as I climbed aboard Northwest Flight 42. I knew some adjustment would be required when I discovered that my seat—2D—was in the first row.

CHAPTER 2
AND HE'S OFF

It was raining when I arrived in Holland after a typical overnight flight to Europe. I quickly discovered that it always rains in Holland in October (and November, and December, and...) I was impressed by the Shell standard of business class, but I was concerned about being in the midst of another move. I already missed the family, and I had to get settled. I checked into the Pullman Centraal on Spui Street in the centrum (center) of The Hague. My clever plan to avoid jet lag—taking a few days to settle in before going to work—was in a shambles because I had fallen asleep at noon on the first day. I spent the next two weeks trying to sleep at night and stay awake during the day. I wondered what kind of impression I was making at the office.

I tried to make myself at home. The family was still in Hanover, but at least I had a computer. It wouldn't work without power, though, so I made my first foray into the Dutch shopping scene.

IT'S AN EXTENSION CORD

The walls of the hotel room at the Pullman Centraal in The Hague were crushing my spirit. I was alone and bored. I checked the television. BBC1 was showing a special on fern cultivation in the Scottish highlands. BBC2 had the international snooker championships. The Dutch, German, and French stations were broadcasting in Dutch,

German, and French. I had read the books that I brought with me. I needed new reading material.

Unfortunately, it was Sunday. In Holland, stores aren't open on Sundays. In fact, it's a point of pride that stores are only open fifty-two hours a week. Fifty-two hours isn't much, especially when forty of them span normal working hours. (Another five cover the average commute time.) I had blown Saturday by going to Amsterdam. I would have to pay.

It was cold, gray, and rainy, but I decided to go to the beach. I stepped out onto Spui Street, which was strangely devoid of people. I crossed to the tram *halte* and huddled under the flimsy roof. Tram nine arrived promptly.

"It seems I'm not the only one going to the beach," I thought as I jammed myself onto the tram. Squashed, I endured the trip to Scheveningen in silence. I had been wondering if I'd recognize the stop, but I needn't have worried. When we arrived, I was popped out of the tram like a cork from a well-agitated bottle of champagne. I was pushed, against the wind, into the Palace Promenade, a shopping mall that fronts the North Sea.

Imagine my thrill when I found an open bookstore. Imagine my dismay when I discovered that the English newspapers and magazines were sold out. I plunged through the crowd and made my way to the sea. Heavy winds and rain drove me back inside. I dashed back toward the tram, Spui Street, the Pullman Centraal, and my room.

The snooker championship was still in progress on BBC2. BBC1 was showing a documentary on the cane toad: "The cane toad, imported into Australia in the '30s to control the sugar cane beetle, met a sad fate. The cane beetle can fly. The toad can't." I napped and resolved to take Monday morning off. Eventually, I realized I had a major opportunity. I had the computer and Darius was stuck in the States. It was an unprecedented chance to beat his high scores in *all* of the games on the computer. I only needed to pick up a European power cable. Shopping on a Monday morning wasn't a grand idea. Like weekday nights and Sundays, most shops in Holland aren't open Monday mornings. I passed the time by mumbling to myself. After work, I secreted the office computer's power cord into my briefcase and happily headed to the Pullman.

After a futile search for a power receptacle, I decided to check the TV offerings. BBC2 was showing a retrospective on the snooker championship, and BBC1 had part one of a three-part documentary called *Fungi—from Champignon to Athlete's Foot*. I decided to initiate a more thorough search for power.

I found an outlet—in the bathroom. The one-meter power cable was just able to reach to the floor. It wasn't too bad. The mouse rolled smoothly over the tiled floor in the bathroom. "It wouldn't have worked on the carpet anyway," I told myself. "And when I beat Darius's records, I can claim that my victory was accomplished under extremely adverse conditions."

After a few hours on the floor, the verdict was in: The conditions were too adverse. Darius's Crystal Quest score was still two million points higher than mine. My legs were asleep and I banged my head on the vanity every time I tried to stand. "I've got to get an extension cord," I said to myself. (There was no one else to talk to.)

I waited anxiously for Thursday—shopping night! Flushed with anticipation, I planned my approach, but knew that I was unprepared. I was a knight entering battle without armor. Shopping wasn't my forte— but "shopping night" demanded professional prowess. I needed Nazy.

I had to reconcile myself to the fact that I was alone. While I had mastered the trams, begun to establish myself at the office, and mapped out the city, I didn't feel at home. I took advantage of the subsidized canteen at work and the free Pullman Centraal breakfast. I had located a pizza place, several McDonald's hamburger emporiums, and a Chinese restaurant. But I wanted to have a few snacks in the hotel room, I needed more books, and I had to have an extension cord—I was still more than two million points behind Darius.

Thursday evening eventually arrived, and I mentally mounted my steed and prepared my cash. (They don't "do" personal checks or credit cards in Holland.) I left work early, dropped my briefcase at the hotel, and strolled toward the Passage, a nearby shopping district. Everyone who lived within forty kilometers of The Hague joined me. Describing it as crowded is like saying that the Indians outnumbered Custer.

Surely finding an extension cord wouldn't be a problem. "Besides," I reminded myself, "everyone in Holland speaks English."

Well, sort of. Everyone speaks conversational English. "Extension cord" isn't a conversational term. Nevertheless, I was certain that Vroom & Dreesman, a large department store called *V en D* in Dutch, must have them. I was determined to succeed as I marched toward the clerk.

"It's a power cable thing," I explained to her. "You know, you want to plug in the microwave here, but the receptacle is way over there."

"What's a microwave?"

"You know, microwave. It's used to cook things fast. It's small, goes in the kitchen."

The clerk's face brightened. "You mean a magnetron. Those are on the fourth floor."

"No, I don't want a magnetron. Forget about magnetrons. Say you want to plug a lamp into the wall. But the receptacle is far away. You need to get something that goes from the lamp to the wall."

She was confused. "But the magnetrons have lights inside them. You don't need a light."

"But I do need something that carries the electricity from the wall into the light."

"That comes with the magnetron."

"Forget the magnetron! The problem is a lamp. Now, suppose…"

"The lamps are on the third floor."

"I don't want a lamp. My computer is sitting on the floor in the bathroom. The power cord…"

DANIEL PAUL MARTIN

"Bathroom items are on the fifth floor. We don't sell computers."

"Let's just start all over again. I'm new here. I just arrived from America. Now, the hole in the wall where you get electricity is in the bathroom."

"Home repairs—second floor."

"Electric receptacles! Wires! Where?"

"They're right over there. Are you feeling all right?"

I eventually found one. They're called *verlengsnoeren*. I bought two (three-meter) *verlengsnoeren* and decided to look for magazines, then took several escalators and wound up in the grocery section. "Well," I thought, "I do need some snacks. Besides, I can't see any way to get out of here without passing through the checkout line." I grabbed several cans of Coke, a box of cookies, a few bags of potato chips, a couple of apples, and some plums.

Standing in the lengthy line watching the checkout process, I noticed that everyone else had brought their own bags. I dropped out of line and selected what I hoped was a container of garbage bags. I reentered the line, paid, and opened my purchase—sandwich bags. I ripped open the plastic bag that contained the *verlengsnoeren*, draped the extension cords around my neck, pushed the Coke cans into the vacant bags, stuffed the fruit into my pockets, and wrapped my jacket around the chips and cookies. I trundled off toward the hotel.

Dropping everything off in the room, I dashed back into the fray. I couldn't think of anything to buy, but I certainly wasn't going to waste a shopping evening. I walked to Centraal Station and the Babylon shopping mall. I browsed through the stores and bought a couple of books and a box of garbage bags. I stopped at the flower store, amazed by the variety of cut and potted flowers. I was even more amazed by the reasonable prices. I bought four African violets (five guilders), stuffed them into the hotel laundry bag, and headed back to my room.

STUMBLING THROUGH THE TULIPS

There, I popped open a can of Coke and a box of cookies. I checked the TV. BBC2 was showing a special called *Ten Years of Snooker*. BBC1? *Rock Gardens in Yorkshire*. I plugged in the extension cord and began a serious attack on Darius's Crystal Quest score.

And so passed the first few weeks. I always remembered to bring a garbage bag when shopping, which could, in an emergency, serve as a raincoat. I acquired a huge variety of African violets. My culinary pursuits branched out as I discovered Dutch appelflappen and a Mexican restaurant. My Crystal Quest score climbed higher and higher, but never exceeded Darius'.

My problems with conversational English were relatively minor. A friend tried to purchase a nightstand. The clerk, he discovered, didn't know what a night stand was, but she had heard of a "one-night stand" and wasn't amused.

Having taken care of the emergency needs—a computer power cable and junk food—I was ready to attack one of the more routine needs. I required money. Not greenbacks (the green ones were only worth five guilders here), but blue, yellow, red, and purple banknotes. Banking in Europe? Not a problem for Mr. International.

DON'T BANK ON IT

Moving is my least favorite thing—with the exception of home renovation projects. In spite of unanimous family agreement on the subject of moving, we continued to inflict the pain of it on ourselves. We're not proud of our sordid record of relocation. We have, however, transformed moving into a conditioned reflex, allocate tasks with finely honed skills. I end up with a lengthy list of arduous tasks—renting a post office box, changing the insurance policies, canceling the book clubs, and paying the final bills. Nazy has a short and easy list. She deals with the movers and sells (or rents) the house.

True to form, while Nazy was in Hanover, I was about to begin an almost impossible quest in The Hague. I wanted to open a bank account. This meant that I would be introduced to the Dutch banking system.

I should have been aware of potential problems. Money is always a Martin problem—not one of our moves has gone through without some banking foible. When we moved to Canada, for example, it took ten weeks to get a card for the ATM. (We had to file a comprehensive application, which included copies of my income tax forms from the previous five years.)

The situation in Houston was even worse. I strolled into the local Texas Commerce Bank with my first paycheck. I was working for Schlumberger, a huge multinational oil field services company, but the bank wanted to wait ten days for the check—drawn on their bank—to clear before opening the account.

In Hanover, it appeared that things would go more smoothly. The bank knew my new company and instantly set up accounts and cleared checks on the very day they were presented. Everyone knew everyone else. It seemed to be an ideal arrangement—until I tried to switch a car loan from the credit union in Houston to the bank in Hanover. The loan was turned down.

The bank officer frowned. "I'm sorry, Dr. Martin, but there is something questionable in the report from the credit bureau."

"Well, what is it?"

"I'm afraid I can't tell you." She was obviously distraught. This kind of thing simply did not happen in Hanover. I could tell that she thought we were bogus "flatlanders."

"Why can't you tell me? It is *my* credit report, isn't it?"

"No, sir. It is the bank's credit report about you. New Hampshire law prevents me from showing it to you or from telling you specifically about the problem."

Lesson learned: Don't get on the wrong side of a credit bureau. The problem turned out to be their fault and was eventually (and I mean *eventually*) cleared up.

Considering my background, I approached the European banking system cautiously. I had brought a few American dollars with me that I converted to Dutch guilders. I didn't think I'd need much, since my employer, Royal Dutch Shell, was to pay a lump-sum moving expense amount. Besides, it would be payday within "two weeks."

As a veteran international traveler, I was prepared to deal with colorful Dutch money, and it didn't take long to remember that even if it looked like monopoly money, it was, nevertheless, real cash. (And given the way the U.S. dollar was moving, the guilder was becoming more real every day.)

As usual on an international trip, I accumulated lots of change. It's always difficult to figure out foreign coins. The problem was exacerbated in Holland because their coins are worth more than I expected. One-guilder, two-and-a-half-guilder, and five-guilder coins were commonly used. (These represent about fifty cents, a dollar twenty-five, and two dollars and fifty cents, respectively, so I had a lot of guilders tied up in a massive coin stack.)

As part of settling in, I opened a bank account with ABN, one of the largest banks in the Netherlands. I quickly discovered a few differences from the United States. First, you don't need any money to open an account. (Nice touch.) Further, all Dutch employers pay you by directly depositing funds into your account. (Even nicer.) But there are no checking accounts. When you get a bill, you also get an *acceptgiro* (essentially a deposit slip) that lets you transfer money to the biller's account. You simply sign the slip and drop in the mail in a postage-paid envelope. Most business is transacted through these transfers. For paying bills, this seemed different, but okay.

I wondered about shopping without checks. No problem! The bank gives out Eurocheques, guaranteed for as much as three hundred guilders (abbreviated Dfl three hundred. The "D" stands for "Dutch," the "fl" means "florins." I assume "florins" means "guilders.") If you want to buy something that costs more than Dfl three hundred, you use more than one Eurocheque. The system seemed simple.

So what's the catch? Well, for one thing, you can only get fifteen Eurocheques at a time. Further, you don't get new ones until all the old ones have cleared. (Don't tear up any checks you fill out by mistake or you'll never get new ones.) It takes two or three weeks to get each batch of fifteen cheques.

What about credit cards? There weren't any. (I could have gotten a EuroCard, which is really a sliding debit card—meaning that at some random point during the month the bank will debit your account for any outstanding charges.) I could have used my American credit cards, but then I'd be taking the risk of adverse foreign currency movements.

You might wonder how people keep the amounts in their account straight with no checks, direct deposit payment, and various card suppliers randomly debiting[1] amounts. The banks send out weekly statements. Additionally, they send a special statement any time a "significant" change occurs. The bank even provides a nice little folder for keeping statements together.

The upshot of this messy banking system is that Holland has a cash society. (The marginal 72 percent tax bracket that kicks in at really low levels might be a contributing factor.) I had brought enough money to live comfortably for two weeks. I figured by then I would start receiving paychecks and then could begin spending Dutch guilders.

Payday arrived, but money didn't. (I should have guessed that things would be complicated when the company sent me to a half-day session on deciphering the three-page pay slip that comes in the pay envelope.)

---

1 . Or, more infrequently, crediting.

The bottom line was that I wouldn't be paid until the second pay period, but Shell claimed they had transferred the lump-sum moving expense into my account. Daily trips to the bank ensued, accompanied by ongoing shrinkage of my stack of guilders. Increasingly strident and worried calls to the company's central office finally determined the problem. The money had been transferred to the wrong account number.

I called the bank and they confirmed that my money had arrived. They were open until four o'clock. At half past three, I walked into the bank to get some cash.

The clerk was less than helpful. "There is no money after two o'clock."

I was ready. "But I called. You said the bank was open until four."

"The bank *is* open. We just don't have money after two."

The guilder has been replaced by the Euro, which is not nearly as colorful but does eliminate some of the conversion challenges we faced during our adventure. The Euro isn't universal, however. We now live in Switzerland and travel mostly to the UK and the Far East—Euro-free zones.

We eventually learned to live with (and actually appreciate) the Dutch banking system. Paying bills was relatively easy, but in spite of an increasingly thick pile of bank statements, I didn't feel in control of our money. (Though as a married man, I was used to not having control.) Moreover, using cash limited a tendency to accumulate credit card debt. ATMs became more prevalent (although there were still long lines at the ATMs on weekends). When we lived in the Netherlands, a typewriter was still used to send money, and I was totally dependent on the only person at my branch who knew how to transfer funds to the States.

After I'd tripped over the extension cord for the umpteenth time, it occurred to me that the family wouldn't survive at the Pullman Centraal. I was getting cramped even on my own. I had to find a house, but Nazy had always found our homes. Was I up to it? Is it possible to downhill ski on Mt. Amsterdam?

THE DRAWING ROOM—OF COURSE

The Pullman Centraal had its charm—free breakfast. And it had lots of rooms—but no room. I was concerned: The full complement of The Martin Family would soon arrive in Holland. The thought of us being stuffed into Pullman Centraal chambers was simply too much to bear. The hotel wasn't ready for the Martins—there wouldn't even be enough space for the luggage. I was forced into the world of residential real estate.

I cautiously began house hunting. I wanted something close to the trams, something European, something in the city, and something big enough for the family. I knew the housing market in The Hague could meet these needs. Unfortunately, I had one further requirement: I wanted something we could afford on the Shell rental allowance.

Remarks from friends buzzed around in my head. "The rental market is very tight in The Hague." "You're thinking of getting a house before Nazy arrives? Are you crazy?" "There are thousands of houses available in The Hague." "Frankly, Dan, I prefer Amsterdam." "What about Wassenaar?" "Have you thought of Leiden?" "Just get an apartment and take your time looking." "Wait until the family arrives." If there was a coherent message, it wasn't getting through.

I had other concerns as well. While Shell had agreed to transport twenty cubic meters of household belongings, the rental allowance was designed for a fully furnished house. Even though I had no concept of twenty cubic meters, Nazy trusted me to advise her on which twenty cubic meters we should bring. I had to discover what furniture came in a "fully furnished" house.

I began by reading up on the subject. Homes and apartments in Holland came in three distinct flavors—unfurnished, partially furnished, and fully furnished. Fully furnished—I thought I understood that. But since we were allowed to bring twenty cubic meters, perhaps I could get more house for my dollar by going the "partially furnished" route. I made an appointment with the Shell housing specialist.

"Remember, Dan, don't say anything about the house to the owner. Say nothing. Verbal contracts are valid in Holland. If you say 'I like it,' you've got it."

"Got it."

"That's right. You've got it."

So I zipped my lip, met the recommended *makelaar* (real estate agent), and made my foray into housing in The Hague. I quickly decided that partially furnished would not meet Martin family requirements. In Holland, partially furnished means carpets and curtains (and maybe not the curtains). Now that I understood partially furnished, I wondered what unfurnished could possibly mean. I asked my real estate agent.

"Unfurnished means a shell house," she said. "Not 'Shell' like the oil company, but 'shell' like vacant. There are no light fixtures, no appliances, no sinks, no carpets, no drapes—just bare walls."

"Bare walls?"

"Bare walls."

"But if I rented such a house, I'd have to put in everything."

"That's right. You'd also have to take it back out when you left."

"So who rents that kind of house?"

"No expats, Dan. Unfurnished houses are subject to rent control. Landlords don't want to lease them and the terms are usually so bad that people don't want to rent them either."

"I see," I said. "It's clear that neither partially furnished nor unfurnished will do for us. What choices do I have in the fully furnished arena? I want something uniquely European in The Hague, close to the tram, with at least four bedrooms."

"Are you on the standard Shell rental allowance?"

"Of course!"

"Oh. Too bad."

It wasn't really that bad. There were exactly two fully furnished houses that appeared to meet my requirements. One greatly exceeded the allowance; the other moderately exceeded it. We went to see both.

The first house—the expensive one—was on the corner of a busy intersection. It had five bedrooms. Three of them were the size of a walk-in, eh, crawl-in closet. That wasn't so bad (the children are small). However, the kitchen posed a problem: It wasn't as big as a closet. The house did have quaint European charm—the original, sixteenth-century kitchen and bathroom fixtures. "We can't leave granite countertops for this," I worriedly thought.

The second house was more promising. It had two bedrooms of walk-in closet dimensions. But it also had three huge bedrooms, a large kitchen, a completely remodeled master bathroom, and several sitting rooms. (The furniture was a bit strange, but I thought I could get used to the wild boar's head in the entrance hall.) The owner wasn't there, but I didn't say anything to the real estate agent. I decided to ask the advice of friends who had recently moved to Holland. I wanted this one!

I grabbed Cormac, my boss, at the office later that day. "What about it, Cormac? You and Maggie spent a lot of time looking for a house. Will you come and take a look at my favorite?"

"We'll look at it. But you're crazy to even think about getting a house before Nazy gets here. Why not just move to a company apartment for a few months?"

We had lived in an apartment in Houston for a few months. The Martin Family in an apartment? Yuck! Not much better than the Pullman Centraal.

Maggie replicated Cormac's advice during the drive to the house. We arrived at Prinsevinkenpark 42 a bit late.

Cormac was impressed as he boomed his initial appraisal. "My God, Dan! It's a freestanding house. That's not done here."

Upon entering the home, Maggie observed that the house was "enormous" and we'd "have to do something about that boar's head." Cormac and Maggie grew more and more impressed as we moved through the rooms. The kitchen was modern (not granite, but modern). I even noticed a TV in the study. Thank God! We'd be able to watch the BBC.

By the time we'd reached the second floor, their advice was changing. "Dan," Maggie began, "are you sure the rent meets the Shell allowance?"

"Just about."

"If this fits your allowance, then I should renegotiate *my* contract," Cormac interjected. "This house is a vast symbol of European decadence. Room after room of enormous space. Nobody can afford to make things like this any more."

As we stood in the second-floor living room, Cormac strode across to the marble fireplace and rested his elbow on the mantle. "A magnificent drawing room. This corner is an excellent place to hold court and make pronouncements on the state of world affairs. Get it. Now!"

Cormac had just sealed the deal for me. "The drawing room, of course!" I thought. "I've got to have a house with a drawing room."

We checked the rest of the house. Everyone was dismayed by the green closets in the master bedroom, and we all thought the fence needed painting.

I called Nazy that evening. "Make sure to bring the art supplies, Nazy, we're going to have a drawing room."

"A drawing room?"

"Of course!"

> *In spite of my preparation with the makelaar, there was a fly in the otherwise unsullied ointment. I had signed a two-year rental agreement with an option to extend the term, subject to a diplomatic clause that entitled the owner to assume possession if he returned from an overseas assignment. Since our assignment was for two years, I wasn't worried. I should have been. Appropriately for an oil company, things moved at a geological pace—the project I thought would take two years took five. After two years, the owner, a Shell employee, returned home and we were (diplomatically) ejected. We hadn't anticipated having to move again in two years.*

I had been lucky to find a house so quickly. The Belgian ambassador's wife had also wanted the home and was willing to pay more than the owner was asking. She had demanded that the green closets be painted white, though, and I, being color-blind, had made no such request. (I did wonder what Nazy would say when she saw them. It was a strange color—something like an overripe avocado.) I had a few more weeks in the hotel while the owner completed work on the heating system.

We were quite happy in the house, although it did have a few idiosyncrasies. The heating system gurgled and the clothes dryer screeched. I also found out (the hard way) that quaint European toilets, the kind with the water tank suspended eight feet above the commode, have drawbacks. When you flush, the water, propelled by gravity, is catapulted through a narrow pipe into the toilet. Physics laws vaguely remembered from college (water will seek its own level) were clearly demonstrated in an unplanned experiment. The Martin Family recommends the following:

Rule: Don't flush quaint European toilets while you're sitting on them.

I'd done, in appropriate order, all of the really important things associated with our new homeland. My home computer (and game-playing machine) was now functional, thanks to the verlengsnoer. I'd opened a bank account. I'd found a place to live. It was time to attack one of the more minor problems—my new job. It couldn't be too hard to get the computer at the office to work. After all, I had a PhD in computer science and years of experience. Shell had an entire division that could help. Moreover, I'd solved my personal computer problem; any office problems had to be a piece of cake.

WELL, NOT EXACTLY

I told the family that it was "just a small career adjustment" when I broached the subject of a move to Holland. "I know Shell is a bit larger than DTSS (130,000 employees rather than 100) and I know there's no vertical relief in the Dutch landscape. But the Hanover spring is 'mud season'; the Netherlands spring is 'bud season.' Besides, we'll be living in Europe." And, I told myself, "We'll even be able to pay the bills." Nevertheless, I had been reluctant: I had made a promise to myself to never again work for a company large enough to require security badges. Now here I was—with a badge. I compromised by carrying it rather than wearing it.

"At least getting set at the office won't be complicated," I thought. "Shell can surely meet my small computer needs." Indeed, the pre-move formalities went smoothly. A representative of the computer center, SNI (*Shell Nederland Informatieverwerking*), called the States to ascertain my computer preference. Here I made my first mistake—I chose Macintosh, a system that was tolerated but not preferred. My new department, more aware than I of the imposing nature of a Dutch bureaucracy, placed my Mac order several weeks before I arrived.

My first few days in the Netherlands were full of extension cords, monopoly money, and jet lag. They had nothing to do with delivery of my new Mac. I used a loaner.

While I waited for delivery, I was reduced to using a mainframe terminal that (in)conveniently linked me to IBM's PROFS e-mail system. PROFS on an IBM terminal is real culture shock for a Mac aficionado. It's like handing an oar to a fighter pilot.

Three weeks *after* I arrived, Informatieverwerking acknowledged the Mac order placed five weeks before my departure. Nothing was in stock. I would be "informed if delivery would take more than four additional weeks." I thought my preference for Macs had caused the problem—I later discovered that this was standard procedure.

What was I to do? "Surely, Dan isn't old enough to know how to work without a computer," you might be saying to yourself.

I'm not! Fortunately, someone had been able to find a replacement power cord for my loaner. (For some reason, the original had gone missing.) My department had ordered a Macintosh IIcx and an associated bundle of software. The loaner was a Macintosh SE. I knew the SE. My own personal SE—complete with extension cord—was working in the Pullman Centraal. It should have been smooth sailing.

Well, not exactly. This SE had a European keyboard and a desk accessory called SmartKeys. Collectively, these conspired to wreak havoc. A few keys—shift, caps lock, control, return, and option, were in a different place on the European keyboard. Every time I tried to press return or shift into uppercase, something problematic happened. Unwanted things like calling up the spell-checker were merely annoying. Unwanted things like restarting the system (and erasing my work) were decidedly disgusting.

But I'm adaptable. I learned to live with this problem. I'm also a program director who writes lots of reports and memos. Although I had mastered the pencil, fountain pen, and Selectric typewriter, a word processor was an absolute necessity.

My request for a *woordeninformatieverwerkingsmachine* (word processor) predictably resulted in a visit from a representative of the Shell Standards Bureau. I could use any word processor that appeared on the Shell Standard's list. The list was short (it had one entry): Microsoft Word. Naturally I had no experience with Word. Aware that an agonizing decision had been prevented, I discovered that Word was already installed on the Mac. I was initially nonplussed by the European SpellCzecher, but then thought I would sound very erudite using words such as *organisation*, *colour*, and *labour*. (As it turned out, I had to use a lot of *labour* to get anything out of my Mac.)

I created my initial memos smoothly, but without a printer, sharing my creations was awkward in the international, decentralized environment at Shell. I couldn't simply gather the audience in front of my machine. The alternative, Polaroid photos of the screen, lacked sophistication.

My issues could have been resolved if the departmental printers were installed on a network. They weren't. The network proposal was being reviewed by the Infrastructure Selection Board, the Compatibility Council, and the Committee on Workstations (COW). My only option was to borrow someone else's machine for printing. Initially this went well. I was new; it took a while for me to create (and modify, and modify, and modify) my reports. Neighborly visits to my coworkers were rare.

Informatieverwerking had put Word in an obscure folder on my loaner computer, and I couldn't find any documentation on how to use it. "But I'm using a Mac," I thought. *"Documentation is unnecessary."* Well, not exactly. Documentation may not be needed to create routine memos, but it is essential for generating truly elegant documents and reports. I borrowed documentation from Brigit next door.

My confidence in my technical ability began to flag. The documentation didn't match the screen. The problem was eventually diagnosed as the dreaded version incompatibility syndrome. The SE had Word 3.02; the documentation was for Word 4.0. The features I wanted to use were not supported in Word 3.02. Company procedures left me in quandary, but a copy of Word 4.0 had been ordered. While I waited, I discovered that my neighbor's 4.0 documentation included original diskettes. Temptation mounted and conquered queasiness. I installed Word 4.0 on the loaner and resolved to eliminate it when my real copy arrived.

Breaking my standard procedure, I actually read (part of) the Word manual and began work. A few false starts later, I had created a table that looked good on the screen. Eventually (i.e., several printing trials later), I managed to put together a table that looked good on paper, but had completely exasperated my colleague, Brigit, who had the printer.

Finally I was ready. Cormac had a printer in his office and he was away on an American tour. His system was available. I would no longer have to bother Brigit. I could simply plop down in the vacant office with my beautiful, elegant, meaningful memo. Life would be splendid again. Or so I thought. Unfortunately, the vacant, available, and beckoning machine had Word 3.02! I was reduced, once again, to pleading with friends for printer access.

In the meantime, a partial shipment of my order, the mouse pad, arrived. Informatieverwerking promised full delivery within two weeks. (The promise of "two weeks" filled me with fear—I kept having visions of a granite computer.)

I was cursing Microsoft's Word program when I discovered WordPerfect hidden on the SE, and decided to switch for the duration. At least with WordPerfect, I could copy the file I wanted to print along with the application on a single diskette. "Nothing can go wrong," I thought as I erased Word 4.0.

But I had forgotten Murphy's Law. And I needed to create graphics for my reports. Surprisingly, SuperPaint, software I was familiar with, was installed on the SE. I created a bushel basket full of pretty pictures. (I was in Europe where they don't understand bushel baskets, so I should say that I created a vast forty-liter vessel full of exquisite illustrations.) I carried them to the vacant machine, where I was cautiously predicting success, but was soon dismayed to discover that SuperPaint is not "MultiFinder friendly" (whatever that means). Nor is it Mac IIcx friendly. I would have to ask Brigit for help (again).

No longer unfazed, and anxious to accomplish something (anything!), I humbly stumbled into Brigit's office. She broke the unpleasant news.

"We don't use SuperPaint anymore, Dan. The European version doesn't work on the Mac IIcx. You should use MacDraw II."

I went back to the physical drawing board armed with templates, rulers, and pencils.

With my hand-drawn pictures and WordPerfect supporting literature, I sauntered back to the vacant Mac IIcx. I hoped to get beautiful, laser-quality output. By now, I expected problems. I wasn't disappointed.

Every Mac is not equipped with the same fonts. My first choice—Times—wasn't the company standard and, accordingly, wasn't installed on the Mac IIcx. The standard font collection had a few unpleasant features. Even in the same point sizes, they used more space than Times. Documents could begin looking like this: Crafty optimized layouts became a surreal exercise in futility.

My Macintosh IIcx finally arrived. The shipping company had dropped the monitor, but it worked. A replacement had been ordered; they were to let me know if delivery would take more than four weeks. The company also ordered various software, including Word (4.0) and SuperPaint(!). The system arrived with all of the software installed on the hard disk (thereby filling most of the available space). The Macintosh network was still not operational, but I ordered my own printer. The order was slowly digested deep in the fearsome bowels of the Informatieverwerking support group.

In the meantime, a departmental color laser printer arrived. And, because I didn't have a printer, the new printer temporarily resided in my office. ("If it can do color, Dan, then surely it will suffice for a few colorless memos.") But the color printer used special, shiny paper that is generally not available in Holland. And my initial efforts dedicated to presentation materials resulted in the formation of a committee to create "color standards" for presentations. I guess I should have told them I am color-blind.

I'm not the only person with strong feelings about word processing. In Houston, I had to introduce a new word processor to the administrative staff. I entered a large meeting room facing scores of glaring people. Caution—and humor—was required.

"I know this is disruptive," I began, "but we had no choice. The company that made our old system has gone broke. We have to change."

There was no reaction.

"But you will be happy. We've completed an extensive evaluation. You will love the new system. It has the latest technology—a telepathic user interface. There is no keyboard. You simply think at this machine and it automatically puts your document in the company format. It spell checks it, it grammar checks it, and, if necessary, it translates into multiple languages. Then it sends it to all recipients and files a copy for you."

"That won't work," someone shouted from the back of the room.

"Why not?"

"I can't concentrate that long."

I resolved to muddle through. My personal printer would eventually become part of my twenty cubic meters. By now, though, I was beginning to understand the need for European-style vacations.

I kept hearing from Informatieverwerking. The Mac simply did not meet corporate standards. (It was usable.) They wondered if I'd like to switch to an IBM PS/2. They also noted that they had received my order for a printer, and would let me know if delivery would take longer than four weeks.

This was my first foray into the world of Dutch bureaucracy—a finely tuned organizational structure that astounds me. The Dutch have procedures for everything. If you know the procedures (and follow them), things will get done—but it will take a long time. You'll notice this theme as you read on.

Now, however, I had figured out money, located a house, and created a working environment. I had even moved out of the Pullman and into the estate on Prinsevinkenpark in The Hague. I was tired. I wanted to sleep in my "fully furnished" home.

BEDS: DON'T TAKE THEM FOR GRANITE

The Pullman had been easy to find—it was right next to the DANS (Dance) Theatre, which had a huge neon sign that even I, new to the tram system, could hardly miss. Hotels are nice for short stays. Mine had been l o n g. I collected my belongings—which had grown to greatly exceed suitcase space—and checked out. Since Prinsevinkenpark 42, the "vast symbol of European opulence," was *fully furnished*, I was sure I would be able to survive until the family (and our famed twenty cubic meters) arrived.

I dropped my cowboy hat on the boar's nose and went upstairs to check out the bed. I knew immediately I would need to purchase linen for the king-size berth in the master bedroom. I had avoided the V & D since the extension cord debacle. "But what could be difficult about buying sheets?" I thought.

It would have been easier if I had understood the sheet-sizing situation. They don't have "king-size" sheets in Holland. (I'm not complaining. I'm sure the Dutch are confused by our "twin" beds that are designed for one small person.) Bed sizes don't have names in the Netherlands; they have numbers. Sheets are purchased by the size, in centimeters, of the bed. For example: 100 cm x 200 cm, 90 cm x 210 cm, 50 cm x 50 cm (maybe that was a pillow case). In short there are thousands of combinations). I ignorantly walked into a shop to buy king-size sheets. I returned home dejected, but armed with a centimeter-marked measuring stick. (At first I asked the clerk for a yardstick. It didn't translate.) I measured the bed and rushed back just before closing time for a set of 200 x 200 cm sheets. I also noticed, as I departed with fewer guilders than planned, that linen prices are high in Europe—and I hadn't even been able to find fitted bottom sheets.

Back home, the bed was beckoning. I was tired. The sheets were too big, but I didn't worry. I made them fit. In the process of making the bed, back strain brought the realization that European beds are close to the floor and don't have box springs. I jumped into bed and was instantly reminded of home (New Hampshire—the granite state). "Perhaps a firm bed is good for posture," I thought. Well that may be, but sleepless nights are not good for your mood.

After deciding that the bed was (marginally) preferable to the floor, I reminded myself that I was on an *adventure*. I tried to sleep, but just couldn't drop off. Fortunately, I was prepared for this kind of an emergency, and carried the TV from the study into the bedroom. BBC2 did the trick. (They were showing an educational program: *Dover Chalk: From Cliff to Classroom*.)

This uncomfortable state of affairs lasted for a few weeks until the family arrived. I did make one emergency telephone call home.

"Nazy, *please* make sure the beds are part of our twenty cubic meters," I plaintively wailed

I was still suffering from back strain when I decided to brave the rigors of the Dutch washing machine. (Clean sheets were the least I could do to prepare for the forthcoming family arrival.) I discovered that while all Dutch people speak English, Dutch washing machines have Dutch instructions. It was impossible to fit the top sheet, bottom sheet, and two pillowcases into a single load (appliances are a bit small in Europe). I was initially impressed with the washer's energy-saving feature of heating its own water, but it really would have been nicer if the concept of "preshrunk" cotton was standard in Europe.

It wasn't a total loss. Now both sheets (and the pillowcases) fit into a single washing load. Unfortunately, we had no need for the crib they shrunk to fit.

> *I was settled but lonely as I rattled around in the vast estate. My worries were building. What would Nazy think about the house? Would the children like their new school? What about that green closet? Would they make the trip without problems? When would the beds arrive? And would the family be happy in Europe? We soon found out that no move is problem-free.*

CHAPTER 3
CULTURE SHOCK

I was here and they were there, but over there they knew they were coming here. Nazy was fighting last-minute battles. Shell wanted a complete physical, but our hometown doctor refused to give cardiograms to the children. Darius's computer program and Melika's meticulous measurements verified that what they hoped to bring with them wouldn't violate the golden twenty cubic meters.

Actually, worries about the twenty cubic meters were unfounded. The American moving company was metrically challenged. Aware that we were moving to Europe on a two-year contract, we decided to store everything in excess of our twenty cubic meters in a spare room upstairs. The movers, eyeing the narrow stairs and granite ledge, decided it would be easier to transport the piano to Holland than to move it to the second floor.

There was also concern about cars. Having mastered the trams and trains, I wasn't worried. I knew they sold cars in Europe. Accordingly, I recommended that we dispose of the Nissan 280Z and the Taurus station wagon. Nazy was happy to rid herself of the Z; it had proven to be less than stable on ice. For the Taurus, she considered my advice, then called Maggie, Cormac's wife.

"Of course you can buy a car in Holland, Nazy. But bring yours. Local taxes make cars very expensive," Maggie explained,

"and even if you can afford a car, every car in Europe is small. Very small."

Somehow Nazy discovered that the standard shipping container was actually forty cubic meters, and that Shell had paid for half. Nazy convinced the moving company to sell us the other half for three hundred and fifty dollars. Luckily, weight was irrelevant and the Taurus fit nicely.

Everything else was packed or relocated to the second floor. (As it turned out, the people who rented the house wanted use of the spare room, so we later arranged to have everything put in storage. The two-year contract stretched to five years. You would not believe the things we paid to have stored.)

Back in The Hague, I was preparing the house for The Martin Family—cleaning up empty soda cans and purchasing interim sheets. I even embarked on an expedition to the third floor—which I hadn't seen since the first day. I bought presents for everyone. I was really excited as I left for Schiphol Airport to meet the novice Europeans, and hoped everyone would be excited and happy.

LET OP DE HONDE POEP

Darius hasn't liked dogs since Maximillian, a Doberman, left him sprawling in the mud. Darius not only dislikes dogs, he also dislikes loud, sudden noises. He *really* dislikes loud, sudden noises generated by enormous dogs running directly toward him. Darius, who was four years old when he had his experience with Maximillian, was eleven when he arrived in The Hague. He still didn't like dogs. Unfortunately for him, Holland is dog-friendly.

My own carefully planned career program (directed by corporate asset sales, ill-timed company bankruptcies, and falling oil prices) had made Darius a self-confident, international traveler. Frequent family relocation, however, was not on his list of fun things to do. When the Shell offer arrived, Darius demanded a family vote. (This episode illustrates the disadvantages of schooling. Democratic principles can't always apply in family decision making.) In deference to Darius, we did vote. Darius still believes that someone stuffed the ballot box, tampered with the results, and cheated on the count. Darius may have a case. The vote was five for the move, one against. (There are only five members in The Martin Family.)

On his arrival at Schiphol Airport in Amsterdam in November with Nazy, Mitra, and Melika, Darius appeared to have reluctantly accepted the situation. He had become the family geography whiz and this was a chance to collect a passport stamp. But the arrival didn't go well: Dutch passport control failed to stamp his passport. Large numbers of *large* dogs joined The Martin Family in their wait for luggage. Darius wanted a recount.

When the family finally cleared customs and dashed through the crowd to meet me, Darius had made up his mind.

"Hi, Dad. I liked Hanover better. Let's just forget this move, okay?"

"Why, Darius?"

"Hanover has *hills* and my friends are in Hanover."

I was stuck—there weren't easy answers to these complaints. "But Darius," I said, "there is a hill in South Holland. We'll go see it. I miss my friends, too, but we'll make friends here. Maybe we should just give Europe a little more time. What d'ya think?"

"Okay. But they didn't even stamp my passport and there are too many dogs in the airport."

Now we had a real problem. In Holland, dogs not only show up in the airport, they show up everywhere—in restaurants, in trams, in trains, in the street, in yards, in shops, on the beach, in parks. The Dutch think of dogs as part of nature.

Darius quickly learned the most important Dutch expression: *Let op de hond poep!* (*Let op* means "pay attention to," *hond* means "dog." I'll leave the rest to your imagination.) While Darius learned the expression, it took personal experience to drive the point home.

The experience occurred on the first day of school. The American School of The Hague sent a tour bus to pick up the children. Nazy and I were at the door to see them off. The bus departed, but stopped one hundred meters down the street. Darius got off.

Nazy dashed across Prinsevinkenpark to see what was wrong. When she got within fifteen meters of Darius, her nose detected the problem. Darius had been ejected with instructions to scrape his shoes. The task wasn't easy, since sneaker treads have lots of little groves. The best that could be done was to scrap, rather than scrape, them. On this embarrassing note, Darius began his academic career in The Hague. But he does *let op de honde poep!*

Over time, Darius began to like Holland and his passport started to look impressive. He still wanted family votes on all important matters. (I've tried to explain that we have a *representative* democracy. *I'm his* representative.) Nevertheless, his innate curiosity and interest in foreign cultures was being satisfied in Europe.

He enjoyed the pastries, the beach, and especially the flowers. The Dutch have flowers everywhere. Cut flowers are available year round at very good prices. Darius liked to buy flowers for Nazy during school lunch breaks. He helped me select and plant one hundred pansies in the Prinsevinkenpark courtyard. He always wanted to carry the weekly fresh flowers to the house.

One Friday, Darius made the flower run with Nazy. Company was expected and Darius was carrying the roses. A tempestuous Yorkshire terrier with a squeaky bark dashed out of a neighboring house. Darius jumped and then froze. The terrier raced directly toward him through the rain.

Darius had just learned an important and applicable lesson in science class—the principle of action and reaction. In this case, the terrier was the action. Darius's reaction? Flying flowers. Darius threw the roses at the terrier and took off for home. The flowers missed the dog but hit a puddle, and the ensuing splash frightened the terrier. Darius made his escape.

At home, a democratic family meeting was convened.

Darius began. "I move that we move back to Hanover."

I was quick. "The chair does not accept that motion. You can't use the word 'move' twice in one motion."

Darius was annoyed. "All right! Then I move that we write a letter to the queen."

"Queen Beatrix has a poodle, Darius," Mitra responded.

"Fine! I move that we buy hand grenades!"

It was Melika's turn. "In Social Studies, they said that hand grenades are illegal here. It's not like America, Darius."

Nazy jumped into the fray. "I move that we collect money for replacement roses from Darius's allowance."

"Hey, Dad," complained Darius, "you said financial matters were beyond the scope of the family democracy meetings."

I reluctantly ruled Nazy's motion out of order and moved on to new business.

Melika interjected, "I've got a motion. I move that we buy a dog."

The motion was defeated in a close vote. I resolved to have a serious talk with Nazy; I had to resort to creative chairmanship when I noticed that there were three pro-dog votes.

After the meeting, Nazy told Darius that dogs are really afraid of him. "If you don't act frightened, the dogs won't bother you." In an intellectual and philosophical sense, this was correct, but Darius had problems developing an emotional acceptance of the principle. Besides, as he told Nazy, "I'm not *acting* frightened." In fairness, I think Darius used italics on the *not* rather than the *acting*.

I told Darius dogs were just like bullies. "They're really afraid of you. Why don't you just bark back and run toward them?"

Darius was unconvinced. "Are you crazy, Dad?" But he tried this plan and it worked. (I hope he doesn't try it with a Doberman.)

Darius began to happily (and bravely) bark at dogs. He still doesn't like big ones, but he has been willing to touch familiar dogs even if they are big and especially if they don't bark. He keeps his eyes open, watches his step and, just in case, always carries a bouquet of flowers.

Not only has Darius has gotten much braver in dealing with the dogs, everyone in the family quite carefully watches their step. You can go around honde poep.

Somehow, we had arranged The Martin Family arrival so that I, who had been living in Holland for two months, rather than they, who had just arrived, suffered jet lag. They had a week to get acclimated before going to school. They were excited. They wanted to stay up late and get up late. Since I wanted to be with the family, I stayed up late, too. But since I had to go to work, I also got up early. This marked difficulty continued until the daily trek to school began. Then they slowly worked their way into Dutch time. Rain, fog, drizzle, and generally cold weather marked their first week in Europe. The Martin Family was unprepared.

THE RAIN IS NOT IN SPAIN

The Eskimos have scores of different words for "snow." Therefore, there should be at least twenty-three different Dutch words for "rain." There's the soaking rain of a summer thundershower, big-dropped "ploppy" rain, drizzle, and fog so thick that it sticks to you. We had lived in Vancouver; we thought we *knew* rain, but The Martin Family had never been to Holland. (I've just noticed that there are an inordinate number of American words for rain: deluge, downpour, shower, thunderstorm, mist, drizzle, cloudburst, precipitation, sprinkle. Perhaps our language had its origins in the British Isles.)

You never see a Dutchman without a raincoat. Ten consecutive days of rain convinced me that the natives were correctly attired. I fondly remembered the good old days in the States when I used to create rain by washing my car. Perhaps an analog approach would work: I bought a raincoat. (My own raincoat was in America. Nazy thought I had lost it; I thought she had forgotten to pack it. In reality, my father had borrowed it.) My simple ploy worked initially. There were five consecutive days with neither rain nor clouds. The spell wore off just as the family arrived. (They had been delayed by "foggy rain" at Amsterdam's Schiphol Airport.)

After settling The Martin Family into the Prinsevinkenpark Estate, I pointed out that they might notice a bit of precipitation. A week later it was still raining.

At the office one day, I noticed that the wet fog had morphed into a steady downpour, and purchased a seven-guilder umbrella at the Shell Shop. The umbrella, a standard black model, was not a fine example of European craftsmanship (the appropriate American word is "cheap"). The soaking rain soon changed to wind-blown precipitation. Walking across the bridge to the tram, I was able to save my hat from the gale, but my new umbrella was quickly reduced to tatters.

Back home, I advised the family to avoid the "seven-guilder umbrella." That weekend, the precipitation changed from shower to deluge and finally back to steady rain. Mitra convinced me to purchase a colorful, fifteen-guilder umbrella complete with shoulder strap at *Centraal Station*. The shoulder strap, she said, would prove to be handy.

"You know, Daddy, it doesn't always rain, sometimes it's just foggy. It changes fast. I can easily carry this one." (I'm still not sure where in the course of the conversation *my* purchase became *her* umbrella.)

Nazy was skeptical. The new umbrella was too small. Nazy wanted a *big* one. Later that weekend we were at *Madurodam*, a local site touted as the "smallest city in Holland." *Madurodam* features miniature models of all the famous Dutch buildings and a really cool model railroad layout. At the park, Nazy found the umbrella of her dreams. It was the jolly green giant of umbrelladom (the thirty-guilder model) and could easily cover the whole family—and most of the population of Western Europe. It also appeared to be quite sturdy. My brief experience with Holland weather had made it clear, though, that *Noordzee* (North Sea) gales easily drove the rain horizontally and I was convinced no umbrella could offer adequate protection.

The fifteen-guilder umbrella quickly succumbed to the rigors of the *Noordzee* weather. Even Mitra should have known that opening an umbrella at *Scheveningen Strand* (a beach) in the middle of a storm is an invitation for disaster. (She still has the nifty strap.)

Seeing that disaster, Nazy was determined that I acquire a good umbrella. For some reason, it bothered her to see me in a (gasp!) wet raincoat. The family embarked on an excursion to the Passage shopping district to get an umbrella for Daddy. Nazy wanted a stylish but functional model. With this mission in mind, we invaded an exclusive shop. I quickly chose a sturdy-looking thirty-guilder model. The shop owner didn't want to sell.

"That umbrella is junk. You should expect to pay at least eighty guilders for good umbrella," he said as he took Nazy's arm and directed her to the special green-and-gray model that his contracted craftsmen assembled in Italy. These recommended umbrellas cost two-hundred guilders.

We knew better. We demurred and finally found our way out of the store.

"Two hundred guilders for an umbrella?" Nazy was outraged. "That's absurd!"

A few days later, Nazy came to Rijswijk to have lunch with me. To get to my office, she had to walk across the bridge. As luck would have it, a cloudburst, accompanied by strong winds arrived just as she hit the bridge. She managed to hold on to her umbrella (the green giant) with two hands and kept it from winding up in the canal. It didn't remain convex, however, and a concave umbrella doesn't offer much rain protection. This experiment showed us that the thirty-guilder umbrella is also an inadequate match for the Dutch climate.

We weren't sure what to do. There was clear danger associated with a sturdy umbrella. Nazy might have been lifted off the bridge and dumped into the canal. And there were economic considerations: Sturdy umbrellas started at eighty guilders and climbed to exceed three hundred guilders. (We'd be really mad when a three-hundred-guilder umbrella disintegrated.) A full complement of three-hundred-guilder umbrellas for a family of five? You can buy a lot of door-to-door taxi rides for fifteen hundred guilders. Besides, even if they were sturdy, someone (e.g. Darius) was sure to lose one. There was also an ongoing controversy to consider: Is an umbrella really useful in Holland? If the rain is falling sideways, who cares about an umbrella?

On the plus side, everyone now understood the need for precipitation virtuosity in the Dutch language. We just couldn't figure out why there is a Dutch word for "sun."

There are so many things to learn when you move to a new country. Clothing sizes are different. You may have mastered ounces, pints, quarts, and dollars, but they sell things in grams and liters—and expect you to pay in guilders. TV is different. (Believe me, the BBC is different.) Luckily, Dutch TV had a lot of American films with Dutch subtitles. "Normal" medications aren't available, and it's not easy to make yourself understood.

"I've got a cold," I told the pharmacist one afternoon. "Do you have Tylenol?"

"If you're cold, you need a blanket."

"Actually," I said, rubbing my forehead, "I'm hot. I need some Tylenol."

"Are you hot or are you cold?"

"I have a cold." I sneezed.

"Here," she said, handing me a package of Rhinoblast.

"That wasn't so difficult," I thought. Back in my hotel room, I discovered that I'd purchased the local version of Vicks VapoRub, except that it smelled like effluent from a manure manufacturing facility. I wasn't even sure how to use it. It seemed to me that the mere threat of holding the stuff close to my olfactory system would scare the germs into submission.

Food is also different. Everyone has some basic, fundamental requirements in the food area. We expected food differences in a new country. Dutch food presented the usual surprises. Beef was basically inedible. It turned out that the butchers cut the meat differently because most Dutch cooking is done on the stove, not in the oven. Pork and chicken seemed to turn out as we'd expected, but we had a nagging feeling of emptiness. Everyone wanted a simple American dessert—ice cream. But coming from New England, the home of Ben & Jerry's ice cream, we had high quality standards.

CHERRIES—BY BEN & JERRY'S

The rigors of the move to Europe were behind us; after a few months, the family was semi-settled. While we enjoyed the culinary treats of Holland, there was universal dismay with the ice cream. We couldn't honestly complain about all Dutch ice cream. Sorbet, for example, was quite good. We wondered if it was a coincidence that this stuff—called *ijs* in Dutch—was imported from Italy.

When the family joined me in Holland, they were distraught by the lack of ice cream in The Martin Family fridge. An early attempt to rectify the problem met with disaster. I cruised through the grocery store and located the freezer section. I knew the family craved Ben & Jerry's Cherry Garcia, but I also knew it would be impossible to find the Vermont brand in Holland, so I decided to look for any recognizable brand name. A quick scan convinced me that no brand contained less than forty-five letters.

Quickly moving to Plan B, I resorted to the Nazy Martin product selection methodolyg: buy the most expensive—it's surely the best.

It wasn't the best. The cheerful, expectant, happy faces of the Martin children quickly turned sour as the first taste of Dutch ice cream stuck to their palate. "Stick" is the operative word. To say that this ice cream had an aftertaste is like saying that Houston is humid. Darius wanted to use sandpaper to scrape the remains off his tongue. Melika tried a tall glass of water, but was disappointed when it simply spread the aftertaste all the way down into her stomach. Nazy, who had been slow to move spoon to mouth, was immediately skeptical.

"Are you sure this is ice cream?"

A brief family discussion was finally resolved through the use of the English/Dutch dictionary. The label on the container unambiguously indicated that what I'd bought was "something like" ice cream. At least it gave us a chance to add a new word to Mitra's vocabulary: purportedly.

All members of the family discarded the excess and dropped their spoons into the sink. Nazy, for some inexplicable reason, returned the—unfortunately—not empty container to the freezer.

There was a surprise the next morning when the sink was examined. Each spoon had been deposited in the sink with a near-full complement of Dutch "ice cream." Normal ice cream would have melted overnight. The Dutch ice cream failed this basic test of quality. The uneaten but rotting carcasses of unfinished spoonfuls had formed a chemical bond with the stainless steel of the spoons. (You're now prepared for a Trivial Pursuit question: Name one chemical component of Super Glue.) Extremely hot water, a hammer, and vigorous activity with a scouring pad reduced the offensive remains to pebble-sized chunks of rubble. Typically American, we washed the rubble down the drain. The next day, we had to learn the Dutch word for "plumber": *loodgieter*.

For the next few months, The Martin Family lived a squalid life without ice cream. It was into this environment that friends from Hanover arrived. They had heard of our plight and taken it upon themselves to provide nourishment. Accordingly, they packed a picnic cooler full of Ben & Jerry's in their checked baggage.

As the baggage sailed through the X-ray machine at the security checkpoint, they became uncomfortably aware that frozen ice cream looks remarkably like plastic explosive. It's not easy to convince airport security that you really are bringing ice cream across the ocean.

There was much rejoicing and happiness as The Martin Family gobbled the Cherry Garcia, Heath Bar Crunch, Chunky Monkey, and Mint with Oreo Cookie. The visitors were amazed by how thrilled we were until we offered our "ice cream" to them. I don't have to go into the gory details, but the sink was clogged (again).

> *It turns out that what I bought wasn't really ice cream. (We're still not sure what it was, but I suggest you avoid the frozen-food section of the little store in Babylon.) There are edible Dutch ice creams available at the Konmar. Italian Ice—ijs in Dutch—is quite good. We continued to experience adjustment problems in the food arena. (My kingdom, such as it was, for an Oreo, a bowl of Cheerios, or a lemon chiffon birthday cake.) There were other things from the States that we took for granted. Things like ice cubes.*

THE CARE PACKAGE

Although the day was gray, cold, and wet (i.e., typical), there was a silver lining. I had an afternoon meeting at Central Office in The Hague. I could walk home from work and wouldn't have to take the tram from Rijswijk. Even the walk through the gloomy winter didn't dull my spirit. I had my raincoat and looked typically Dutch.

As I arrived at the house, I was struck by a palpable feeling of excitement and euphoria. An emergency care package had arrived from America. My parents, aware of the desperate situation of a family in need, had braved the forms necessary to send parcels from Atlanta to the continent. The family, bursting with anticipation, had waited for my arrival before tearing the box open.

Like a huddled group of refugees, we demolished the wrappings in an exuberant attack to reach the goodies therein. When we discovered the contents, the children broke into a spontaneous cheer that picked up momentum as the entire family joined the celebration.

Mitra articulated the appreciation felt by each member of The Martin Family: "Ice cube trays. Oh, Daddy, they do care about us. We can have real American ice. Oh, I'm so happy!"

The family's unquenchable spirit had been severely tested by an unquenchable thirst caused by the lack of adequate ice. Ice cube trays in the "fully furnished" home created *miniature* cubelets that degenerated into a pile of submicroscopic flakes in the rare times they could actually be extracted from the tray. The alternative, a disposable cellophane bag of ice, had similar problems. Every bag we tried leaked. And we had to heat the bag to peel the cellophane from the ice. (By the time we disengaged the cellophane, the ice had disappeared.)

There were tears of joy as water was ceremoniously poured into the trays. The next morning, we were able to

(1) Easily extricate the frozen cubes from their constraining receptacles, and

(2) Hear a satisfying *clunk* as the cubes tumbled into a glass.

There was a deafening thunder of applause as iced tea was triumphantly poured over the solidified water. The family gathered to observe, in awe and wonder, the massive, American-sized ice cubes that refused to melt before the ice tea was tasted. I quickly finished my tea and was able to achieve nirvana in the simple, but almost forgotten, joy of crunching the satisfying icy debris that remained after the tea had been consumed.

Importation of these high technology devices into Holland had not been accomplished without some problem. Our refrigerator, like most in Europe, was not frost-free. And the freezer thermostat was permanently stuck in the "Antarctic" position. The extreme cold of the freezer, over time, made the American ice cube trays brittle.

Most annoying, however, was an energy-saving feature of the freezer compartment: After the door was opened (and then closed), an automatic sealing mechanism locked it in place until the thermostat-controlled internal temperature returned to its preset frigidity. It was impossible to open the freezer door more frequently than once every five minutes. However, the sealing mechanism was not perfect. The door could be opened—with a determined effort. But, since European appliances are smaller than those in the United States, the determined effort required two hands. (One to wrench the door open; the other to hold the refrigerator in place.) Members of The Martin Family, like most human beings, come equipped with only two hands. If one hand is, for example, holding an ice-cube tray full of non-congealed water, there are insufficient remaining hands to open the freezer. The usual result was a small (or more frequently large) puddle of water on the floor. The Martin Family worked on a solution to this problem. The children suggested a "buddy system" arrangement.

These issues were mere bugs on the windshield of life. The Martin Family was no longer deprived of a basic necessity for civilized life. We were now prepared and ready to face new challenges and adventure in a foreign land.

Ice cubes—the mark of Western Civilization. Do you think Attila the Hun had ice cubes? What about Genghis Khan? The Vandal hoards sacking Rome? I was quite happy to crunch away, and I was adjusted. (Later, Nazy discovered real ice-cube trays for sale at Blokker's in The Hague.)

I thought it was quaint and European to ride the tram to work and do the daily grocery shopping in the Bankastraat shopping district close to the house. Of course, I didn't have to carry the groceries home. Nazy, who did carry the groceries, had a different opinion.

SHOP! AND YOU'LL DROP

I was sure that Nazy, the consummate shopper, would be enthralled with the wonder of European shopping. Her insatiable spirit had been somewhat dampened by lack of variety in Hanover, but here in The Hague, I knew that would change. I imagined ecstasy would replace all thoughts of home as she discovered the pleasures of the Passage and the Denneweg shopping districts. Centrum was a veritable bazaar of wonderful little shops. I did expect a few minor "settling in" problems—I didn't know how Nazy would cope with the crowds and anticipated comments about the limited hours that the stores were open.

My worries were misplaced. Nazy happily explored the vibrant shopping districts that I recommended and discovered many more on her own. She noticed that there are small areas about every eight blocks. (It seemed to us that the limited shopping hours, coupled with the high population density, mandated distributed stores.)

She was quite happy with the Bankastraat shopping area, which was within walking distance of our house. She made friends with the *winkeliers* (shopkeepers) and became quite European in the realm of grocery acquisition. She picked up fruit and vegetables from the *groente-winkel*, fish from the *vishandel*, bread from the *bakker*, and meat from the *slager*. She even resurrected a memory from my youth—the *melkboer* (milkman) who delivers. She was getting quite fit by making the daily trek toward Bankastraat.

For other shopping, she took the trams to the Passage or Stevinstraat and was able to walk to the Denneweg shopping area. She found potters, jewelry, antiques, and more different kinds of clothing stores than I imagined possible. It looked as though everything was under control.

The Thanksgiving holiday loomed. The Martin Family was determined to celebrate a traditional American Thanksgiving, complete with all the fixings. (It didn't matter to us that it's not an official Dutch holiday—the children were out of school and *we were going to celebrate*.) But Thanksgiving dinner requires a complete assortment of ingredients. Nazy, while healthy from the daily strolls to Bankastraat, was not interested in carting a complete Thanksgiving dinner home, one bag at a time.

"Come on, Dan," she said. "This is Europe, not some backwater dump in the middle of nowhere. I'm sure they have supermarkets."

I supposed there must be supermarkets in The Hague, but my simple needs had been met in Bankastraat. "We're in Europe," I replied. "Let's do things the European way. They buy groceries every day, why can't we? It's worked so far, hasn't it?"

Nazy was unperturbed. "Yes, dear, it has. But from now on, I'll expect you to help carry the daily groceries home."

"Let's get out the *telefoon* book and see if we can't find a supermarket. I suddenly understand the urgency of the situation."

We couldn't find anything in the *Gouden Gids* (Yellow Pages). Do *you* know the Dutch word for supermarket? While I was scanning the Dutch/English dictionary, Nazy was being more inventive. She called Maggie O'Reilly and found out about the Konmar Supermarket. Thanksgiving grocery shopping was scheduled for the next day. I would be at work. Nazy would brave the wonders of the European supermarket with the children.

When the group arrived at the Konmar, they were astounded. The store was a vast edifice with wide aisles, huge shopping carts, and a complete selection of everything even marginally related to cooking or food. Melika observed that the store was a bit crowded, but she solved her problem by walking *underneath* the cart. It was a dangerous gambit—the carts had an interesting steering mechanism: All four wheels, rather than just the front two, could be used for steering. This meant that Darius, the official Martin family cart pusher, could make an immediate perpendicular jog. Whenever he did this, Melika banged her head and was ejected into the crowd, where she quickly disappeared.

These minor problems notwithstanding, Nazy and the children plunged into the fray. Darius inched (okay, they were in Europe, so he millimetered) forward. There are always problems when you shop at a new store. Since you don't know where things are, you run the risk of missing something. These problems were exacerbated by not speaking Dutch. Well-known brand names weren't available. ("Mommy, we *have* to find Life Cereal or at least Honey Nut Cheerios.") The language barrier caused a few other difficulties.

We needed cinnamon, but when sent on the expedition to the spice counter, Mitra couldn't find it. (Do *you* know the Dutch word for cinnamon?) Mitra assumed that since everyone spoke English, she wouldn't have a problem. (I hadn't told her about my adventure with the extension cord.) While almost everyone did speak conversational English, "cinnamon" is rarely used in day-to-day chats.

After Mitra had worked her way to the cart to confess failure, Nazy sent her back with new instructions: Unscrew the lids and smell the spices. "And remember, Mitra, cinnamon is red, so you won't have to unscrew them all."

The idea was good—cinnamon does have a unique smell—but the plan was foiled. Konmar spices came in sealed plastic bags. An American expatriate rescued Mitra. (The expat knew the Dutch word for cinnamon: *kaneel*.) Mitra grabbed several envelopes and looked for our cart.

By now, Nazy and the rest of the group had made their way to the meat counter. Ordering ground beef was not straightforward. What did we want? *Tartaar? Rundergehakt? Gehakt?* Nazy solved the problem in her typical manner—she bought the most expensive.

The projected one-hour trip stretched to two as they picked up fruit, vegetables, milk, juices, and twenty-three-hole notebook paper. (The school mandated twenty-three-ring binders for the elementary and middle schools. Why twenty-three? I don't know. It must be a magic number in the metric system.)

The weary explorers were, by now, anxious to depart, but a quick exit was not in the cards. The crowds had grown steadily thicker as the family made its way through the store. They got stuck in a gridlock in the middle of the toilet paper section. (Considering the way they felt, it was appropriate.) Nazy sent Darius ahead to scout out the problem. He returned with the bad news.

"This is the line to pay, Mommy. There are forty-seven carts in front of us."

The disgusted family was now introduced to European queue courtesy: If there is a millimeter of space between you and the cart in front of you, a fellow sufferer will attempt to shove himself in the unused space. Disgruntled shoppers behind Nazy were upset when she "let" someone cut in. They expressed their dismay by shoving their carts into Nazy's back.

Darius was particularly unamused and used the opportunity to trumpet his fine grasp of the new language. (You don't want to know what *klootzak* means.)

Eventually, they made it with the cart, heaped full of Thanksgiving cuisine, to the cashier.

There was an evil grin on the clerk's face as she explained to Nazy, "Eight items or less." It was the express line. (Do *you* know the Dutch word for express?)

All was not lost. Nazy had to back the cart out of the "express" lane. In the ensuing tumult, she was able to take advantage of a dumb American who had left not a millimeter, but an entire meter, in his queue. Checkout was in sight.

The checkout process was amazingly automated. Super-efficient scanners read the bar codes and totaled the prices. Then the cashier tightly stacked the groceries, without bags, back into the cart. (Baggers haven't made it to Holland.)

This was a modern supermarket, though. They recognized the problem. They sold bags (ten for three guilders) in an anteroom behind the checkout area. Darius bought the bags and the entire family unpacked the cart and filled them. When they were done, they placed the bags back in the cart. (This makes a lot of sense. The cart had now been filled three times: It was empty at the beginning and Nazy filled it in the process of shopping. The family emptied it onto the conveyer belt at the checkout counter, and the clerk filled it back up after each item was scanned. The family emptied its contents into bags and put the bags back in the cart.)

The immense feeling of accomplishment was tempered by the three hours that the mission took. And it wasn't over. A final chamber at the store contained cheese, flowers, and chicken. For some reason, these items are purchased separately. Nazy, in a foul mood, bought some fowl and some cheese. They had used up the bags, so Darius stuffed the cheese into his pockets. Melika bought a bouquet of lilies. (Nazy hoped she wouldn't have to use them.)

They called a cab and made it home.

STUMBLING THROUGH THE TULIPS

I was there watching the BBC (*Cricket: From Insect to Wicket; Part 1 of a Special Documentary*). Worried, I proceeded to pour oil on the fire.

"What happened, Nazy? Where were you?"

"We spent the last four hours at the Konmar."

"Grocery shopping, eh? How could you possibly waste four hours at the grocery store? Oh, well, it doesn't matter, I'm hungry. Let's eat." (I should have taken heed of Mitra's frantic hand motions.)

"Get your coat, Dan. We're eating out tonight."

"Why? We've got all these groceries."

Quick to the rescue, Mitra interjected, "Just get your coat, Daddy."

A quick, pre-Thanksgiving meal at McDonald's soothed everyone. Later that evening Nazy and I put the groceries away. There were some strange items. The yeast, for example, didn't come in little envelopes, it came in a plastic bag. (It was alive, and it was multiplying—the bag was about to explode.)

As we put the last item in the cupboard, Nazy discovered that someone had forgotten the pumpkin.

"Dan, dear, could you run down to the Konmar to get some pumpkin for me?"

"Sure. What time is it?"

"It's nine o'clock, dear."

"I'd love to, but the stores are closed now. *You* can get it tomorrow."

The bag of yeast exploded against the wall, very close to my ear.

> *Thanksgiving wouldn't have been complete without a turkey. We ordered a fresh bird from the slager (butcher) on the Bankastraat. But as novice Europeans, we were metric-challenged.* Mixing up the pound to kilo conversion, Nazy had ordered *an eighteen-kilo turkey. I took my bike to the Bankastraat to pick it up.*

Imagine my surprise when the butcher hopped on a forklift when I arrived. Consider the look on my face when I was confronted with an ostrich-sized turkey that weighed more than Melika. I couldn't get it home on the bike, so I called a local moving company.

Nazy had similar problems. Not only did the bird did not fit in the Dutch oven, we had problems wedging it into the Dutch kitchen.

Grocery shopping remained a big pain. Nazy located a store specializing in American items—at three times the prices we were used to in the States. Happy with the Dutch cuisine, we really didn't use it very much. Dutch food must be healthy—it has no preservatives. (We soon learned why preservatives are used—it preserves the food. Dutch bread, sans preservative, might be fresh when you get it to the house if you take a fast train. If you don't? Then the bread crusts transform into road-paving material by the time you get home.) Other shopping items remained elusive until Nazy conquered the city. Arm & Hammer baking soda? Available at the Chinese restaurant shop. Chamomile tea? The drug store.

So The Martin Family celebrated Thanksgiving. Christmas wasn't far behind.

SINTER WHO?

Melika was convincing: "It's true, Sinterklaas will come—with presents—on December fifth."

"Sinter who?" I asked.

"Sinterklaas! I learned all about it in school. He will come to our house and give us *presents*. We leave our wooden shoes (can we get some wooden shoes?) outside and he puts candy in the shoes every day. And then on the fifth of December he leaves a bag of presents. He also leaves poems about people."

"But if Sinterklaas comes on December fifth, Santa Claus probably won't come on December twenty-fifth."

"Daddy! That's the stupidest thing you've ever said."

"I'm sorry, that *was* a pretty stupid thing to say. What about these poems?"

"Sinterklaas leaves poems for everybody. It's like a joke. You're supposed to figure out who the poem is about."

It looked as though there would be no choice. Sinterklaas *had* to visit The Martin Family. His appointment had to be kept secret: We didn't want the competition—Santa Claus—to feel slighted. I wondered about these Sinterklaas poems. They were rumored to be sarcastic.

> The homework, good grief, it's found everywhere!
> Some pieces are here. Some parts of it there.
> It's even been stuffed in Mellie's Brown Bear.
> Science papers clutter the bath and the hall.
> Math projects linger and down the stairs fall.
> French assignments? Scattered hither and yon,
> Picking up after is simply not fun.
> Photography projects? Stuffed in pink files.
> History Essays? In little blue piles.
> Green notebooks with cartoons—thought to bring smiles.
> To get past the mess, you have to walk miles.

The holiday season was upon us, but we were away from friends and family. It didn't feel like Christmas. It was cool, cloudy, dark, dank, and drippy. There wasn't any snow. We weren't quite at home. Our car, our clothes, our toys, and our beds were still in transit somewhere in the North Atlantic. When we selected Mayflower Transit, I thought we were picking a moving company. Elapsed time indicated that I had actually chosen a ship. I wish I'd picked one with a motor.

Christmas decorations were slow to appear in The Hague, but Sinterklaas did make a ship-borne arrival in late November. The family took the tram to the second harbor. Actually the family, letting me lead, took a tram to the *vicinity* of the second harbor. We joined thousands of other merrymakers. Sinterklaas, surrounded by hundreds of *Zwarte Pieten* (his

Spanish helpers), arrived in a huge boat. He even brought his great white horse. He was wearing his bishop outfit and carrying a long staff.

Zwarte Pieten danced around giving licorice and candy to all the children who were strong and determined enough to barge to the front of the crowds. Everyone (except The Martin Family) was singing traditional, seasonal songs in Dutch.

Introduced to Sinterklaas, we were now in the holiday spirit. All our friends recommended a Christmas shopping expedition to Germany. Well-informed sources indicated that the Düsseldorf shopping district was really nice. Nazy booked a day trip by bus, which left Centraal Station very early.

The trip was uneventful (except that Darius did manage to get his passport stamped). Düsseldorf was amazing. Our bus was parked with hundreds of others in a paddock outside the city, and we took the (typically efficient) German train into town. The center of the city was festively decorated. We divided our deutsche marks and separated for some serious shopping.

> Someone here is the geography whiz,
> But I'm getting sick of taking the quiz.
> The U.S.A. capitol? Washington DC.
> Honduras, Mongolia? Please don't ask me.
> The geography notebook is clever and neat,
> Unlike his room, where you can't see your feet.
> Clothes are thrown all over the room.
> The only thing useful? Something called VOOM.
> But when he has lost it, no ONE can find it.
> But while they're all looking, he'll sure have a fit.
> He knows where it is! He remembers it well.
> It'll lay there and rot, till we find it by smell.

Nazy and the girls were a bit more serious than Darius and I. They bought Christmas presents; we found things to eat. (Why do the Germans sell fifteen-inch hot dogs in a two-inch bun?) We did fast-food comparisons. Did you know that beer is on the McDonald's menu in Düsseldorf? We even found Coke Classic.

By The Martin Family measure of shopping, the day was a complete success: We were totally bereft of deutsche marks. We hopped on a punctual train and returned to the acres of buses parked outside town. Everyone from Holland was shopping in Germany, and they had all arrived by Dutch bus. The Germans were busy shopping in Amsterdam.

I was sure we would never find the bus. I conveyed my feelings to Nazy. "This is incredible! There are more buses in Düsseldorf than there are documentaries on the BBC."

Nazy was quick to put things back in perspective. "That's the biggest exaggeration I've ever heard, Dan. There are probably only a few thousand buses here." She was right. We located the bus and made the trip home. It was a good thing it was a tour bus; The Martin Family's packages could be stored below.

> Someone insists that we shop
> Till we drop
> Every last guilder in a bottomless pot.
> A scandalous plot. A burial spot
> Can't be afforded if she simply won't stop.
> Who cares? Have a great Christmas here in The Hague.
> And about the expenses? Be customarily vague.

Sinterklaas Dag was gray, wet, and rainy. We didn't have a Christmas tree. They hadn't yet arrived in the city. Dutch transportation authorities did their best to foster the holiday spirit by dressing the tram police in Sinterklaas costumes.

The Martin Family's efforts to foster the spirit were more traditional. Nazy baked sugar cookies, the children wrote letters to Sinterklaas, and I made sure the roof was clear and the damper was open. (Sinterklaas sometimes shares the chimney with Santa Claus.) I assured Melika that Sinterklaas knew about Nikes and Reeboks. "We don't need wooden shoes, Melika." The children stuffed notes into their sneakers; I stuffed my note into my cowboy boots. Nazy, less confident about my advice, used a real pair of tourist clogs.

Because we were new, we weren't sure just when Sinterklaas would make his appearance. The family retired to the drawing room to read. We briefly considered watching the finals of the World Sheepdog Championship on BBC1, but heard a bell and dashed downstairs. The curtain was still fluttering, but the saint had made his getaway. Melika had been right—Sinterklaas had come to visit.

> Reading a book, with glasses so smashing,
> This little girl looks mighty dashing.
> She's reading, she's thinking, she's sleeping, she's dreaming.
> We wonder what kind of a plan she is scheming.
> For everything must be ordered and planned
> That, you see, is her minor demand.
> She's organized, careful, cautious, and calm,
> But if you get in her way, you'll need some lip balm.

Following the successful Sinterklaas day, we began The Martin Family Christmas plans. Mitra, excited by the triangular Dutch Christmas stamps, artfully developed a way of applying them to look like an angel. She then set up a business (Christmas stamps, professionally applied by Mitra K. Martin Enterprises, Ltd.) and handed me an invoice for her personal assistance. Darius and I, having squandered our day in Germany, had to arrange some serious Christmas shopping expeditions. Nazy resumed work on Mitra's needlepoint Christmas stocking (expected completion date: the turn of the millennium). Melika, predictably efficient, had completed her shopping and wrapped her gifts. She couldn't understand the confusion, panic, and distress of the rest of the family.

Christmas, of course, is not complete without a Christmas tree. The Martin Family had grand plans in this area. Where would we put it? The drawing room, of course. We stopped by the Malieveld Christmas Tree Winkel after enjoying the Circus van Moskou.

The drawing room sported a high ceiling—about five meters. We wanted a Christmas tree worthy of the vast residence we were enjoying in Holland. Unaware that the "ceiling" in an open-air shop is really (really!) high, we bought a truly grand tree. Delivery would take place the following day.

The next day brought a few problems. The tree was not only grand, it was six meters high. Moreover, the Prinsevinkenpark home accoutrements (supplied by the landlord) didn't include a Christmas tree stand. And the only way that tree would make it up the stairs to the drawing room would be if an earthquake brought the drawing room down to ground level.

> Someone moved the whole family
> To Holland, my dear!
> He told everyone there was nothing to fear.
> He's always filling the house full of smoke.
> (We breathe, we cough, we rattle and choke.)
> My God! What on Earth is wrong with this bloke?

We decided to install the tree in the dining room and I sprang into action. I walked to Bankastraat to buy a saw (we needed to eliminate one meter of tree) and a tree stand. My excursion was a partial success—I got the saw. I couldn't find the stand. Back home, we carefully apportioned out the remaining work. Nazy agreed to locate a tree stand, Darius and I would cut the tree down to size, and Mitra and Melika would make a trip to Babylon for Christmas tree lights. Our lights, air-shipped from New England, were one hundred and twenty volts. Plugging one-hundred-and-twenty-volt U.S. Christmas decorations into the two-hundred-and-twenty-volt continental current would have been a (briefly) enlightening experience.

Nazy was somewhat dismayed to find out that Christmas tree stands are not a Dutch staple. After she checked the Bankastraat (she didn't believe that I'd looked), the Passage, Scheveningen, Denneweg, and the Konmar, she dropped into a neighbor's house. Emma told her that the Dutch simply nailed a wooden cross to the bottom of the tree. (Mixing up Easter and Christmas perhaps?) Nazy pointed out that tree stands provide water for the tree, but Emma was not convinced.

"Water, Nazy? Why water?"

"Well, the water keeps the tree wet so it won't catch fire from the lights. Isn't a dry tree dangerous?"

"There's no real danger. Just keep a bucket of water nearby."

Nazy envisioned conflagration in spite of the "bucket solution," so she located a tree stand at Babylon. Unfortunately, the stand was more appropriate for a Christmas twig. My proposed solution—a garbage can filled with concrete—was vetoed and Nazy departed for a more extensive search of the local shops.

Meanwhile, Darius and I hacked the bottom meter off the tree. We moved the dining room table into the back yard and set up a block and tackle to transport the tree into the dining room.

Nazy finally returned with a German Christmas tree stand made of wrought iron. It was built to withstand Armageddon and had a long German name: *Christbaumständer*. It didn't provide for a water supply, so we decided to spray the tree frequently. (I walked to Bankastraat for a bucket.)

The tree finally looked wonderful. The Russian blue spruce dominated the dining room. This tree was so large it would have dominated Sequoia National Park. Festively decorated presents were stacked in the hall, as there was no space left in the dining room. We succumbed to the Dutch wrapping practice of attaching thousands of colorful ribbons to every package.

Christmas morning dawned early (The Hague is on European time—six hours ahead of Eastern Standard Time). Santa Claus had indeed made a special visit to the Netherlands. There was one small problem: The Russian blue spruce had been hacked from Siberian tundra the previous July. The German stand and the lack of water had taken their toll. At precisely noon on Christmas day, The Martin Family Christmas tree underwent explosive and spontaneous decomposition. Every needle dropped off. It didn't matter. The family was happy, festive, and cheerful.

Later that day, we checked out the traditional Christmas TV viewing. The BBC had an address from the Archbishop of Canterbury. This was followed by a documentary on BBC1 called *Hadrian's Wall: Stone by Bloody Stone*. BBC2 had a seasonal program, *Crocodile Dundee*. It was better than the counter-programming on Nederland 2—*Carla Does Christmas with Carlos: A Pin-up Club Special Production*.

That evening we dragged the tree into the courtyard, and it disappeared that night. The Dutch collect old Christmas trees for New Year bonfires.

Christmas festivities were fun, but they marked the end of the beginning. We had to stop acting like tourists and begin acting like natives. That meant that having to venture into the dreaded and frightening land of Dutch bureaucracy. Holland was physically created by the Dutch. Polders (parts of low lands reclaimed from the sea) were constructed and windmills were built to pump water into the canals. Historically, the Dutch handled the tasks of maintaining and controlling the pumping process through very careful organization and procedures. This ability has become a national trait. The Dutch are organized, the Dutch are proceduralized, and the Dutch have created a massive, awesome, impenetrable bureaucracy, one that The Martin Family, unprepared, was about to collide with. We were babes in the woods.

BUT THAT'S NOT A NUMBER!

It was seven-thirty in the morning, and the *telefoon* at Prinsevinkenpark Estate was ringing. I was in London. Nazy, whose cheerfulness and quick wit aren't operational before ten a.m., was the unwitting answerer.

The voice on the other end was direct. "*U spreekt met Smits. Waar zijn de papieren voor uw auto?* Where are the papers for your car?"

"What papers?"

"You cannot import an automobile without papers."

And so began the import saga. It seems that Mayflower Transit had safely stored the papers for our Ford Taurus in Indianapolis. The car was in Rotterdam. Several days later the papers arrived. We anxiously awaited the next dialogue with Smits.

"*Met Smits. Deze papieren zijn slecht.* These are the wrong papers. You cannot import an automobile with bad papers."

Another *telefoon* call to the States set additional square wheels into finely tuned, but bumpy, motion. Nazy was blustering. I was calm. (Once again, she was in The Hague and I was in London.) The semi-correct papers finally arrived. Smits arranged a meeting with customs officials for eight-thirty the next morning. Unfortunately, the meeting was in Rijswijk and the children attend school in The Hague. Nazy couldn't be in both places at the same time. There wouldn't have been a problem if we had a car, but…

Nazy postponed the meeting. Smits was incredulous.

"We have worked very hard to arrange all of these appointments. You cannot cancel. It's not possible."

Possible or not, a new meeting was arranged for the following Tuesday. Nazy was warned to bring plenty of cash. She was also told that the process would take two hours. The cash part worried me; we were living in Holland. Papers, not bribes, had seemed the order of the day.

Months of careful observation of Dutch traffic had convinced me that insurance was absolutely necessary. So, in the interim before the grand meeting with customs, I contacted the Kröller insurance agency. Car insurance in Holland is not cheap. I knew the risk I was taking by walking into to an insurance sales office. Nevertheless, I did. I left shortly thereafter. I was bereft of guilders, but fully covered.

The following morning was announced by the familiar jangle of Smits's *telefoon* call. The *telefoon* is on Nazy's side of the bed. Sometimes I do think ahead; she had to deal with the problem.

"*Met Smits. Wat is het nummer voor uw auto?*" (What is the license plate number on your car?)

Proud of our New Hampshire vanity plate, Nazy was quick. "-BRRR"

"*Dat is geen nummer! Wat is uw nummer?*"

"DASH B, then three Rs."

"What is 'DASH'?"

Things continued along in this vein for a while. Finally, Smits agreed to enter "-BRRR" as the license number. He still wasn't happy, and he had a final arrow to sling.

"Live free or die. What does that mean?" he asked as he broke the connection.

"Smits just doesn't 'get' the New Hampshire state motto," I thought.

The next morning, Nazy and I arrived for the two-hour session with customs. At ten a.m. sharp—they are punctual in Holland—Smits arrived.

His demeanor was grave. "We have a bad problem, Mr. Martin."

I cringed, but I wasn't surprised. "What is it?"

"We need your date of birth, Mr. Martin. Also, does this automobile have a two- or a three-liter engine?"

"September 27, 1946. Three liters."

"Okay, 27 September, 1946, three. I'll just be a minute."

Three and a half hours later, he returned with the announcement that the papers were ready and we could drive over to customs.

During the extended wait in the customs office (there was only one computer terminal shared by the fifteen agents), Smits explained the remainder of the procedure.

"Your Taurus is a very expensive car in the Netherlands. Because you owned it for several months before you moved, you don't have to pay duty. I spent this morning computing the amount of duty you don't have to pay."

"Why would you do that, *Meneer* Smits?" I asked, cleverly injecting my only Dutch word into the conversation.

"In a moment. The duty is 34,743 guilders. You must be very careful not to sell your car before January 15, 1991. The customs police can call at your house any time between now and then. If you are not able to produce the vehicle, they can immediately collect the duty. This is a lot of money, so they probably will show up at your house."

"A lot of money! That's no joke," I thought. "It's more than I paid for the car when I bought it three years ago." Now I was sure to sell it as soon as it was "legal."

Smits was still talking. "After the customs agent inspects the car—which he'll do as soon as he finishes entering the forms I filled out into his computer—you must take this green paper to a post office. Give them 276.50 guilders and ask for the yellow form. They will send your green form to the Department of Transportation.

"In about five weeks, you'll get a letter from the Transportation Department with the appointment for your technical inspection in Rotterdam. Before you go to the technical inspection, go to a Ford garage and change your lights to the 'E' configuration."

I interrupted. "What's wrong with the lights?"

"American cars have sealed beams. Sealed beams are not legal in Holland."

"Why not?"

"Tradition. Perhaps in five or ten years they'll be made legal. Anyway, about two weeks after the technical inspection, you'll receive parts one and three of your registration form. Place part one on your front windshield. By the way, you have to give twenty-four guilders cash money to the postman to get this package. Take Part three to the post office with one hundred and thirty-five guilders and get the application for Part two. Send completed Part two application, with an *acceptgiro* for two hundred and fifty-two guilders, to the Bureau of Motor Vehicles for road taxes. In return mail, you'll receive the accepted application for part two. This will contain your Dutch license plate number. And, Dr. Martin," he snootily commented, "it will be a *real* number. Take the accepted part two application to any garage. They'll make your Dutch license plate. When that arrives, staple a copy of part two to your copy of part three and store those in your house. Take the original of part two and store that in the glove compartment of your car with a duplicate copy of the blue appendix of part three. If you want to drive outside of the Netherlands, go to any grocery store and get an 'NL' sticker to place on the back of your car. Glue it just to the right, and a little above, the Dutch license plate. Don't forget to call your insurance company to change the number on your insurance to your new Dutch license number…"

He was still going strong, but the customs people were ready for the inspection.

They asked me to pop the hood while they checked that the vehicle identification number stamped on the engine block matched their paperwork. (It would have been amazing if it hadn't. Smits had stamped the number onto the engine block just before we left for the customs office. The American custom of a little plate on the dashboard is inadequate in Europe.)

"Everything looks fine, Mr. Martin. Tell me, does this car have cruise control?"

I was in a quandary. I knew that if I said yes, the paperwork would have to be redone. (I had read the list of options on his copy of the papers.) Nazy, who was too short to see the forms, was quick to respond.

"Yes, it does have cruise control."

Customs and Smits sighed simultaneously. Smits was quick to intercede. A brief conversation in Dutch created some compromise. The forms would be completed tomorrow, but the car could leave now.

The drive home was uneventful. We didn't hit any bicyclists and we didn't get lost. We were lucky to be finished just before rush hour, and our luck held when it came to parking.

Nazy had spent the previous week scouting Den Haag for the only parking place large enough to hold an American station wagon. Miraculously, that space was directly in front of our house.

So we had begun the certification process. Our car was both here and drivable. All we had to do was collect enough courage to actually use it. It wouldn't be easy. There were too many things to keep track of in

The Hague. In the States, you worry about other cars. Here, you worry about cars, drawbridges, trams, trains, bicycles, pedestrians, buses, and a plethora of traffic rules that everyone else seems to understand. But if we were actually able to get a Dutch license plate—with a real number—we had probably demonstrated that we were clever enough to drive the car.

I was still a bit worried. Smits called to explain the procedure for getting a Dutch driver's license. I got lost somewhere between the blue attachment to part six and the yellow copy of my passport photo.

We like vanity license plates, but they don't do that in the Netherlands. Now we live in Switzerland. Unexpectedly, they gave Nazy her choice of license plate number. She chose the "best one": ZH 631 721—because both 631 and 721 add up to ten (digit by digit). Unimpressed, I asked if she could have found one with prime numbers. It was an unfortunate comment; Nazy had spent a few hours in the queue.

Eventually, we got a Dutch license plate. It took nine months, but we did it! The first technical inspection appointment was missed because we couldn't read the note announcing it. We were late for our second appointment when the car wouldn't start, but you can't blame that on the government.

Our New Hampshire vanity plate continued to receive stares until we passed the inspection. We got parts one and three, but Smits hadn't told us about the problems caused by wanting a non-standard license plate. The standard yellow Dutch plate won't fit in the standard Taurus license plate slot. But not to worry! There is a procedure for this problem. You get a notarized engineering drawing of the front and rear license compartments, take a color photograph of the back of the car, and get approval from the city police. Can the automatic cameras that trap you when you speed readably photograph the registration number on a smaller license plate? Finally, file and application with the Ministry of Exceptions...

For us, the inspection process was actually rather simple. After we found the station, we acted ignorant. In the end, the only thing we had to do was disable the center brake light at the rear of the car. It turned out that acting ignorant but pleasant was a good strategy. A German woman behind us didn't act ignorant, she was ignorant. And she wasn't pleasant as she wheeled her giant Mercedes into the inspection station.

"Get on with it," she shouted. "I'm in a hurry."

"Kan niet,"[2] replied the clerk as he began to dismantle the car. He was weighing bolts when we left.

License plates aside, we had a more pressing problem. Nazy's driver's license was about to expire. Another voyage into Dutch governmental wilderness was necessary.

---

2 . "That's not possible."

THEY'RE DRIVING ME CRAZY!

Nazy's cheerful demeanor, ebullient nature, and innate optimism would all be needed in our upcoming foray into Dutch officialdom. The task ahead seemed simple enough. All she wanted was a Dutch driving license. However, The Martin Family had already been initiated into the intricacies of Dutch bureaucracy. We knew it wouldn't be easy, but it couldn't be too tricky: A quick view of the traffic in The Hague made it clear that millions of people had licenses. Our Dutch friends comforted us with the news that "it used to be really complex but they've simplified it."

It should be noted that it was Nazy, not me, who made the initial trek. Discussions, ratified in a family meeting, confirmed the idea that she had the "right personality" for the task. Besides, I like to wait until the last minute. Nazy was early—her New Hampshire license wouldn't expire for at least two weeks.

Buoyed by the knowledge that the process was "simplified," Nazy made the trip to the town hall. An impressively brief (two hour) wait later, she was talking with a clerk. The form, in Dutch, was indecipherable. After an attempt with the Dutch-English dictionary, Nazy asked for help.

The clerk was alert. "Can you not read the form?"

Nazy was just as quick. "Of course I can read it. I just don't know what it means."

The clerk was unimpressed. "Are you healthy? Is anything wrong with you?"

"I'm fine. There's nothing wrong with me."

The clerk filled out the form for Nazy, a matter of writing *nee* (no) fifty times on the half-meter long document. "Now you have to take the form to Rijswijk."

"What do they do in…" Nazy began, but the clerk had left. Town hall was *gesloten* (closed).

On the tram to Rijswijk, Nazy was able to translate enough of the form to know it was a medical questionnaire. She was relieved to discover that the clerk thought she was healthy.

In Rijswijk, I met Nazy for lunch and for the trip to the various bureaus there—it was the least I could do. We made it to the *centrum* (city center) and handed the form and six guilders to the clerk. She placed the form in an envelope and filled out a receipt for the six guilders, and we were directed across the street to another division. (I'm convinced the function of this particular bureau was to agree that the initial form had been filled out correctly. Apparently, they, too, thought Nazy was healthy.)

The next division was the sole occupant of a building that was under construction. We had been directed to room 341, so we took the elevator to the third floor. Because we were in Europe, it was really the fourth floor. However, since the third floor was only a concrete skeleton, and surely not adequate chambers for an official government division, we began a systematic search of the building. We finally located room 341 on floor zero. Additional clerks took the forms, our payment voucher, and two guilders, and proceeded to type our responses onto a duplicate application. After the expected wait, we signed a few documents (in Dutch, so we really don't know what they said). We obtained an envelope full of additional forms, and Nazy was directed back to the town hall. It suddenly became very important for me to return to my office.

The following day, Nazy decided to call the town hall to make sure she had everything she needed. "That was a good decision," she thought as she dashed downtown to get passport photos. Then she collected her birth certificate, passport, and certificate of town registry and, confident of impending success, she drove to the town hall.

The situation, like the weather, looked gloomy. Nazy grabbed a number—435—and noted with dismay that they were currently "serving" number 106. But we had lived in Holland for five months; Nazy was a veteran. She had a book. She made the mistake of partaking of the free coffee.

The Dutch do know how to make coffee. It's fresh. It's perked. It's strong. The cream? Another story. The Dutch think cream is for wimps. It is not replenished at regular intervals and is not refrigerated. It caused Nazy some tummy dismay.

While reading her book, she wondered if she might throw up all over the town hall. Several chapters later, her number appeared on the scoreboard-size display. Nazy worked her way through the crowd. She arrived just after two Dutch ladies who were also tired of waiting. Nazy, who had the magic number, had to stand back and let the clerk fight it out with the interlopers. She finally made it to the desk.

Quick with people, Nazy listened to the clerk's introduction. "*Ik ben Mw. Auldham-Breary. Verstaat U Nederlands?*" Nazy thought she remembered the name, but nullified this strategic success with a tactical blunder.

"*Nee*, I don't speak Dutch, Mrs. Old and Dreary, I just want my driver's license. Is this my final stop?"

The subsequent conversation showed that it is possible, even when everyone is speaking English, to have a communication breakdown.

"Well, Mrs. Martin, you give me all of the papers and your American driver's license and the passport photos and we will mail you a Dutch license."

"Mail me a license? When will I get it?"

"It usually takes about two weeks. But we're rather busy, so it will take six weeks."

"Six weeks?"

"Normally two weeks."

Ms. Auldham-Breary was scrutinizing Nazy's New Hampshire license. It was with a grave demeanor that she spoke up.

"You have a problem, Mrs. Martin. Your license has expired."

"My license has not expired."

"It has. It says the expiration date is 04-01-90. Today is March 17. January 4 has already passed. You have an expired license and must fill out an alternate set of documents."

An alternate set of documents. The very idea threw Nazy into panic. "But in the States, they write the dates differently. This license expires on April 1, 1990."

"They all say that, Mrs. Martin."

"I'm saying it again. Can you ask your supervisor?"

Forty minutes later, that minor problem was resolved, but a major problem remained. Unyielding (and uncomfortable), Nazy waded back into the fray. She wasn't completely satisfied with her small victory. She wanted a license and she wanted it now!

"You want to take my old license. But if you take my old license and don't give me a new one, I won't have a license for six weeks. Isn't that right?"

"That is correct."

"Can I drive my car without a license?"

"Yes. But if the police stop you, then you will have to pay a fine."

"Can you give me a permit indicating that I have applied for a license?"

"That's not possible."

"Is there some way I can keep my old license?"

"Naturally. But you must fill out this alternate petition in triplicate. We'll take your license and mail it to you in…"

"Yes, I know, six weeks."

"That is correct, Mrs. Martin."

"Let me try this again. I want to keep my New Hampshire license until I get my Dutch license. Is that clear?"

"That is perfectly clear, Mrs. Martin. But it's not possible."

"I have my car parked outside. Should I leave it here until my Dutch license arrives?"

"You can't leave it here, it's not possible. You'll get fined. You must drive it home."

"Can I drive it without a license?"

"Of course, but if the police stop you…"

"I know, I'll have to pay a fine. Isn't there something you can give me to show the police so that I won't have to pay a fine?"

"That's not possible, Mrs. Martin. In six weeks, when you get your license in the post, please have forty-eight guilders to pay the postman."

"What about my New Hampshire license?"

"Fill out that form, then take it to Rijswijk…."

"*Kan niet!*" *(It's not possible) is taught to government employees in the course "Basic Bureaucracy 101: Befuddle, Bewilder, and Bedazzle the Citizen." I do not miss this expression. Perhaps we really shouldn't complain about Dutch bureaucracy. The American government, for example, gave us a form to import edible fowl when we tried to bring Canadian parakeets into Houston. A friend from Nigeria claims that the process in the Netherlands is amazingly simple and quick. And it does seem to work, if you know the process and have developed European patience. Besides, Nazy got a driver's license that was valid for twenty-five years! And we found out that it's really not that complicated. If you apply early, you can do everything in one visit. (Well, there is an extra form to fill out to bypass all the visits to various other offices.)*

It really doesn't matter anyway. You don't need a license. Public transportation is completely reliable and always available.

DE TRAMHALTE NIET

It was (indeed) a dark and stormy night. The thunder was loud and the lightning was bright. Melika wasn't scared; she just couldn't sleep. After making sure we were awake (and aware that she was *not* scared), she climbed into bed with us. It was three a.m. The storm continued. At six, Mitra arrived with a simple message.

"The alarm clock went off, Dad. I'm awake."

"That's wonderful, Mitra. Is it time for me to get up?"

"No, I'm going to take a shower and then I'll wake you."

"Thanks for that news bulletin. I'll see you in a few minutes." I tried to go back to sleep, but kept wondering why Mitra had woken me up to tell me it wasn't time to get up.

Mitra was proud of herself for actually responding to the alarm clock and decided that she had plenty of time before school. She returned to bed. She fell into a deep sleep, dreaming of her awesome ability to rise and shine.

At seven forty-five, Darius arrived.

"Hey, Dad, it's almost eight. Don't ya think we should get up?"

Turning an eye to the alarm clock (which Mitra had turned off), I was quick to respond. "Go bounce Mitra out of bed and tell her I'm mad. Thanks for waking us up, Darius. How long have you been awake?"

"Gosh, Dad, I've been awake for almost an hour. I was waiting for you to come and tell me it was time to get out of bed."

"Thanks, Darius."

Breakfast was rushed. The family was not in a good mood. (Everyone was tired from the effort required to lift Nazy to her feet.) We all needed a good shot of pure caffeine. Nazy took coffee with her to the tram stop.

Things did not brighten during the mad dash to the *tramhalte* (tram stop). I had to go south toward the office; everyone else had to go north to school. Both the north- and southbound trams passed within sight of the family. Everyone had just missed theirs. Disgust was added to insult and indignity when another southbound tram zipped past before I got to the stop. The trams, scheduled to pass every seven minutes, had bunched together. That meant the next would probably arrive in fifteen minutes. We all took our places at the *tramhaltes*.

Melika opened the new forty-guilder umbrella. A *Noordzee* gale turned it inside out. The tram arrived just as she dropped the (now useless) umbrella onto the track. Nazy and the children departed in a cacophony of catcalls from fellow passengers.

On the northbound tram, as Nazy was cautioning Melika to be careful with what remained of the umbrella, a Norwegian wolfhound decided to take a sip of her coffee, which she'd set on the ground. The wolfhound was not expecting a hot liquid. It burned its tongue and began a sorrowful wail.

Mitra's stop was first and she quickly exited the melee. She couldn't believe her luck. The number fourteen bus, which goes directly to the school, was waiting. She jumped on and relaxed. Then she remembered that on Tuesdays, her first class, photography, met at the art center. It was Tuesday. The art center would have been the next stop on the tram. Mitra got off the bus and walked back toward the *tramhalte*.

Meanwhile, my tram had arrived. I had an eventful ride to Spui Street: Striking ambulance drivers had blocked the road at Mauritskade, a very pretty area with canals. And disgruntled farmers had parked their tractors in front of the Binnenhof government buildings. I arrived just in time to see my connecting tram, number one, leaving. I walked across the street to get a newspaper (I simply must have something to read during these lengthy waits). I returned to the *tramhalte* just in time to see another number one tram departing. Thirty minutes later, and fifteen minutes after I finished the newspaper, the final number one tram arrived.

Back at Kanaalweg, Mitra's tram had (re)arrived. She got on and was on her way to Duinstraat when she remembered she needed film for photography class. It was at the school. She exited the tram at Duinstraat, crossed the track, and waited for a return tram. She had to go back to Kanaalweg.

Nazy, Darius, and Melika were in fine fettle. The dog left at Kaizerstraat, but it was replaced by a large Dutch lady carrying an enormous suitcase. Darius dutifully left the tram at his stop (the *VVV*). Nazy and Melika weren't so lucky. Melika tried to climb over the suitcase but was stopped by its owner. A bystander began complaining to the suitcase wielder about the impoliteness of blocking the exit. The doors closed and the tram departed. Darius was on the curb. Melika and Nazy were not.

At Spuistraat, I was finally on my way. It was an entertaining trip. I was so late that the tram was almost empty, but not completely devoid of passengers. A single passenger, a refugee from Suriname, yelled at me for the entire ride. (She hated Holland. She hated white people. She spit on the country….) I was trying to learn Dutch and had been pleasantly surprised when she started to speak to me. By the time I got to Rijswijk, I was sick of it.

Nazy and Melika left the tram at the first stop after *VVV*, the Kurhaus, and ran back. Darius remembered family rules about waiting if he got separated. Remarkably, he had been waiting, but now he was late, and it "was all your fault, Mommy." At this point, Nazy remembered leaving her coffee cup on tram seven. Melika was relieved. It would be difficult for Mom to complain about the umbrella. It, too, was on tram seven. Perhaps Mitra would find them—she was having lots of experience on tram seven.

Mitra finally arrived at school. She retrieved her film and headed back to the *tramhalte*. A tram was just arriving. It buzzed right by the *tramhalte*. Mitra was mad. The tram driver had even waved at her. She plopped down on the bench, determined to wait it out. Unfortunately, there was no newspaper stand nearby. (Given what had happened to me, "fortunately" may be a better choice of words.)

Melika and Darius were eventually delivered to school. Nazy wearily got on bus twenty-three. Unfortunately, it is bus twenty-*two* that passes Prinsevinkenpark. She might have gotten to see the town of Zoetermeer if it hadn't been so foggy. She made it home just in time to leave to pick up the children.

When Mitra (re)arrived at Duinstraat, she was greeted by her friends returning from photography class. She crossed the tram tracks and joined them in the wait for the trip back to the school.

I took a taxi home.

There was little cheer in the Martin household that evening. The umbrella was gone, and the family was beat. Beat, perhaps, but not broken. Besides, as Scarlett O'Hara says, "Tomorrow is another day." (It began at three a.m. with a crash of thunder.)

You're not really at home until you've mastered the language. The Martin Family had linguistic experience: We'd learned to say "y'all" in Memphis, to end every question with an "eh?" in Canada, and to disregard the letter "R" in New England. Now we were in Holland. Surely we could master Dutch. Maybe! My initial forays into Flemish linguistics convinced me that the human vocal cords were unable to replicate the necessary phonemes. (The only way I could generate some of the sounds was to place a hot potato in my mouth.) To make matters worse, the grammar was complex and convoluted. I explained the situation to Nazy.

"Don't argue, Nazy," I said, "No human being can ever learn Dutch. It's impossible."

"That's absurd. About two hundred thousand children under the age of three learn to speak it every year."

Observing our efforts, many people explained why it wasn't necessary to learn the language. These opinions fell on deaf ears. (Q: Why learn Dutch? It's only spoken in Holland. A: But we are in Holland. And it's also spoken in Suriname.) More importantly, Shell was paying for a tutor named Ron; they expected me to learn Dutch.

Some of us, it turned out, have a natural affinity for languages. Some of us could even pronounce the Dutch sounds. Others? Well, the title of the next episode translates as "I don't know."

IK WEET HET NIET

It was crunch day for The Martin Family. A boisterous family meeting the night before had resulted in passage of Mitra's motion demanding a "concerted family effort" to master Dutch. Everyone had agreed to *really try* to use Dutch today.

At the office, struggling with the Dutch language homework Ron had assigned, I was waiting for Shell's coffee lady to appear. The coffee lady is a traditional Dutch benefit. Three times a day, a fresh cup of coffee is brought directly to each employee. A minor enhancement—tea instead of coffee—had been arranged by the (astounded) Dutch especially for me. Today I had determined that I would speak Dutch to the coffee lady. Ah! There she was.

"*Ik wil één kopje thée met suiker*," I intoned, thinking how continental I sounded. The response was completely unexpected.

"Yeah, look, buddy, do you speak English? I just moved here from California and I don't understand a word you're sayin'."

"Right-o," I said. (Perhaps a British accent would suffice to meet the spirit of Mitra's proposition.) "I'll have a rather light cup of tea. And, ahh, don't forget me mates down the hall. Cheers."

This ill-fated first attempt turned out to be the harbinger of things to come. I turned back to the Dutch lesson and the clever concept of separable verbs and strangulation syntax. Separable verbs break into pieces that can be scattered anywhere in a sentence. The sole purpose of such a construct is to foil efforts of novice translators who have to find, and sequence, all of the pieces. Strangulation syntax further complicates the problem by pushing all the verbs (except for their separable pieces) to the end of the sentence. In practice, this means that an incredibly good short-term memory is necessary to understand spoken Dutch; by the time you get to the verb, you've forgotten the subject. An example might be in order.

English	Dutch
Watch for the tram.	*Let op de tram.*
We watch for the tram.	*Wij letten op de tram.*
We had watched for the tram.	*Wij hebben op de tram gelet.*

Notice that the Dutch verb *opletten* is scattered all over the sentences. The "*op*" appears in many different places. The more complicated the sentence, the more likely the verbs are to congregate at the end.

The pages of my dictionary were crackling like pinecones in a forest fire as I raced through the translation assignment. I had to finish so I could start memorizing verbs and working on my short story. I was interrupted by the *telefoon*. A Dutch friend was inviting us to dinner. In the spirit of the day, I carried on the conversation in Dutch.

"*Ja, Bert, dat kan. Waar wonen jullie?*"

I just wanted to know where he lived. I had forgotten that not only can you lose track of a sentence while you're waiting for the verb, you can also get completely lost in the middle of a single word. Bert lived on Schiermonnikoogestraat. I compounded my mistake by asking him to spell it.

Spelling is tricky because the letters, in particular the vowels, are not pronounced as they are in English. "A" is pronounced like the "ah" in "ahchoo," "E" like the "a" in "ape," "I" like the "e" in "reed," and "U" like the sound you make when someone sticks their elbow in your stomach. Just to confuse things, the "O" is pronounced the same as the English "O." The "V" and the "W" sound exactly alike. (The Dutch claim they don't, but…) As Bert was spelling, I was mentally trying to transcribe all the "I's" into "E's" and vice versa. I was hopelessly confused.

I interrupted and asked for nearby streets. More information: "Scheveningseweg, Beekbergenstraat, Delpratwoningenlaan, and Nassauzuilensteinstraat." How many of those will you remember tomorrow? Pronouncing them isn't difficult—just imitate a 1952 Studebaker with an engine knock.

Resigned to my fate, I spilled my tea in my lap and began work on my Dutch short story.

The rest of the family was having similar problems. Nazy was at the *slager* (butcher) trying to buy ground beef (in Dutch). The conversational contest was one-sided victory for the natives.

"*Ik wil graag vijf hondred kilo tartaar.*"

"You want ground beef?"

"A*lstublieft.*"

"Five-hundred kilos? That's the size of a house."

"*Uh, zo. Ik will graag vijf hondred gram tartaar.*"

"Making those famous American hamburgers?"

"*Nee, ik will een vleesballen.*"[3]

"Meatballs!" Nazy shouted, then muttered something unprintable to herself in Persian. It is literally unprintable: I don't have the proper character set on my computer. You can see the problem. Nazy was speaking perfect Dutch—take my word for it. The butcher was responding in English. He didn't want us to learn Dutch—he was too busy practicing his English on Nazy.

Darius and Melika were similarly challenged. Melika marched into the PTT (post office) to get stamps ("*Ik will graag één, één, één*, ah... STAMP!"). Darius was speaking Denglish at the stores ("I vant von ov de *apfelfarten.*"). Well, we were trying.

I arrived home just after Ron's Dutch lesson had begun. We reviewed the basics—the colors. This was useful for me, the only colorblind member of the family. If I got the answer wrong I could always blame my eyesight: *Ik dacht dat het rood was.* (I thought it was red.)

We practiced Shakespeare—*Zijn of niet Zijn? Dat is de vraag.* (To be or not to be? That is the question.) Personally, I think it loses something in the translation. We thought up sentences to drop into conversation: *Dat is een tafel.* (That is a table.) We handed in our assignments.

---

3 . *Vlees means meat and ballen means balls. Unfortunately, vleesballen means testicles.*

Phil, our Shell colleague in the Dutch lesson, joined Nazy and I in appalled disbelief as we eyed Mitra's "short" paragraph. Phil broke the ice.

"Was it really necessary to have your 'essay' printed and bound, Mitra?"

"Oh, phooey, Phil. I just did it on Dad's Mac."

Now I was concerned. "Do we have any printer paper left, Mitra?"

"You guys are just jealous. I just wrote a short story. You should buy us a Dutch spell-checker, Dad."

Ron interrupted our harassment of Mitra with his commentary on our last assignments. *"Het werk was heel slecht omdat u de taal niet begrijpt. Maar het werk van Mitra was heel goed. Prima, Mitra!"* (Mitra wanted me to translate Ron's comments here. I declined. If you really want to know, ask her. *She's* the expert.)

Hearing Ron's commentary, I quickly interjected a tricky Dutch verb ("to work your fingers to the bone") to explain mistakes: *"Maar, Ron, ik werk me kapot."*

Later that evening, we reviewed the events of the day. We all agreed that we had done "great" and decided to celebrate with ice cream (*ijs*) at Scheveningen. We left the house and walked to the *tramhalte*. ("*Wij liepen naar de tramhalte.*") Mitra decided to buy the *strippenkaart* (i.e., pay for the trip) completely in Dutch.

She boldly marched up to the driver. *"Ik wil graag één grote strippenkaart voor mijn ouders."*

"Sure, ma'am. Do you miss the States?"

"How'd you know I'm American?" said Mitra in shocked disbelief. How could anyone detect even the faintest hint of American in her flawless Dutch?

"Actually, I'm an Aussie."

"Oh. Well, I need a *strippenkaart* for my parents. And g'day, mate."

Mitra was in high school when we moved to the Netherlands. As this story conveys, she was very precocious. She entered college at Princeton while we were living in The Hague. She objects when I claim that precocious is not the same as practical.

My mother told me that "Mitra is a dreamer and she will follow her dreams." Mom was right. It took Mitra a while to find her passion. Based in New York, she toured the world while working on a marketing project for Exxon She discovered tango in Argentina, and her world changed. She spent a few years becoming a great tango dancer. [Disclaimer: Mitra objects when I make this kind of statement because: "How do you know, Dad?"]

After 9/11, Mitra moved to Los Angeles, where, with her partner, she opened the best tango school in the country. Check out www.oxygentango.com. At the time, it didn't seem practical to me. (As Cormac observed, "Tango? Couldn't she think of something a bit more obscure?") However, unlike many of us, Mitra is doing exactly what she loves. Perhaps precocious and practical are linked.

The idea behind Dutch lessons was that we'd be able to read the newspaper, watch television, and understand Dutch government forms. We learned to read the newspaper—sort of (De Telegraaf is the easiest). A lot of TV, except for the BBC, is in English with Dutch subtitles. (The BBC is in British, without subtitles.) Even the Dutch can't understand Dutch government forms.

We made progress. Mitra and Nazy ordered things in a store without having the clerk switch to English. There were a few minor stumbles. When you purchase bread, for example, you have to ask for it to be sliced. We learned to do that, but we also asked for locked, chopped, grated, pureed, and circumcised bread. Some words really sound alike. In fact, the Dutch words for strawberry (aardbeien) and hemorrhoid (ambeien) are remarkably, and embarrassingly, close.

Subsequently, I attended an intensive Dutch language course at a convent in Den Bosch. (My teacher was Attilla the Nun.) While my Dutch got better, I never became fluent. I was good enough, though, to understand Shell colleagues who switched to Dutch when they wanted a private conversation. Several other nifty things happened: Americans complimented me on my "fine grasp of English" (they just barely detected my accent). And I myself all the verbs at the end of the sentence find putting.

Food, language, shopping, and government—we'd handled it all. The long, dark, winter days had come to an end. The famous Dutch flowers were springing up all over the city, and the weather grew warmer. We (and everyone else on the planet) headed for the beach. We weren't quite ready for European swimming attire.

HE IS WEARING A TIE

Freezing, I repeated myself: "I'm telling you, I *did* see the bunkers with Cormac!"

Nazy and the children, trudging through the sand, didn't care about bunkers. They didn't care about the historical significance of our new home. They were cold.

I still had memories of my first view of the bunkers. Cormac, Maggie, and I had been walking down the beach on a typical Dutch autumn day—gray, bleak, dreary, foggy, and chilly. As I looked along the sea, I could see the bunkers emerging out the fog. It was a scene straight from *The Longest Day*. I wanted to share it with the children and Nazy, but none of them had seen the movie. They hadn't been excited by the news that recent storms in the North Sea had deposited World War II mines on the beach. They were cold and wanted to go home.

In fact, I was cold, too. It was time to call off the expedition.

"All right, guys," I said, sounding reluctant, "if *you* want to just give up with victory in sight, then we can head home now."

"What d'ya mean, 'victory in sight,' Dad? We can't see anything."

"Darius, when Daddy says 'victory in sight,' he's using an idiom," Nazy said. "That's an expression like, uh, the early worm catches the egg. Right, Dan?"

"Yeah, right, dear. Besides, Darius, you're supposed to see the bunkers through the fog. It's impressive that way."

"Okay, if it's so impressive, we'll continue on." Nazy was calling my bluff.

"That's all right, dear, I can accept the fact that you guys just don't have the interest, stamina, or enthusiasm necessary for us to complete our journey."

Spying my short-sleeved T-shirt, Nazy wasn't about to let me off easily. "I'm interested. But aren't you cold?"

"Me? Cold? I revel in frigid conditions. I laugh at the wind. I just think that if the children aren't having fun, then…uh… Well, we should call it a day."

"Only if you insist, dear."

I pointedly nudged Mitra. She obliged by insisting that she and her siblings were ready to go home.

We executed a sharp, one-hundred-and-eighty-degree turn and headed back toward the pier—and McDonald's.

This, like our other bunker pilgrimages on the *Noordzee*, ended in failure. We huddled together in the warmth of McDonald's, each in our own private world. I was annoyed that this particular McDonald's didn't offer Quarter Pounders. Everyone else was too wrapped up in their own thoughts. A dog grabbed Darius's hamburger.

Displaying energy unseen since his ancestor ("The Great") had conquered the known world, Darius jumped five feet in the air. When he landed, Melika's fries and Mitra's McNuggets were in my lap.

Nazy was able to negotiate replacement foodstuffs. She also asked the manager why he let dogs in the restaurant.

"Dogs are Dutch."

"Dutch? That was a *German* shepherd."

"I mean everybody has a dog in Holland."

"We don't have a dog in Holland."

"Dutch people like dogs. They take them everywhere. If I prevent dogs from coming into the restaurant, I won't have any business. Besides, dogs are small compared to the problems we have in the summer."

"Oh, yeah?" I interjected, "What d'ya have in summer? Elephants? Or is it just the smaller pachyderms?"

"No, sir, in the summer we have people without clothes."

"Without clothes?"

"That's right. Especially the Germans."

"Hey, Dad, ask him if they bring their shepherds," Darius said.

Spring materialized in The Hague the following weekend. The Martin Family returned to the *zee*, determined to forge our way to the bunkers. It was an appropriate weekend. Scheveningen looked as if it was under invasion. There were so many people we couldn't even see the sand.

We did, however, see a few German tourist families marching—in straight lines—to the beach. I even overheard the parental admonishment, "Ve are on ze holiday and you *vill* haf a goot time!"

Shoving our way to the waterline, we noticed that topless attire was not an exception. We also noticed that not everyone was pinup material. Darius subtly pointed out an especially bad example of the human condition.

"HEY, DAD, LOOK AT THAT."

"Darius! Keep your voice down," I admonished. But I had to admit, "She does look a bit like a relief map of Europe, doesn't she?"

"Hey! You're right! I can see Mount Blanc and Mount..."

Maybe Darius and I were looking at different examples.

Nazy had also been quick to observe the nonstandard attire. Everything from Sunday suits to holy—er, holey—underwear. People were walking the beach in six-inch-high heels, wet suits, suede skirts, silk blouses, no blouses. It was certainly different.

"This really blows my head, Dan. Look at what these people are wearing."

"What he's looking at is what they're *not* wearing," Darius said.

Gazing to the north (just past the young couple feverishly intertwined on the sand), Nazy saw the bunkers.

"Look at that, kids. I can't see how we missed them last time. Let's walk up there and get a better look."

Interestingly, there wasn't a lot of enthusiasm for the journey. The bunkers looked as if they were far off in the distance. They also looked—in a word—boring. Nevertheless, we worked northward.

Unbeknownst to us, the bunkers are the backdrop for the nude beach. As we got closer and our view of the bunkers cleared, so did our view of the natives.

Nazy went bonkers (in front of the bunkers) as a gentleman wearing only a hat, shirt, and tie walked toward us.

"Hey, Dad, look at that," said Melika. "It's bouncing up and down!"

"Melika!" I yelled, none too subtle myself. "It's not polite to yell. Besides, it's not like he's naked. He *is* wearing a tie."

"He may not be naked, Dad, *but look at her*!"

"Darius! Melika shouldn't yell and you shouldn't point."

"Yeah, okay. It's just that Mount Blanc and…"

"Darius!"

But Darius couldn't be interrupted. He had spotted another anomaly. "Melika, look at what that guy's doing over there," he cried.

"I see that. It reminds me of the old idiom 'look before you leak,'" I quipped.

Mitra, our budding teenager, was quietly taking notes. "I thought the idiom was 'a bird in the hand is…'"

"That's enough, Mitra!"

The trip was, shall we say, revealing.

We passed the bunkers and started up the stairs for the walk home. Nobody had been impressed by the bunkers and everybody thought I had known about the beach.

We ran into Cormac and Maggie at the top of the stairs walking their dog, Paddy. Nazy told Cormac about the state of affairs on the dunes below.

"Yes, I know. It's frightfully embarrassing for me. You see, Paddy has a rear-end fetish. He runs up to people and sticks his cold, wet nose up their…"

DANIEL PAUL MARTIN

CHAPTER 4
FRIENDS

No matter where you live, it's important to have good friends. We wanted to go about finding friends in the Dutch way—or at least close to the Dutch way. It wasn't easy. People are organized (I wonder if there's a form to fill out to have a party). We tried to avoid inviting people to dinner several months before the actual event. The result was dismal—no one was ever available. We learned to keep an accurate agenda for ourselves, and Dutch friends invited us well in advance of any parties. Of course, getting invited (or getting someone to accept your invitation) is only part of the work. But there would be no problem—The Martin Family knew how to have...

A LUNCHEON PARTY

Nazy had been remarkably busy. We had Mitra's play on Friday, company on Saturday, a luncheon party on Monday, and my parents' arrival on Wednesday. I missed the carefully choreographed luncheon event—I was in Aberdeen. (After reading these stories, Nazy has observed that I'm often somewhere else at times like these.)

The menu was constructed directly from Martha Stewart's *Entertaining*. Keeping with tradition, Nazy was up until two a.m. cooking and cleaning the night before the party. As usual, she had prepared enough food to feed the crowd gathered at the Super Bowl. She thought she had invited seven people. She prepared salad niçoise and mounds of fruit, and subcontracted napkin folding to Mitra, who created miniature linen models of the Peace Palace. Casks of wine had been flown in from France. The first crop of white Dutch asparagus was featured and there was a collection of fine European cheese. Darius had acquired rare Belgian mushrooms from a classmate.

On the morning of the event, Nazy woke up a little late, skipped breakfast, and dashed off to drop the children at school. Well, she was more than a little late. She rushed home to "spiff up" the house, finish the last-minute cooking, and get dressed for her party. She had every minute planned—coffee from 8:52 a.m. until 9:01, last-minute cooking from 9:01 until 9:42, table setting from 9:42 until 9:59, last-minute cleaning from 10:00 until… Well, you get the picture.

At nine o'clock, a potential guest called to say she would be a little late. At quarter past nine, another guest called and said she, too, would be late—she had to drop her child off at school. At nine-thirty, our neighbor, Hilary, called and asked Nazy to help her start her car.[4] Nazy volunteered both herself and our jumper cables. (It never occurred to her that there might be an automotive problem that can't be solved by jumper cables.)

Once she got the two cars nose to nose and figured out how to open the hoods, Nazy realized she didn't actually know how to use the jumper cables. She knocked on a nearby door.

Jan, appropriately pronounced *yawn*, was the reluctant neighbor. He arrived at the front door in his underwear, his glasses semi-balanced on his nose. His hair looked as if it had been combed by a North Sea gale. We *think* she woke him up.

"Oh, Jan, I'm so sorry. Do you know how to use jumper cables?"

"Yeah. red to red, black to black. Call me if it doesn't work."

---

[4] . *Asking Nazy for automotive assistance is like using a windmill in a vacuum chamber.*

"Thanks, Jan." Jan didn't hear Nazy's thanks. He simply ambled back into his house, forgetting to shut the door. At least it would be easy to get him back if there were more problems.

Armed with Jan's useful information, Nazy approached the disabled vehicle. Jan forgot to tell her to be careful to not touch red to black. After a brief fireworks display, Nazy made the connections, but it didn't work. Hilary's idea—"Let's ask Jan for more help"—was discarded just after the front door to Jan's house slammed shut. We *think* it was the wind.

Nazy volunteered to take Hilary to work.

"Oh, thank you, Nazy. Can we also stop by the hairdresser? Pushkins has an appointment for a shampoo."

"Pushkins?"

"Yeah, Pushkins, the dog."

"The *dog* has a shampoo appointment?"

"Yes. And we're already late," Hilary said as she grabbed a barking ball of fur from the back of her inert coupe. "Pushkins looks like a large rodent," Nazy thought as she climbed into the driver's seat of the working automobile.

She drove to the hair (fur?) salon and then dropped Hilary off at work at the Mauritshuis gallery. She dodged construction, the striking farmers' tractors, the parading ambulance drivers, a march against extended shopping hours, and Lithuanian silent vigil near the Russian embassy.

She arrived home at eleven, just in time to get a call from a third neighbor who couldn't come. ("My daughter injured her knee and none of the sixteen physicians who have examined her know what they're doing.")

Nazy carefully set the table for eight people—the seven guests and herself. It was then that she remembered she'd only invited five people. Moreover, one of the five wasn't coming and two were going to be late.

Nazy just had time to dash upstairs and enter the shower when the first guest, a punctual Dutch lady, arrived. Nazy might have been ready if her hair hadn't been wet. Another guest showed up a few minutes later. The three of them sat upstairs for ninety minutes before the final two visitors trickled in. By the time they were ready to eat, everyone had to dash off to pick up children. It wasn't a total disaster—guests could take cheese for the drive.

There was a golden lining. The Martin Family enjoyed acres of asparagus, alpine-high piles of fruit, and scrumptious salad niçoise. The extra three napkins became Mitra's art project and Darius started a mushroom collection. However, words that inject fear into the heart of any husband had begun to be heard in The Martin Family home: "Perhaps we should have a dinner party." (If this were a movie instead of a book, there would be ominous background music.)

The luncheon was simple; the dinner event promised to be much more complex. Provisions had to be acquired, and because the invitation count exceeded the place setting count, accoutrements had to be obtained. A shopping spree was mandatory. Was The Martin Family up to the challenge? Ha! Was the captain of the Titanic a great navigator? Is an IRS audit fun?

As this was happening, I was busy at Shell. Busy in the sense of holding meetings, writing minutes, generating proposals—all with the aim of achieving a necessary but increasingly illusive consensus. Hired to retire the telex, I had made the mistake of announcing the retirement in a company newsletter. All ten thousand printed copies were retrieved because my note, "Shell telex to be pensioned," was too direct. I was told, "You can't say that, Dan, people might think we're going to retire the telex. Consensus will be harder to come by." In spite of this, an RFP (Request for Proposal) for the replacement system had been generated, and responses were about to be evaluated. I expected the dinner to be a welcome diversion.

THE CASCADING DINNER

Our Dutch friends attempted to explain European appliance superiority to The Martin Family. Small refrigerators are energy-efficient: They force you to shop often and consequently assure that you will eat fresh, wholesome food. Small, energy-efficient stoves encourage smaller portions: your intake of fattening, calorie-laden food is limited. Small washing machines are energy-efficient: They heat their own water.

The washing machines do heat their own water—to an incredibly high temperature. This feature means that all disease-causing germs are eliminated in the wash cycle. As noted before, this would be more impressive if the concept of pre-shrunk was recognized in Europe. Personally, I think the most interesting part of the washing machine is its front-loading mechanism. I have fond memories of my sister, Wendy, standing in front of the old family front-loader, watching her blanket spin around.

We weren't trying to be ethnocentric, but we did discover yet another reason to prefer the craftsmanship of the American appliance makers. If the door pops open on a top-loading washing machine, nothing happens. It's not the same with a front-loading European washing machine.

We had company due to arrive in twenty minutes. The laundry room was crowded with sorted piles of clothes, and Melika started the washing machine. Water filled the (seemingly) small drum, and the heating cycle began and ended. The agitation cycle, complete with scalding water, began. The door bypassed seven safety mechanisms and popped open, and the curtain was lifted on World War III. The washing machine flung hot underwear and scalding water all over the laundry room. The flood inexorably worked its way toward the kitchen, where The Martin Family sprang into action. A mop handle was used to shut off the machine. Massive portions of the spill had been lapped up by the various piles of laundry (the European "pre-wash" cycle?). The remainder was pushed out the back door, and order was miraculously restored just after the company arrived.

The dinner party was a normal Nazy Martin event. Food fit for the queen and sufficient for an occupying army had been prepared. The week leading to the undertaking was fraught with the usual preparatory work and occasional missteps. The bulk of the food shopping took place during a thunderstorm—and Nazy forgot to bring her own bags to the Konmar. Melika and I had to make several trips to Bankastraat to collect ingredients that had been forgotten in initial forays into the shopping district.

The family provided the usual assistance: Mitra had homework, Darius was visiting a friend, and Melika had "done the laundry." I polished the silver and cleaned up my desk.

A standard complaint ("We don't have enough dishes") was heard frequently because the Dan Martin rule of thumb of "Don't invite more people than dishes" had been violated. Nazy, unfettered by practical concerns, was forging ahead with the following:

(1) A Dutch potter had been employed to replicate The Martin Family stoneware;
(2) A comprehensive and sophisticated public relations effort was initiated with the simple objective of getting me to agree to the purchase of a new, European set of china; and
(3) For the party, the children were to be migrated elsewhere.

In combination, these strategies were mostly successful.

Although the potter didn't finish the plates before the party, she did agree to return the ones taken as patterns. As for relocating the children, Mitra attended a performance of *The Miracle Worker*. She had no choice—she was in the cast. Darius could spend the night at Josh's house, and Melika agreed to be my colleague Lucas's date. (For some reason, Lucas was unable to bring either his wife or girlfriend.)

The new china initiative proved unsuccessful when Nazy was unable to find sufficient place settings for the planned company complement. This is not to say she didn't try. She took the tram to Babylon Station and tried the shops there, she taxied to Denneweg and tried the shops there, and she drove to Scheveningen and tried the shops there.

Nazy thinks shopping is fun. The variety of stores and shopping districts in The Hague are like heaven for her. The contrast with Hanover's two-block Main Street is immense. In Hanover, Nazy had memorized the inventory of each store. It was impossible to give her a surprise gift while we lived in the Upper Valley. Whenever we bought something, Nazy immediately noted its disappearance from the local shelves. She knew, before she unwrapped the package, where it had been purchased and whether we had been able to get it on sale.

In The Hague there are thousands of stores. Even Nazy hadn't memorized all their inventories (yet). European stores are, however, a little bit different. Space is at a premium, so they are crowded with priceless items (artfully displayed). Limited shopping hours mean the stores are *always* crowded. Imagine a very little store packed with people and a variety of expensive plates. It's the kind of store you wouldn't let small children enter—an island of crystal serenity in the stormy ocean of people flooding the Scheveningen promenade.

It was Nazy's last stop. Although her mission of acquiring dishes had not been a success, she had accumulated a rather large load of ancillary stuff. Naturally, the Scheveningen shop didn't have what she wanted, but Nazy always has a second objective in a shopping mission. She wanted to know exactly what they did have and the cost.[5] She picked up a plate, turned it over to ascertain the price, and placed it back on the stand. Unfortunately, the stand had been meticulously balanced on a crystal ball. The plate, the stand, *and* the ball rolled to the right—directly into a collection of forsythia branches. The flowers slid into an assortment of porcelain boats, the boats sailed into safe harbor in a city constructed of pewter thimbles, the thimble city exploded into a vast vase of porcelain flowers, and the flowers "de-petalled" themselves on the floor. The accompanying crash brought instant clerical attention.

Nazy's cheery good nature, fumbling command of Dutch, and graceful apologies smoothed the troubled waters while a broom smoothed the floor. But now Nazy felt as though she had to buy something. After glancing around, she asked the clerk to let her look at some Little Prince

---

5 . *It was a miracle day. Nazy actually inquired about the price before making the purchase.*

plates that were displayed high above the carnage. The clerk climbed a ladder and grabbed a stack. A minor gravitational anomaly combined with limited surface tension caused ensuing chaos. The clerk dropped five of the six plates onto the floor. The floor was hard. The plates were not. Nazy decided to buy the last Little Prince plate. She imagined thunderous clerical applause as she left the shop, and the devastation, behind.

The party was wonderful. Individually skewered shrimp wrapped in snow pea pods were stuck into a head of cabbage and served as appetizers with endive and cheese. The main course was a classic leg of lamb, stuffed tomatoes, and shirin polo—a Persian rice dish with de-stemmed currants, slivered pistachios, almonds, carrots, and shredded orange peels. It was a culinary delight.

We were soon working on the next event—an upcoming parental visit. My father had been to Europe before: "I occupied it, Dan." I told him there had been minor changes. The family was getting ready. Darius was preparing a geography test, Nazy needed more dishes, and Melika wanted to finish the laundry. I was collecting my courage for a drive to Schiphol. Mitra? She had homework.

The washing machine had caused a lot of problems. You've read about the shrinking sheets and the flood. The agitation cycle had also failed: The washer filled and drained, but it refused to move between the two events. Agitation did occur when I kicked it, however. It could have been worse. We have friends whose washer suffered a thermocouple breakdown. The thermocouple tells the washer when to stop heating the water. When it breaks, water is heated forever! Of course, water can't be heated forever—it boils away. The water boiled, vaporized, and disappeared. The heat that was generated annihilated the underwear and melted the washer door. In comparison to this, The Martin Family had it lucky!

It's important to establish new friendships in the new country. It's also important to maintain old friendships from the old country. I'm a bit confused at this point. Is the United States the new country? Or was that Europe? Maintaining contact with our friends from the States wasn't easy. People kept acting as though we'd moved to another continent. Letter-writing skills, atrophied by the "reach out and touch syndrome," weren't replaced by the international telephone call. Luckily, our friends didn't forget us. Somehow, people who had never been able to find the time to visit us in Houston or Memphis were able to make it to Holland. Friends and family came. John, my Georgia Tech roommate, even made Holland his first international destination.

THAT BELL WILL NEVER RING

John's arrival was unmarked by any major problem. Well, okay, his flight was an hour late, all of the Schiphol parking lots were under repair, and Shell had decided to *re*think, *re*tool, *re*organize, review (and, hopefully) *re*new my project and my contract. Perhaps this was Shell's first step toward staff *re*deployment.

John, unlike any member of The Martin Family, had prepared for his foreign trip. He was determined to foil jet lag by staying awake until at least ten p.m. local time. This meant he would be awake for about thirty-five hours straight. John didn't sleep on the plane; he flew economy class—there wasn't room for him to shut his eyes.

The Martin Family did its best to help. Knowing that a *re*capitulation of my career moves would put him to sleep, I left for the office to attempt to *re*create consensus. Melika challenged him to a game of Monopoly, Darius asked him how to do the four-ace trick—John is a magician—and Mitra played the piano at high volume. It was to no avail.

At this point, Nazy sprang into action. "What about a visit to the topless beach?" she innocently asked.

"The topless beach?" said John, instantly alert.

In point of fact, all of the beaches in The Hague are topless, so it wasn't hard finding one. The unique happenstance was that it was warm and sunny enough to warrant a visit to the *Noordzee*. Nazy was happy to point out all the sights to John. Additionally, she offered a running commentary on the costumes of the crowd.

"*Look* at that, John. Hey, there's another one over there. Look at that outfit—straight off a Barbie doll. Did you see the guy wearing leather pants and purple hair? There's a delightfully dignified outfit—suspenders attached to a string bikini bottom."

The visit to Scheveningen was sufficient to double John's mental alertness coefficient. When I got home, we all went for a walk around the neighborhood, and decided to stop by the Iraqi embassy to shout slogans. On the way, however, we passed the American ambassador's residence. Darius was busily explaining the difference between America and Iraq.

"See, John, they have barbed wire at the Iraqi embassy. They have video cameras and ugly guards who don't speak English, and they won't even let you take pictures. Our embassy is different."

"I see that. Let's stop here and get a picture by the American ambassador's residence. I'll just stand here by the sign…"

John was interrupted by an ugly guard who didn't speak English and didn't want us to take any pictures. John was unamused. He asked Darius to explain the difference between the Iraqis and the Americans once again.

Having made it through the first day, John was able to adjust to Europe time without any trouble. I continued trying to make sense of office reorganization. I *re*peated my plans, *re*iterated my objectives, and *re*capitulated my procedures. I was not *re*warded with *re*cognition. The whole thing was getting *re*diculous (sorry). By the weekend, I was *re*ally tired. I can't *re*member when I needed *re*juvenation so badly.

But the weekend wasn't entirely restful. On Sunday morning, Darius knocked the lid off Nazy's new teapot and onto the floor. It broke. (Not the floor, the lid.) Melika, happily observing how clumsy Darius could be, then dropped a full honey jar on the kitchen floor. It, too, broke. Melika and Darius thanked John for visiting. "You saved my life, Uncle John. If you weren't here, Mommy would have killed me."

John, in trying to adjust to children, asked me how we were able to cope with the ongoing calamity. I started to explain, but just then John dumped his glass of Coca-Cola all over the lace tablecloth. He thanked Darius for saving *his* life.

Having destroyed the house in The Hague, we decided to take on Belgium. We drove to Bruges, an ancient city in which every building is a museum. All the buildings, even those from the eleventh century, are in excellent shape. Bruges likes to call itself the Venice of the North (it does have canals). It has an advantage over the Venice, though—the mildew that stains Venetian buildings doesn't grow in Belgium.

John agreed to climb the Bruges Belfry with the children. He likes to show the children, and us, that he is in good shape. Climbing four hundred and twenty-nine stairs in one-hundred-degree weather takes good physical conditioning. *Willingly* doing it generates queries about mental conditioning.

John and the children arrived at the top of the Belfry a few minutes before five o'clock. Gigantic bells, in sight a few meters above their heads, generated lively discussion.

Darius began the conversation. "John, do you think these bells will make us all deaf?"

"Deaf? Of course not. I don't even think the bells will ring."

"Those *huge* bells will bust our eardrums!"

"If the bells could bust your eardrums, Darius, the museum people wouldn't let you up here. Besides, the bells won't ring."

"Of course the bells will ring, John, it's a belfry. Bells ring in the belfry."

"No. Bats fly in the belfry."

"Bats?"

"Bats!"

"In the belfry?"

"Right. In the belfry!"

"What about bells?"

"Darius, the ropes connected to the bells are frayed. *Anyone* can see that the bells don't work. They probably don't even have clappers. In fact, the last time the bells were used was to announce Columbus's discovery of America."

"Well, Uncle John, I heard the bells when we drove into town. Didn't you? We have to get out of here. Our eardrums will be busted."

John was totally exasperated by this point. "Darius! I personally guarantee that these bells will never…"

BONG! BONG! BONG!

After a few notes on the carillon, John and the children began the trek down the stairs.

"So, Uncle John, no clappers, eh?"

"Speak up, Darius, I can't hear you. I think my eardrum is busted."

"Wait until Mom and Dad hear about this! I didn't see any bats, either."

Nazy and I greeted the children, immediately noticing that they seemed to have lost the ability to speak in a conversational tone.

"YOU WOULDN'T BELIEVE IT, MOM! THE BELLS WENT OFF WHILE WE WERE STANDING THERE. JOHN THOUGHT IT WOULDN'T WORK, BUT…"

When we spoke, they didn't understand us.

"Melika. You don't have to yell. We can hear you."

"WHAT DID YOU SAY? THE BELLS WERE REALLY LOUD UP THERE. DID YOU SEE ANY BATS?"

Over time, the children's hearing gradually returned to normal. We took a canal ride and then had a pleasant drive back to Den Haag.

During the last week of his visit, John saw lots of Holland. We went to Amsterdam, where we tried for a late-night canal ride to see the lights. Unfortunately, a marketing blunder resulted in a strange departure schedule: The "night" canal boat left and returned before dark. John and the family went to Utrecht to see the train museum and the mint, and to Delft, where we had lunch in an outdoor cafe that was floating in a canal. John took the children to Madurodam, the miniature city with the super electric train set. He has always liked electric trains.

These were nice visits, but he wanted to try out the Holland Casino. Darius thought it was a great idea. But Darius also thought the casino would let John, the professional magician, shuffle and deal.

John, Nazy, and I went to the casino, and John described the "Miller system." I explained how, mathematically, he was sure to lose, and he told us it had always worked in the past. I said there was as much chance of that system working as there was of a meteorite landing in the garden; John was unconvinced. I played my trump card by explaining that the government owned the casino.

"Think about it, John. The people who own this casino are the same ones who collect taxes. They are *not* going to lose money."

John, working the Miller system, made three hundred and sixty-five guilders. Nazy and I, using the Martin method, were somewhat less successful. I'm now careful to step over the meteor crater in the courtyard. Maybe I'll even get a refund check from the IRS.

We took John to the airport in plenty of time for his flight back to the States. On the drive to Schiphol, John told us how he had carefully chosen his departure time to avoid the crowds because "no one flies on Monday."

There were lots of "no ones" at the airport. I didn't understand, but according to John it was extremely unlikely that he was wrong. Those people must have been left over from Sunday flights. To compensate for the crowded conditions, Schiphol airport authorities had closed the short-term parking lot. Anyone wanting to park was routed to a suburb in Denmark.

A line of cars stretching back to The Hague marked the suburban parking garage. We inched our way to the entrance gate, where we met a computer-controlled, mechanical ticket-spitting-gate-opening machine (TSGOM). The TSGOM was broken. We were fortunate—the silicon computer chips that controlled the TSGOM were augmented by a carbon-based, analog computer system (CBACS)—a human being.

The human being, inauspiciously for us, was trying to fix the TSGOM. He was able to get both the TS (ticket-spitting) and the GO (gate-opening) mechanisms to work. He couldn't, however, get them to work in sequence. The gate would spring open, but the machine wouldn't spit out a ticket. When the machine did spit the ticket, the gate wouldn't open. The repairman kept walking back and forth between the GO and the TS, muttering in Dutch about the host computer. I think that among the civil things he said was that the computer wouldn't stamp the date and time on the parking ticket.

I suggested that he get a ticket from the next aisle—I needed a ticket to get my car back. He said that was not possible because the machine only gives one ticket at a time.

There were two things wrong with this statement: (1) He was holding a stack of fifteen tickets that "our" TS had deposited in his hand during the last test; (2) I only needed one ticket.

Eventually, having tried everything else, he blocked traffic behind me and helped me sneak into the adjacent queue. While all of this was happening, the beautiful, sunny day had turned to a stormy, cloudy night. We had to face a lengthy trek to the airport terminal.

A soggy family arrived in the Schiphol departure hall. We located the ticket counter in a new wing of the airport. The rearranged parking had put us on the extreme northern side of Schiphol, but the new counter was on the extreme southern side. It was like walking from New York to Atlanta through a Mumbai monsoon surrounded by millions of fleeing refugees. John was lucky: He could leave. We had to fight our way back to the parking lot.

The Martin Family trudged through the Schiphol arrival hall, marveling at how many people could be packed into such a small area. We arrived—soaked—at the parking lot. The computer money collector was broken: It wouldn't give change and it wouldn't return the ten-guilder note that it had digested. Several alternatives, including crashing through the gate Rambo-style, were considered and discarded. Nazy located a human being who took our money.

We stopped at the office on the way home. Shell had begun to *re*novate the office space; I was *re*luctant to remain. *Re*legated to confusion, we all headed home.

> *The reorganization effort had taken a toll on Cormac, and he decided to leave the company. The person who had recruited him was furious.*
>
> *"Cormac! You don't understand anything about Shell."*
>
> *Cormac was not moved. "Ben, you don't understand anything but Shell."*
>
> *They glared at each other. Then Ben broke the silence. "Cormac! We're both right."*
>
> *This didn't appear to bode well for me. Consensus seemed to be a mirage. My efforts turned to contract renewal.*

STUMBLING THROUGH THE TULIPS

Meanwhile at home, we were using all of the traditional methods for meeting people. Our determination was influenced by Nazy's experience. When she was in college, she was astounded to meet a fellow student who had lived in Iran for three years. In fact, this person hadn't actually lived in Iran. She had lived in the American community. She shopped at the PX, she watched Armed Forces TV, she had never actually met an Iranian, and she had never seen any of the sights of the country. (And she was there well before the Ayatollah.)

We were going to have a different experience. We were not going to be ugly Americans. We chose to live in the center of the city surrounded by Dutch (and expats), and we were going to make Dutch friends. So we invited the kids' friends and colleagues from my office to visit. Local immigration and taxation laws made it difficult for Nazy to take a paying job and therefore make friends at an office, so she embarked on a number of volunteer efforts.

I SECOND THE MOTION

One night I gave up on the BBC's educational offering (*Boron: The chemical element of the week—Part 5 of 103*) and decided to head for bed. Problems appeared as soon as I reached the bedroom. The bed was just barely visible under an enormous pile of books and papers. Nazy, almost buried in disarray, was busily collating information from several thick volumes. The books had the troublesome look of *culture*.

"Hi, Nazy. Isn't that green opus the transcript of a BBC documentary?"

"Very funny. That one's a Dutch commentary on the life of Hieronymus Bosch. Can you translate this passage?"

Always proud of my complete and total grasp of the language, I was quickly able to translate the sentence: Hieronymus Bosch is famous for his [blank] paintings of [blank] and [blank]. The second [blank] looked a bit like the English word "cloud." The third blank looked like the German word that means "sky." "Nazy," I said handing her my card:

Have Dictionary, Will Travel

Wire Martin, The Hague

"I believe it says, uh… 'Hieronymus Bosch is famous for his beautiful paintings of sky and cloud.' I hope that clears things up. What is all this stuff?"

"Remember how I volunteered to help out at the Mauritshuis gallery?"

"Yeah. So?"

"So I'm working on the qualifying essay."

"The qualifying essay? You're a volunteer!"

"Not yet. I can't be a volunteer until my essay is accepted. In order to qualify for the opportunity to volunteer, I have to prepare an essay on the artistic merit, historical background, and emotional impact of four paintings in the Mauritshuis collection. The essay has to encompass the life and times of the artists. Listen to what these instructions say, 'It shall provoke deep thought and foster international understanding of work, the artist, the museum collection. It should…'"

"Yes, I know. It should cultivate comprehension and compassion for cultural differences and promulgate cognizance of beauty and empathy for art among disparate members of the planetary population of the human species. That, my dear, is not an essay. It's a doctoral thesis. Are you sure you want to volunteer?"

"I already did. I've got to finish this essay. It would be very embarrassing to be sacked from a volunteer job. I am going to be much more careful about future volunteering."

"Well, dear, look at the bright side. You may end up with a PhD in Art Appreciation. Right now, though, I'd appreciate it if we could just bulldoze all the books onto the floor."

I shoved the reference material from my side of the bed and began work on my own enrichment program—Dutch language study. Before long I was asleep. Nazy slogged on. Alone.

The Mauritshuis study program continued and Nazy's dissertation got thicker and more erudite. Mauritshuis, however, was merely a thorn on the rosebush of Nazy's volunteer and get-acquainted efforts. She had joined the American Women's Club (AWC) and the Petroleum Wives Club (PWC), and was thinking about joining the IWC (International Women's Club).

These organizations played an important role in Nazy's assimilation into Holland. Our new home had the greatest effect on Nazy. The children and I met people and made friends at work or school. Dutch tax laws don't encourage spousal jobs; Nazy couldn't work until we returned to the States. Fortunately, the various women's clubs enhanced Nazy's organizational and artistic skills. Sometimes the rest of the family also got involved.

"No, Nazy, I don't have a calligraphy program on the computer at the office." I said, responding to her telephone inquiry.

"Can you buy one?"

"I'm sure we can, but why do we need it?"

"Remember when I volunteered to be the hospitality chairman for the PWC?"

"Yes. And do you remember how I warned you to find out what the hospitality chairman does?"

"Yes, yes, yes. You're always warning. Uh…it does seem that the hospitality chairman makes calligraphy name tags."

"I don't have any Mac software for that. I guess you'll have to do it the old-fashioned way, with pen and ink."

"Funny. Just stop at the *V en D* and pick up some ink and a calligraphy set. What color ink do you recommend?"

"Asking me for advice about handwriting problems is like asking the Prince of Wales to be your marriage counselor."

"Just pick up black ink, Dan."

I arrived home with calligrapher implements later that evening. Melika was sorting a vast pile of file cards into alphabetical order, Nazy was reading *Rembrandt: The Early Years*, and Darius was upstairs constructing a computer program. Mitra? She had homework. The wild boar hanging in the entrance hall was hidden behind a wall of wineglasses.

The hospitality chairman, it turned out, was responsible for the three hundred and eighteen PWC wineglasses—most of which were typically on loan to various members. If Darius's program worked, it would track the inventory.

Nazy welcomed me home, put down her book, and began shouting instructions to Darius.

"Okay, Darius, Mary has forty-seven until Wednesday. Mimi has thirty-two until *Donderdag* [Thursday]. Cherri will bring twenty-one to the luncheon on Friday, but don't forget that Alice is hosting Saturday's Git Down an' Stomp party. She'll need two hundred and fifty. I think we'll have to call Brigit; she has fourteen. I also need to take two hundred to the drop-in luncheon on Friday."

"I've got all that, Mom. But how many are they going to break at the drop-them luncheon?"

"It's a drop-*in* luncheon, Darius, not a drop-*them* luncheon."

I stepped over Melika's file, handed my purchases to Nazy, and held my breath. My track record is not impressive—about seventy-five percent of the time that I'm asked to bring something home, I arrive with the wrong thing.

Today I was in luck, but not because I purchased the right items. Quite simply, Nazy was too busy to examine my acquisitions.

Over time, Nazy molded the environment to more carefully match her needs. Mauritshuis accepted her essay and scheduled an oral examination. The PWC had agreed to eliminate wineglass borrowing. Mitra, in a course selection debacle she'll never forget, took Calligraphy. Nazy was able to circumvent Mitra's standard "I have homework" excuse by subcontracting the calligraphy effort. Naturally, as soon as it looked as if everything was under control, the telephone rang. There was a vacancy on the PWC board and..

"I was the only one available. I had to accept."

"But what does a second vice president do? I'm sure you don't just sit at meetings seconding motions."

"I know. But don't worry, they sent me another calligraphy set. I wonder if we can talk Mitra into the Calligraphy II course this semester."

Our conversation was interrupted by the telephone. I headed for the computer and another unsuccessful attack on Darius's Crystal Quest score.

Nazy came into the study beaming.

"Who was on the phone, Naz?"

"It was Mrs. Humphrey. She was "sooo sorry." They drew names for homeroom "volunteers" for Melika's class and my name was *not* selected. What a great day!"

"That's wonderful, Nazy. I had a good day at work, too. Tomorrow we're celebrating my second year in Holland. I wonder if you'd mind volunteering to make a…"

By the way, my translation was somewhat wrong. I had said, "Hieronymus Bosch was famous for his beautiful paintings of sky and cloud." In fact, the passage read, "Hieronymus Bosch is famous for his fearsome painting of hell and damnation." Maybe that's why Nazy had to rewrite her essay.

Nazy's volunteer efforts expanded. She eventually became President of the Petroleum Wives Club, and managed the Extravaganza—a twenty-five-year celebration of the American School in The Hague. She made Dutch friends. And, when we returned home to New Hampshire, she founded the International Women's Club of the Upper Valley. She made sure we made the most of the assignment. We saw more of the Netherlands than most Dutch. And we weren't going to make a faux pas like what had happened to Nazy at college at a dance. Her partner asked her where she was from.

"Iran," Nazy replied.

"Oh, Iran. That's one of those states up north."

"Right," Nazy replied. "It's between Ohio and Iowa."

CHAPTER 5
SETTLING IN

Our efforts to both make new friends and maintain contact with the old ones had been reasonably successful. Nazy was an expert friend-maker. In fact, she was sometimes a bit too good. One weekend, a scheduling fumble resulted in Prinsevinkenpark visitors for both lunch and dinner. Just think of the potential for disaster—a luncheon party and a cascading dinner in one day! The evening ended with a Dutch autumn thunderstorm. We walked our last complement of visitors to the door, which was flung open by the wind with an appropriate flourish. An old Dutch couple was huddled on the doorstep to escape the rain. Nazy grandly invited them in. With cheerfulness like this, how could we fail to make friends?

After a while, the new home became, well, the old home. Problems caused by the "they do it differently in Holland" syndrome began to fade away. Problems never disappear all together—especially for the Martins. Children, as Walter Cronkite used to say, "alter and illuminate our lives." Children make life interesting. Some even become teenagers, capable of committing the ultimate sin: morning cheerfulness.

THE CAMOUFLAGE RAINBOW

Mitra was cheerful even though it was seven-thiry on Sunday morning. "It's time to rise and shine, Daddy." Once again, I placed alarm clock batteries on my mental list of things to purchase. Letting Mitra be in charge of morning wake-up mischief was getting on everyone's nerves.

Gradually, the responsibility for waking us up fell to Mitra, the official Martin family procrastinator. Mitra was in the habit of putting off homework until the very last minute. She even began to claim she liked getting up early to finish, a claim we began to doubt when her initial efforts were foiled—her alarm clock battery went dead after "beeping" continuously for two hours while she slept. She borrowed my alarm clock, and somehow was now in charge of getting the family up.

This new arrangement ruined my carefully crafted early morning routine. When I got up first, I was able to take a shower in peace and quiet. I could wander around before anyone turned on the water or flushed the toilet. Then, I could cheerfully roust everyone else out of bed. Under this new orchestration, Mitra woke up first. She was cheerful. She used up the hot water. And she flushed the toilet during my shower. While toilet flushing may seem innocuous, The Martin Family residence in Den Haag was supplied with city water, which is dispensed in dribs and drabs. Toilet flushing during an in-progress shower created an instant steam bath.

If you're an alert reader, you may have noticed that Mitra cheerfully woke me up on a Sunday morning. "*Why?*" you might say. After all, surely she knew I was sleepy. The family, after visiting friends in Belgium, had returned home late the previous night. In fact, we had really returned home early that morning. The children, and in particular the jolly Mitra, had slept while I drove home. Dutch roads are flat, but they're not straight, so I had to stay alert. Why was Mitra trying to wake me up?

"Ah," I thought, "we're going to Keukenhof park." Keukenhof is home to the annual Dutch flower show, and we had wanted to go early and beat the crowds. Now I wanted to reconsider that decision. After several attempts to ignore increasingly cheerful requests, I opened my eyes and looked at Mitra.

"*Gawagh!*" This is a Dutch word. It translates as "gawagh" in English. A rainbow of color greeted me. "Mitra," I muttered, "what are you wearing?"

A vision attired in a green vest, pink pants, orange shirt, sneakers with rainbow shoelaces, and strange sunglasses smiled back at me.

"Isn't it great, Daddy?"

When I was a teenager, everyone wanted to have the same look. Mitra, the official Martin family teenager, wanted to look different. As she put it: "I just can't be ordinary, Daddy." Her approach was to boldly dress as no person had dressed before. There are more than two million different hues available in the MacColour software for my office computer. Mitra's clothing palette put MacColour to shame.

For Mitra, Holland had been a wonderland. Her first shopping experience was at Sweetheart, a candy store in the centrum of The Hague. Sweetheart wraps every purchase with forty ribbons of different colors, which Mitra collected. Darius and Melika, more sensibly, ate the candy. Mitra spent more money on Christmas wrapping paper than she spent on Christmas presents. She saved the paper and used it to color-code her school book covers. Pink for Monday classes, yellow for Tuesday, etc. Even our Dutch lessons were geared toward Mitra's idiosyncrasies. The first thing we learned were the colors. Unfortunately, we just learned the basics. Mitra wanted to know about puce, lavender, rose, cobalt…

Mitra's outfit was so loud that it bounced everyone out of bed. In short order, we were ready to go. And, since the trams are "boring beige" on the weekends, we elected to drive to the Keukenhof. A minor problem delayed our departure. Mitra didn't want us to carry the lunch in brown paper bags. A compromise—hiding the brown-bag lunches in a Sweetheart bag—was reached and we were ready to depart.

We first had to stop at Holland Spoor Station to pick up Ron, our Dutch teacher. Strangely, Ron had never been to the Keukenhof. After living in Holland for more than a year, we had become seasoned veterans with vast knowledge of Dutch traffic regulations. Indeed, regulations and rules were not our problem. Directions, however, were. We didn't know how to drive to the Holland Spoor Station. We could get there by tram, by train, and by taxi. We could bicycle and we could walk. Driving? No such luck.

I decided Nazy should navigate while I drove; I liked being the blamer rather than the blamee. I dodged construction, bicycles, trams, and pedestrians. Nazy's navigation was slightly helpful—it put us within sight of the station, but we were in Europe, where there are no ninety-degree turns and lots of one-way streets. After the third pass close to the station, I pulled into a trams-only lane. I quickly recognized my mistake. (But gosh and golly, I didn't realize that the trams had foghorns. I thought they just had polite little bells.) I quickly drove over the curb and into a traffic lane—for bicycles. "At least the bikes only had bells," I thought. I drove across the sidewalk, dodged a few parked cars, hopped the curb, and entered a one-way street—the *wrong* way. I executed a finely crafted U-turn while Mitra jumped out to collect Ron.

"I saw Mitra as soon as she got out of the car— Oh yeah, today we must speak Dutch. *Welke kleur is dat, Mitra*? (What color is that?) And why didn't you go down Spui, Dan? Its goes right by the Holland Spoor."

"*Dank u, Ron*," I replied, determined to practice my Dutch.

Finally, we were on our way to the Keukenhof. Flowers are serious business in Holland. The Keukenhof in Lisse is an event where growers from all over the country display their new varieties. Our route to Lisse passed through the flower-growing region. We saw vast fields of tulips, hyacinths, and daffodils. Spring in Holland is unbelievably beautiful and colorful. Wide strips of color, two- or three-hundred meters long, lined the landscape.

Tulip bulbs arrived in Holland in the fifteenth century smuggled in by a Turkish refugee. During the 1700s, tulips were more valuable than gold. In fact, for a number of years, royalty used tulips as personal jewelry. An eighteenth-century flower market crash was as disastrous to the Dutch as the 1929 stock market crash was to the Americans. Tulips have continued to sustain the country. For example, many citizens survived the last winter of World War II by eating tulip bulbs. Today, two KLM 747s, fully loaded with flowers, depart for New York daily. Flowers are a big, big business.

By the time we got to the Keukenhof, we had seen hours of flowers. And it didn't look as though we were the only people who had decided to come early and beat the crowd. License plates in the parking area indicated that a second German invasion was underway. We pushed our way through the multitudes and into the park. It was beautiful.

The grounds were immaculate. There were tulips everywhere and the beds were well prepared. The Dutch had left nothing to chance. As soon as one group of flowers completed its blooming cycle, it was dug out and replaced with another that was just about to bloom.

The Martin Family was astounded. Finally, a practical use for Mitra's color selections: camouflage in the Keukenhof! We wanted to get a family picture, but it was impossible because Mitra kept blending into the background.

While the visit was wonderful, we all agreed that it could have been "a little bit" better. We wanted temperatures "a little bit" warmer, "a little bit" fewer visitors, and weather with "a little bit" less wind. The day would have been perfect if only we had returned from Belgium "a little bit" earlier the previous evening. And on the way home, we discovered that it would have been nice to have "a little bit" more gas in the car.

On the way out, Mitra had to have a flower garland. "Dana's coming tomorrow, Daddy." We dutifully purchased a garland suitable for the winner of the Kentucky Derby.

The next morning, Mitra cheerfully arrived at our bed. "It's six-thirty, Daddy."

"Six-thirty, eh? Isn't that a time that civilized people sleep, Mitra?"

"Come on, we've got to pick up Dana."

A quick shower—actually, a bracing steam bath—and a fast breakfast got us ready for departure.

"Mitra, could you please put the dishes in the dishwasher while I get my briefcase?" I asked.

"I'd like to, but I've got homework."

A few hours later, Mitra's nose was pressed against the glass of the international arrivals hall at Amsterdam's Schiphol Airport. Resplendent in a pink outfit tastefully punctuated with yellow flowers and a green polka-dotted vest, Mitra and I excitedly awaited her friend's arrival. We watched each and every Northwest passenger head through customs. Dana was not among them.

Distraught, Mitra came up with an impossible analysis. "Maybe she didn't see me, Daddy."

"That's absurd," I said. "No one could possibly miss you. Will you go to the information desk and ask to have her paged?"

"I'd like to, but I have homework… Ah, yes, well, uh…I'll be, uh, right back."

Mitra indignantly returned. "Those jerks won't let us page anyone. People flying in can page people waiting, but people waiting can't page people flying in."

I was getting a bit annoyed and a bit worried. I told Mitra we'd find a way around the Schiphol paging rules, then suggested that we check the Northwest ticket counter. They were decidedly unhelpful.

By now, I was concerned. The airplane had been on the ground for an hour and a half. We couldn't find Dana. What would we tell her parents back home in New Hampshire? "Gosh, I'm sorry, Penny, but we couldn't find her."

Mitra and I decided on a stealthy approach at the information desk. I left Mitra at Northwest's ticket counter. Remembering her experience, I planted myself at the information desk and launched into a deceptive description of the problem. Essentially, I lied.

"Hi. I'm Dan Martin and I just arrived from Boston on Northwest Flight 42. Would you page Ms. Dana Zeilinger for me? She's supposed to meet me here."

Mitra and I felt very sly as the announcement was played on the public address system. "Will Miss Dana Zeilinger, meeting Boston arriving passenger Dan Martin, please apply to the airport information desk." Our sly satisfaction should have been tempered. This type of message is only announced in the area outside of baggage claim. We were outside of baggage claim. Dana wasn't.

After a short and nervous wait, I decided to call Nazy for help.

Sounding somewhat confused, I began the conversation. "Has Dana called you, Nazy?"

"What do you mean, has she called me? You're the one at the airport. You're supposed to pick her up, remember?"

"I know that, but we can't find her."

"You can't find her? Were you late?"

"Of course I wasn't late. Mitra woke me up in the middle of the night."

"I bet she's waiting for you at the gate."

"Thanks, Nazy, you're probably right. Any ideas on how to get through passport control?"

"You'll think of something. Call me when you find her."

I took Mitra back to the Northwest counter. The shift had changed and the new clerk was much more helpful. We were assured that Dana had been on the flight in seat 17J. They sent someone on a fruitless search of the gate and asked me to have her paged.

We told them we appreciated all the help, but we really needed to get through passport control ourselves. The reply, "I'm sorry, but that's just not possible," was typically Dutch.

Typically American, I decided to take matters into my own hands. I left Mitra at the Northwest counter and strolled toward passport control. They wouldn't let me through because I didn't have a boarding pass, but the immigration agent had helpful suggestion. An exception could have been made if the missing person had been my child. Otherwise, of course, it simply "wasn't possible."

Fortunately, there are two passport control stations at Schiphol. Agents at the second station, out of sight of the first, were unprepared as I marched up and announced the problem.

"My daughter came on Northwest Flight 42, but she's never flown outside of the United States. I'm certain she is waiting for me at the gate. You must let me through to get her."

"Do you have a boarding card, sir?"

"No, *I'm* not boarding. I just want to get my daughter."

"Do you have a passport, sir?"

"Of course I have a passport, an American passport. At home. But I don't need a passport. I'm not going anywhere. You must let me through. I can't just stand here while my daughter is crying at the gate."

Now, I decided, it was time to play the trump card. "You can't ignore my request. It's simply *not possible*."

"Your daughter is waiting at the gate?"

"Undoubtedly."

"Why didn't she fly as an unaccompanied minor?"

"I was in Den Haag. She was in Boston. I must get in. I'll come back out through this station."

"Normally, it's not possible."

"Thank you for making the exception," I shouted as I dashed past the barricade.

I found Dana patiently waiting at gate C46. Schiphol Airport is large. Gate C46 is in Leiden.

I located a Northwest agent and asked her to send Mitra to baggage claim to meet us.

"Is that the girl in the pink outfit?"

"Yeah, it's pink. It's yellow. It's green. It's purple. It's…"

"Don't worry, sir, they'll recognize her."

We made it. I even convinced Mitra and Dana to get on the boring yellow train for the ride to The Hague. The next day was easy—I just had to get up early for a trip to the dentist.

I still need sunglasses and earplugs when I look at Mitra, but her early morning cheerfulness was short-lived—in due course, she returned to normal. It wasn't even clear that she was alive in the mornings. Unfortunately, Melika had grabbed the fallen gauntlet. Melika can be very cheerful in the morning; it's the afternoon that causes her problems. And as we were ending our second year in the Netherlands, Melika missed her friends.

Finally, the second Christmas came. We weren't prepared, there wasn't any snow, we hadn't bought any presents, and everyone had a cold. In short…

THERE'S NO CHRISTMAS SPIRIT

Darius was despondant. "We're not going to have Christmas this year, Dad."

"Why not?"

"Because no one has any Christmas spirit in this house. No one cares about tradition. Nobody is doing anything. It's sickening."

"Are you a little upset?"

"Upset, Dad? Upset? No! I'm not upset, I'm disgusted. Why don't *you* care about Christmas? Why isn't Mommy doing anything? Why aren't you doing anything? Where are the decorations? Where are the…"

I interrupted. "Darius, we *are* doing traditional things. Mommy has Mitra's needlepoint stocking out and…"

"Yeah, Dad, she's got it out, but she's not doing anything with it. It'll never be finished."

"That's tradition, Darius. Tradition—a wonderful thing."

"Dad!"

"Yes?"

"That's disgusting."

Darius, while typically annoying, was also correct. Prinsevinkenpark didn't have the seasonal feel. Christmas shopping hadn't begun, the tree hadn't been installed, Christmas cookies hadn't been made, and cards not only hadn't been mailed, they hadn't even been purchased. It wasn't as if we didn't have enough warning—the Dutch shops had been promoting Christmas since September. The problem was logistics. We had visitors—parental visitors—who took lots of time. We had colds. We had play practice. We had... Well, we had waited too long. We were behind.

Darius wasn't the only person with problems. Mitra was swamped in schoolwork. A singing role in *Oliver* had her in endless rehearsals. She had volunteered for the speech and debate team before finding about their rehearsal schedule. She was a chem lab assistant and a defense attorney in a mock trial for her English class. Her French book report on the five-hundred-page *Le Fantôme de L'Opéra* was due. (Her friends read things like the fifty-page *Newcomer's Guide to Paris*.) Mitra was reacting to the overload situation by shedding "unimportant" tasks. For many children, this would have meant things like bed-making, clothes picking-up, and other routine household tasks. Mitra had already shed that load. Her response was to scatter homework around the house, and to first forget, and then lose, her locker key, her house key, her replacement locker key, her bus pass, her homework... It was really getting out of control. She was beginning to remind us of Darius.

Nazy was also swamped. While she had enjoyed her parents' visit, she had concluded that daily entertaining chores rapidly ate into her time. She wasn't amused by needlepoint jokes, and she didn't even have time to make Christmas cookies. Everyone could tell it was a major disaster: Even Nazy had been unable to find time to go shopping.

I was overwhelmed as well. Shell was in the midst of its annual reorganization. Cormac, my mentor and the person responsible for the family relocation, wasn't going to be part of the new organization. Shell's Committee of Managing Directors (CMD) would be meeting in an extraordinary session to endorse the continuation of the project and, coincidentally, my job. I wasn't worried. Annoyed, dismayed, besieged, and disgruntled, but not worried.

Only Melika was calm, serene, and totally prepared. She had saved her allowance and had enough money to buy presents. Mitra tried, but her nest egg had been markedly diminished by required and regular purchases of replacement locker keys, house keys, and tram passes. Darius? Let's just say his body contained a chemical compound that created a flammable mixture in any pocket containing money. Melika had selected and wrapped each present. She had even decided on what she wanted from Santa Claus—a real cat.

The good news: The current overload situation was coming to an end. Guest departure, the play, the speech tournament, and the CMD meeting were all scheduled for mid-December. If we could stay alive until then, it would be strictly downhill.

"Dad?"

"Yes, Darius?"

"Melika wants a cat for Christmas."

"A cat?"

"Yeah, a cat. Is she going to get one?"

"A cat is a big responsibility. Where would we put it when we went on vacation? Who would feed it? How could we get it back into the States when we move? Don't you think a cat is an unrealistic request?"

"Maybe. But she *really* wants a cat. Do you think she'll get one?"

"A cat is not a good idea, Darius."

"She's really going to be disappointed. This is going to be a terrible Christmas. Mommy hasn't even made any sugar cookies."

"That's because when we went shopping, we forgot to get all of the ingredients."

"What did we forget?"

"Sugar. We forgot *sugar*."

"Oh. Could I borrow some guilders? I need to pick up a cat toy for Melika. Do you think that would be a useful gift?"

"Darius!"

The mid-December relief date came and the family was almost too exhausted to notice. Mitra provided a predictably brilliant performance in her play. Her French teacher wanted to know if "there was anything Mitra couldn't do." We suggested housework. Nazy and I agreed that Mitra's talent was a simple indication of the importance of genes.

The family tree, a Norwegian blue spruce, was finally acquired and installed. The German *Christbaumständer*, acquired for the giant sequoia of the previous year, met the new need perfectly. Nazy located a not-to-be-missed Dutch event—lighting the city tree in Gouda. The Martin Family headed for Centraal Station for the (newly) traditional trek to Gouda.

The city, famous for cheese in America, is pronounced gHOWda in Dutch. (It is their country; if they want to screw up the pronunciation, there's nothing we can do about it.)

The train was so crowded that we couldn't sit together. We were clearly sharing tradition with others. Darius struck up a conversation with his seatmate. I couldn't hear everything, but I did catch snippets that wafted their way toward me. ("My sister really wants a cat for Christmas but my parents..." "Nobody in our family has any Christmas spirit this year.")

We walked from the Gouda station to the city center, where we discovered we were a few hours early. We located a suitable restaurant on the square and ordered dinner. We discussed the attraction while we waited for our meals to arrive.

"So Nazy, what's the big deal about the tree-lighting ceremony in Gouda?" I asked.

"That's gHOWda, Dan. It says that the ceremony 'should not be missed.' Everyone comes to the town square to see the tree and to sing Christmas carols."

"I said 'Gouda,' dear. Why does everyone come?"

"Yes, you said 'Gouda.' You should have said 'gHOWda.'"

"What I said was, 'Why do they come here?' And that, my dear, remains the question."

"It says that all the stores and houses turn off their lights and all the townsfolk put candles in their windows. Then the tree is lit and everyone sings carols."

"Do they sing in English or Dutch?"

"Good cheer, Dan. Be of good cheer."

I was trying to be cheerful, but I was cold and squished. I was hungry, too. We had been sitting at the table for an inordinately lengthy time. When it arrived, the food was cold and squished. Just as it was placed in front of us, all of the lights in the restaurant went out.

Darius jumped. "Hurry up, Dad! We're gonna miss it. You're gonna mess up the tradition. I'm going outside right now to see what's happening. Why'd you pick this restaurant anyway? We should've just gone to McDonald's."

We wolfed down the meal, the better to disguise the taste, and dashed outside. Actually, we tried to dash outside. The town square was crowded. We joined hands, pushed a few tourists out of the way, and got elbowed by a few natives. We shoved our way to within sight of the tree.

The town square was quite picturesque. The square was dominated by a remarkable town hall. All the lights were turned off, and there were candles in every window. Had there been room to breathe, it would have been a bit better.

As usual, Darius was complaining. "I can't see anything, Dad."

"You're not supposed to see anything. You're supposed to listen. The mayor is talking now."

Nazy interrupted. "Maybe he's talking, Dan, but I wish he'd shut up and turn on the tree. I can't understand a word he's saying. Why does he insist on speaking Dutch?"

"Nazy, he's speaking English."

"Really? I can't understand it. The crowd noise is drowning him out. What's he talking about?"

"He's thanking the Norwegian ambassador for the tree donation."

"In English?"

Just then, the tree lights appeared. Everyone cheered. I lifted Melika over the crowd to see. We began to surge forward for a better look, and the crowd burst into song—in Dutch.

Darius was beside himself. There simply wasn't enough room.

"What kind of a tradition is this, Dad? We sit on a crowded train, we stand in the freezing rain, we see Zwarte Pieten from Spain…"

"Darius! You're real pain. Do not make a rhyme again."

"Yeah, Dad. Well, what's traditional about this?"

"It reminds me of a famous Christmas story. Remember the Grinch and 'all the Whos down in Whoville'? We're the Who Family."

"We're not the Who Family, we're the crazy family."

On the train ride back to The Hague, I sat with Melika and asked about her Christmas wish list.

"I just want one thing, Daddy. A real, live cat."

"A cat? Uh…you have an allergy to cats, Melika."

"We *need* a cat, Daddy. It won't be Christmas without a cat."

"A cat is a very complicated gift. What else would you like?"

"I don't want anything else, just a cat."

"Did you like the tree-lighting ceremony?"

"It was too crowded."

"Just like your Waldo books, eh? Would you like a Waldo book for Christmas? What's the name of the newest Waldo book?"

"It's *Where's Waldo's Cat?*"

We finally entered the holiday home stretch. Nazy was really worried—a week before Christmas and not a present was bought, and to the wish list, we had given not a thought. She was convinced we'd never get everything done. I wasn't worried. All of Nazy's concerns could be resolved by shopping and buying. With Nazy on my team, there was little doubt of success. So we hit the streets.

The final week went quickly, but not without another discussion with Darius.

"She wants a cat, Dad. If she doesn't get a cat she's going to cry."

"That's ridiculous. No one cries on Christmas. There are lots of things that she wants. Don't worry."

"Is she going to get a cat?"

"Darius, she's allergic to cats. Mitra is allergic to cats. You're allergic to cats. Mom is allergic to cats. Do you want to make the whole family sick?"

"We need a miracle. She really wants a cat."

"Did Melika ask you to talk to me?"

And the feline discussions continued.

A miracle occurred before Christmas. Melika made the announcement. "Daddy! Mitra's in the kitchen."

"So what? That's where we eat."

"She's *cooking*, Daddy."

"*Cooking*? Mitra? Are you sure?"

"Mitra's in there cooking, Daddy. Do we have to eat it?"

"Eat what?"

"Whatever she's making. Do we have to eat it?"

It was completely out of character for Mitra. Melika quickly collected Nazy and Darius, and we all tiptoed to the kitchen door and peered in. It was amazing. There she was, actually cooking. It wasn't a complete miracle; she wasn't cleaning.

"Do you want me to go in and find out what's up, Dan?" Nazy whispered.

"Please. And see if she's feeling okay."

"I'm not eating anything Mitra cooks. You can't make me," warned Darius.

"Calm down. I don't remember Mitra ever cooking anything. What are you worried about?"

"Remember the bread she made in Hanover, Dad? We had to borrow Chris Sachs's chain saw."

"You're right. We'll be careful."

Nazy came back out. The rest of the family was huddled in the hall awaiting the news.

"She's just in the Christmas spirit. She's making cookies."

"I'm not eating it, Dad."

"That's enough, Darius. Let's listen to what your mother has to say. If she's making cookies, why has she sliced all those tomatoes?"

"It's a special recipe. I talked her out of using the grated turnips."

"I'm *not eating* that stuff."

The family was treated to Mitra-prepared culinary delights for the next several days. Cookies that were eaten with a spoon. Gingerbread pavement slabs. A disintegrating cake. The kitchen was a perpetual mess, but everybody bravely tried the wonders.

Christmas Eve finally arrived. Melika was despondent and abnormally quiet. She had had a long discussion with Nazy about cats. Nazy, on the other hand, was feeling good. Every necessary gift had been acquired.

We had a great dessert—real sugar cookies.

When we tried to pack the children off to bed later that evening, I caught Darius in the kitchen with a molar in his hand.

"Did Mitra make these cookies, Dad? Look what happened to my tooth."

"Darius," I replied, "that tooth was already loose."

At that point, Mitra joined us. She wanted to know why Darius was trying to eat a Christmas tree decoration.

"It looked like a sugar cookie."

"Well, it's not. It's a tree decoration. I baked it with the gingerbread."

"Oh yeah? Then where's the hole for the hook?"

"Darius you're a… Daddy, do we have a drill?"

"We've got a drill," I replied, "but I think we left the diamond bits back in Hanover."

The children finally trundled off to bed. Darius whispered a final warning about kittens.

Christmas morning was definitively Dutch—gray and drizzly. The children dashed downstairs. Mitra was overjoyed by the new clothes she received—a red sequin hat, a gold sequin purse, and sparkly silver shoes. She gave the Julia Child cookbook to Nazy. Darius quickly conquered his Kasparov chess computer (the first level) and moved on. Christmas dinner, prepared by Nazy, came sans salt. Mitra had disposed of that and any other useful condiments.

For Melika, Santa had left a note—something about a Persian kitten. The kitten, which was real and live, was bounding around the room knocking needles off the tree. Melika was overjoyed.

Darius snuck into the kitchen, grabbed one of Mitra's gingerbread slabs, and crumbled it into the new cat food bowl. He was finally in the spirit.

It turned out that only Darius was allergic to the cat. Asthma, a scourge vanquished when we moved from Hanover, reappeared. We weren't exactly sure what to do. Melika wanted to solve the problem by voting Darius out of the family,

An intercontinental move puts enormous strain on everyone. It's important to maintain family traditions and to have a calm and safe harbor, a rock of solidity in a stormy sea of change. For us, the traditional Persian New Year celebration (which we've performed everywhere but Persia) is our citadel of stability. On New Year's Day, which occurs on the first day of spring, we greet each other with Persian wishes, "Aide shoma mobarack." Some of us can't quite pronounce the Persian.

AID A SHOMA EAT A SNACK

The boy nervously glanced over his shoulder as he slinked into the kitchen. It would soon be dinnertime, but he was hungry. As silent as a stalking cat, he pried open the kitchen cupboard and slyly grabbed a jar of Nutella. A quick, well-practiced twist of the wrist had the cap off. Warily, he stabbed his finger into the chocolate-and-hazelnut concoction before slipping the jar back into the cupboard. He was in the process of quietly closing the cabinet door when the Dutch-designed tension-grip mechanism took control. The door slammed shut and obliterated the silence necessary for his furtive task.

A worrisome voice broke the quiet. "Darius! It's dinnertime."

The boy, an avid reader of spy novels, knew it was actually "desperation time." He dashed toward the back door, sticking the evidence-covered finger in his mouth. He only had time for a quick glance over his shoulder to see how close his opposition was.

Too close! Worse, although several independent events were combining to create a confluence of catastrophe, he was unaware of the hopelessness of his situation.

Melika, conscientiously obeying standing rules to keep the doors closed, had shut the back door milliseconds before Darius began his escape. The door, with its automatic dead bolt, had latched solidly shut mere microseconds before Darius crashed into it. On his rebound from the door, Darius bit his finger.

Nazy watched in awe as her son bounced off the back door. "Are you all right, Darius? What happened?"

For Darius, this was a major mess. It was Persian New Year, the meal was set, his finger was hurt, and, on the rebound from the door, he had knocked a pile of laundry into some trash bags. He was in big trouble. He remembered that the best defense is a good offense.

"Who closed the stupid door? I was just going out to ride my bike."

"Are you all right? Let me look at the finger, I hope you didn't hurt yourself. I thought you might have been trying to sneak a bit of Nutella before dinner."

"Ah, come off it, Mom. I know the rules. My finger's fine. Besides, Melika closed the stupid door right in my face."

"She's supposed to close the door. Let me see your finger. Is it bleeding?"

When Darius exposed his middle finger, he compounded his problem. He hadn't quite consumed all the Nutella. Luckily, it was Persian New Year, and Nazy was in a good mood. After a final lick of his damaged finger, Darius left to wash up for dinner.

The dinner was a traditional meal of *sabzi polo*—Persian rice with dill weed and fresh fish. The family adjourned to wait for the vernal equinox. A ritual table, the *haft seen*, is traditional on Persian New Year. *Haft seen* refers to seven items that begin with the Persian letter *S*, which is pronounced "seen." My English translates it to a table of seven sins.

We had decided to call Nazy's parents at the exact time of the equinox. Melika was busily practicing the New Year's greeting—she wanted to be ready for her turn at the telephone. *"Aide a shoma mobarack. Aide a shoma mobarack..."* The grandfather clock struck ten-nineteen (it's not very accurate), and the family burst into song, impervious to the fact that we didn't understand the words.

Mitra dialed the call to America and began babbling. Listening to her half of the conversation made me wonder if we were getting our money's worth on this particular transatlantic call..

"Aide shoma mobarack, Baba Joon... Yeah, fine. Okay. *Aide shoma mobarack, Mamoon Joon.* Yeah, fine. Okay. Yes. Yes. Oh, *yes.* Fine..." (Translation: I know Darius wants to talk, but it is my turn now!) This went on for several minutes before Darius was able to wrestle control of the telephone, but the litany continued. *"Aide shoma mobarack, Mamoon Joon. Aide shoma, mobarack, Baba Joon.* Yes. Fine..."

Melika finally had her turn. She snuck a quick look at the beckoning dessert and launched into her New Year congratulations. *"Aid a shoma eat a snack."*

Everyone had a good chuckle before I took the telephone. To my dismay, I sounded as inept as the children. Nazy wrapped up the call. In spite of the fact that I work in telecommunications, that she has a master's degree in computer science, and the plainly functional international telephone system, Nazy continues to believe that if the call is long distance, you have to shout to help the system make the transmission. *"AIDE SHOMA MOBARACK, MAMOON JOON! AIDE SHOMA MOBARACK, BABA JOON!"* The neighbors rushed over to see if we were declaring an emergency.

Nazy's dad reminded us of an ancient New Year tradition. On New Year's Day, the family should leave the house by the back door and then reenter from the front. Moreover, to guarantee good luck, they should carry flowers during this traditional trek. When Nazy hung up, everyone grabbed a hyacinth, departed from the back door, and tiptoed through the tulips. I even remembered to grab the keys before we made our exit. It was Dutch weather—blustery drizzle. The Martin Family looked rather ridiculous as we traipsed toward the front door. Mitra and Melika were wearing robes.

When we made it to the door, I triumphantly pulled the keys out of my pocket, but as I expectantly pushed it I remembered the manual dead bolt, which was not controlled by the key. I had set it earlier in the evening. The family tromped through the tulips toward the back door while Nazy serenaded us with the traditional Dutch warning "*Let op de hond poep!*" Inevitably, Darius responded to the warning—a little late.

We made it to the back door, but were dismayed to learn that Melika had shut it—per the standing household rule. Shutting the door activated the automatic lock, and there was no key for it. Melika succinctly summed up the situation.

"We're dead, Dad."

"We should keep an emergency key hidden," Darius opined.

"That wouldn't do any good," Nazy said. "We already have a key. We still can't get in."

I was annoyed. "That's right, we do have a key. So what? Does Persian tradition make a statement about a year that begins like this?"

Everyone was getting cold and short-tempered. The lights were coming on in neighbors' houses—they wanted to investigate the strange goings-on at the Martin residence. The family retired to the bicycle shed to huddle in misery and plan our next move.

After a quick check to make sure none of the downstairs doors to the garden were unlocked, we voted to hoist Darius to the second floor. He crawled in through a window and let everyone in.

At a subsequent family meeting, we decided to let Nazy explain the nocturnal wanderings of The Martin Family to the neighbors. (It was, after all, *her* New Year holiday.) We also decided that our experience presaged an *exciting* New Year. Darius's motion that Melika be a bit less rigorous in her enforcement of the "closed door" policy was unanimously adopted.

While we were in Europe, we tried to keep in touch with both Nazy's and my families. The six-hour time difference made it difficult and, for my parents, the thought of an international telephone call was extremely unconventional. Imagine my surprise when my dad called on July 22, 1992.

"Is everything all right?" I asked.

"Of course. Happy anniversary. Twenty years, right?"

"You remembered. I never knew you were so romantic."

"Yep, 1972. That's the year we bought the Buick."

"Hmm."

"I'm glad your marriage lasted longer than that car."

"Thanks."

"Want to talk with your mom?"

The year was exciting. And the back door was usually unlocked. Unfortunately, mosquitoes were able to fly in. (Why hasn't someone told Europe about screen doors?) We didn't worry about the neighbors, who were a sophisticated group. They weren't even fazed when the local Romanian dropped out of sight after the revolution. Besides, why worry about small things like what the neighbors think?

Residence-wise, things were changing. The spiritless Christmas was our last at Prinsevinkenpark. The diplomatic clause that seemed so reasonable when we moved in was now being used to force us out.

THE BAD HOUSE

It was an ominous development: A letter that required a signature for delivery had arrived at the Prinsevinkenpark home. Full comprehension would require time-consuming efforts involving an intimate relationship with the Dutch/English dictionary, but I immediately detected the phrase "diplomatic clause." Reacting quickly, I made a copy of the letter and asked Mitra for a translation.

"We have to move by the end of the year," Mitra explained after an embarrassingly rapid review of the document.

"The end of the year? That's in three months."

"Who signed a contract with a 'diplomatic clause,' Dad?"

I ignored Mitra's rejoinder, called Shell to arrange for help in locating a new abode, and prepared to explain the challenge to Nazy.

Hendrik Petrus Berlage—a well-known Dutch architect who, after a visit to the United States, increasingly incorporated the approach of Frank Lloyd Wright in his work—had designed the Prinsevinkenpark house. Berlage also designed the Museon, the municipal museum in The

Hague. It was a well-known building in Den Haag: Our house, we discovered, was also well known:

One morning when Nazy dashed into the rain for a quick walk to the nearby Bankastraat bakery, she was met by a tour bus filled with people taking photographs of "our" house.

"I wish I had known," Nazy explained later. "I would have dressed differently."

"Differently?"

"I was in some of the photos and I wasn't dressed properly. And I was carrying a broken umbrella."

"You were walking to the store to get bread."

"You can't live in a house like this and carry a broken umbrella."

We were comfortable and didn't want to move. I called Stefanie, my Human Resources contact.

"We're being ejected," I explained.

"That's what the diplomatic clause means."

"The guy who owns the house is a Shell employee who is repatriating from Norway. Do you think you could, say, 'void' his transfer?"

"*Kan niet.*" (The all-purpose Dutch response.)

Stefanie helped put Nazy in touch with a real estate agent. I shared helpful hints: "I found the Prinsevinkenpark residence all by myself. I'm sure you can do better. Just remember: We need a drawing room."

Nazy explained the "choices" to me:

"Too expensive, too small, too remote, too old."

"Too bad," I replied.

I was convinced we'd have to leave The Hague or greatly exceed the housing allowance. Nazy decided on an alternative approach. She canvassed her friends in the Petroleum Wives Club and the American Women's Club. The clock, which began ticking in September, accelerated. The ticks became louder and soon December arrived.

"You know," I explained to Nazy, "I found a house in less than a week. You've been looking for months and…"

Reader warning: The interests of domestic tranquility are not well-served by accurate, but inappropriate, commentary.

A few days later, Nazy's friend, Susan, called to say that they were being transferred to Paris and that "the landlord is looking for a new tenant."

The house was located on Badhuisweg, about two hundred meters from Kurhaus Hotel and the Scheveningen beach. It was also very close to the Stievenstraat shopping district. We drove over to see and were quickly impressed.

"Look at that, Dad!" Darius exclaimed. "The Bad House."

"Bad house?"

"We're on the Badhuisweg. So this is the Bad House."

In Dutch, *"bad"* means "bath." The Badhuisweg was the old route to the changing rooms at the beach.

"But this house has a name: Adele."

Darius was right. The name Adele was displayed in colorful tiles over the front door. The house was even larger than the Prinsevinkenpark estate. It had a front garden (a bit overgrown) and stained glass windows. Everyone liked Adele and, more impressively, the Badhuis fit Shell's housing allowance. We immediately negotiated a rental agreement that did not have a diplomatic clause. Nazy arranged for a mover to transport our stuff on December 30.

The day before the big move, we packed some of our fragile items into the car and drove to Badhuisweg to deliver them. Before returning to Prinsevinkenpark, we toured the house to reach agreement on room assignments. Our final stop was the family room.

"These windows are really totally tubular, Dad," Mitra observed.

"Tubular?"

"In 'adult' we'd say 'cool' or 'neat' or…"

"Sexy?"

"Or artistically magnificent," Nazy interrupted.

"The windows are very heavy," I noted, returning to the subject. "Mr. Sangster, our landlord, said we should be careful…"

While I was talking, Mitra opened a heavy window just as a gust of wind from the very nearby *Noordzee* (North Sea) rumbled down Badhuisweg. The leaded, stained-glass window, which she had previously rotated into the wind, now acted like a spinnaker. The bolts that connected the hinges to the house were unable to resist, and the expensive window crashed into the front yard. There was nothing to do but complete my sentence.

"…with the window, it may fall out if it's windy."

"Thanks for telling me, Dad," Mitra replied.

"Would you like to tell Mr. Sangster what you did?"

"You can handle that," she said.

Expecting less fireworks if I brought a child, I selected Melika (and the cat) to accompany me for the explanatory meeting with Mr. Sangster. Fortunately, he liked cats (he had several) and he liked Melika. I also learned that every tenant who had rented the Badhuis had dropped a stained glass window into the front yard. He had a large supply of spares in the basement.

My elation was quashed as I recounted the meeting to Nazy. "The windows are not one of a kind. Mr. Sangster has a large supply in the basement."

In spite of the inauspicious start, the move was trouble-free. As much as we had liked Prinsevinkenpark, we enjoyed Badhuis even more. Although not designed by Berlage, it was a well-known residence. We sometimes got mail addressed as simply:

Adele

Scheveningen

The Netherlands

(Scheveningen is a district in The Hague.)

And, by the way, Adele had a drawing room.

Things were still progressing slowly at the office. We had evaluated vendor responses to our tender. Formal procedures had been followed, but with some difficulty. The procedure mandated a finding of technical validity from telecommunications directors in both the UK and the Netherlands. The Dutch response was clear, and the UK response was a masterpiece of prose. It was written so that it could be read as an agreement if the project worked or as a warning if it didn't. Cormac was away, so I asked his Dutch boss, Frans Kooyman, for advice.

"What does it say, Dan?"

"I'm not sure. That's why I asked you for advice."

"It's your native language."

"Actually, Frans, it's English. I speak American."

"We want it to say 'yes,' don't we?"

"Indeed."

"Then let's just assume that's what it says."

The official scribe for the formal process handled the confusion with aplomb: "It appears that a finding of technical validity has been agreed."

But this was work. We had important family problems and complex challenges. We had to get the family out the door in time to see a movie.

LET'S GO!

It was just a simple family outing, but it had the inevitable tension required of any timely departure. "Schedule" and "on time" are phrases that strike fear in the hearts of Martin family members. Unfortunately, we were in Holland, where "fashionably late" means "on time." Besides, we were going to a movie, and at least half of the family wanted to arrive before the show began. We had already factored in the half hour of commercials shown before the film, but were still running late. The departure was continuously delayed.

"Let's go!" Nazy shouted from the bedroom. There was no family response; Nazy frequently shouts "Let's go" when *she's* not ready. I glanced into the room and, sure enough, Nazy was standing there wrapped in a towel, trying to decide what to wear.

"I'm ready," she opined, having seen my skeptical look. "I just have to jump into my clothes. What do you think I should wear?"

At that point, Darius ambled into the bedroom. He was wearing one white and one black sock, his shirt was on inside out, and he was still in his pajama bottoms. "Come on, Mom, you're going to make us all late," he whined.

I went to wrestle Darius into a more suitable outfit, and passed Melika on the way upstairs. She had a collection of hair "thingees" and wanted Nazy to fix her hair. I put on my sunglasses as I passed Mitra's room. Garishly clad, she was "doing homework," well-hidden from the fray. Darius and I found suitable attire and I foolishly left him to put it on himself.

Back in our bedroom, Nazy had fixed Melika's hair and had tried on and discarded several different outfits. She was still wrapped in a towel. "Let's *go!*" she cried to no one in particular. Just as she was donning her final outfit, Mitra appeared with a bunch of hair "thingees" and a request for assistance. Melika, meanwhile, had grabbed a book and begun to read. I went upstairs to check on Darius.

There was no visible progress in Darius's suite. He had partially disrobed, but he been distracted by his stamp album. He was busily sorting through a collection of stamps while simultaneously reading his atlas. I suggested he get dressed and started to leave the room, but, being an experienced parent, quickly glanced back.

"No, Darius! Put on the clothes we picked. Don't put the same clothes back on."

Downstairs, Mitra's hair was fixed, and Nazy had decided on an outfit and was busily applying makeup. Melika had finished one book and was starting on another. "Let's go!" Nazy's voice reverberated against the high ceilings. Mitra, experienced in the process, began reading *War and Peace*. I dashed back upstairs to get Darius. He had finally gotten dressed in the clothes I had picked. Too late, I realized I had made a fatal error: I, rather than Nazy, had picked his clothes. We bravely marched down the stairs to face Nazy's inquisition.

Another "Let's go" was echoing throughout the Bad House as we cautiously entered the master bedroom. "Darius! What are you wearing? Those pants don't fit you and it's the wrong season for that shirt. Where is your belt? Look at your hair. Now go upstairs and wear something reasonable."

"But, Mom, Dad picked…" Darius began just before I jammed an elbow into his Adam's apple. We began the ascent to his room. Melika started to work on her science project, and Mitra, having finished *War and Peace*, turned on the TV. BBC2 was showing a documentary on medieval British history.

Darius and I selected another outfit. I remained in his room to make sure he would actually wear it. We were just about finished when a cheerful "Let's go!" shook the rafters. The tenor of this announcement carried with it the weight of authority. We began our descent to the ground floor.

I put on my jacket. Mitra, less optimistic, had started work on her eighty-page French report. Melika came downstairs and announced that she was hungry and departed for the kitchen. Darius showed up with his stamp collection and library; he wanted to read on the tram and during the movie commercials. Nazy was still upstairs, turning off the lights.

Finally, Nazy, elegantly making her entrance down the curved staircase, noticed a few minor problems. "Mitra, let's go! Darius, you may not bring your books and stamps. And where are your shoes? Where's Melika?"

Melika strolled out of the kitchen. Unfortunately, she was strolling with apple juice all over her blouse. She left to change. Mitra, meanwhile, bounced down the stairs and grabbed her jacket. Darius entered blame mode.

"Where are my shoes? Who stole my shoes? They were right here. Melika hid my shoes. Why can't I bring my books? Come on, Mom, you've made everyone late."

Melika reappeared, only to ignite another fight. "Mitra, that's the coat I was going to wear. Mommy, why does Mitra get to wear that coat? And I didn't take Darius's stupid shoes."

Mitra, reluctant to give up her coat—it clashed with her outfit—pretended to be above the fray. Darius, meanwhile, had found two left shoes and was trying to convince Nazy that it was good enough. Mitra and Melika reached a compromise: Mitra wore the coat, but Melika got to wear Mitra's hair "thingee." Unfortunately, this meant both girls' hair had to be reworked. I sat down on the stairs and began reading *The Complete Works of Shakespeare*.

Darius, ever up to the challenge, finally found a shoe for his right foot. "See, Mom, bringing the stamps was a good idea. I found my shoe in the stamp collection." We were ready.

I, who had been cool as I read my book, suddenly realized I didn't have the house keys. Providently, I was able to cover my misfortune. "Melika, do you have to go to the bathroom?" I inquired as I began to look for the keys. This created a sudden surge in bathroom visits. Just as predictably, there was no toilet paper in the downstairs WC. Mitra left to find toilet paper and I scoured the pockets of my nearby jackets. I found the keys just as everyone was finishing.

"Let's go!" I said as we walked out the door. We began strolling toward the tram.

"Did you turn off the oven, Dan?" Nazy inquired as we passed the ten-meter mark—just before we turned around and walked back.

STUMBLING THROUGH THE TULIPS

The oven was off, but as veteran of these events, I made sure the iron was unplugged. We walked out again. This time, we made it forty meters when a crash of thunder interrupted our quiet merriment. We all turned back toward the house to get raincoats and umbrellas. We left again.

Just as we were turning the corner, I looked back at the house, only to see the window to Mitra's room wide open. With rain threatening, it seemed worthwhile to head back and close the window. We also took the opportunity to turn off the light in Melika's room and leave Darius's stamps in the house—again. We departed for the tram, which we just missed.

Our arrival at the movie theatre was ill-timed. The movie was almost over and the second showing was already sold out. But it was the queen's birthday, and surely there would be something happening in The Hague. We walked across the Binnenhof, where we saw an American-style country fair.

At least it looked like a country fair. They called it the *kermis*. Rides and games of chance were set up in the square.

Darius was thrilled. "Come on, let's go!"

Although there weren't many rides that would permit retention of dinner, I warily agreed. Nazy demurely endorsed the idea but resolutely resolved to not ride. We walked to a nearby *kassa* (booth) and purchased a bundle of ride tokens.

It was a mistake. At American country fairs, you buy tokens that are good on every ride. In a *kermis*, you buy different tokens for each ride. I had purchased thirty rides on the carousel, which was aimed at the under-two set. Our children were quickly bored.

Mitra and Darius set up a cut-rate shop to resell our surplus tokens, and Melika spotted the cotton candy machine. I was trying to convince Nazy that the carousel token fiasco was her fault.

Having cut our losses to forty guilders, the children were ready for adventure. Besides, as Mitra observed, "We can keep the rest of the tokens as souvenirs."

Given the way the evening had gone, the family found a completely appropriate ride—the bumper cars. Primal urges for destruction, coupled with extensive experience driving real cars in Europe, had readied us for the challenge. We purchased our tokens and took our place along the ride boundary. There were no lines. Instead, there was chaos.

When a bell rang, the cars stopped and a surging throng of bodies dashed for open vehicles. Thirty seconds later, there was another bell. Those not safely ensconced in a bumper car had five seconds to race to the perimeter. A final bell rang and the games began.

After several fruitless dashes into the bumper car arena, The Martin Family gathered to plot strategy. Darius had noted the numbers of the cars that had the best performance, Melika asked passing vehicles to stop next to us, and Nazy thought the whole thing was stupid. I craftily pushed the children out of the way so I could get a running start. We had *lots* of bumper car tokens.

As luck would have it, the bell rang just as a Los Angles–sized traffic jam ground to a halt directly in front of us. We all grabbed cars and settled in.

There's something about bumper cars that brings the instinct for devastation to the fore. The Martin Family was ready. We thought the Dutch couldn't touch us in bumper car warfare. We were wrong. The Dutch drive bumper cars the same way the Italians drive real cars—wildly. We escaped with minor whiplash and made our way to the Ferris wheel and rides called the Maze, Octopus, and Galicticon.

The crowds were thick, but we were having a good time. Nazy suggested a trip to Scheveningen for ice cream and the queen's birthday fireworks. "Let's go," she trilled, unthrilled by the *kermis*.

"We're having fun, Mom. I don't want to go to stupid fireworks. Let's ride that one," Darius said, eyeing a ride that seemed to simultaneously rock, roll, rotate, revolve, and revolt its passengers.

I quickly browsed through my pocket Dutch/English Dictionary. "Darius," I said, "I refuse to ride something called the Vomit Machine."

A quick family meeting was called to decide whether we would walk or tram to the fireworks and ice cream. Nazy wanted to walk. "It's healthy."

I suggested the tram. "It's quick, and besides, we pay taxes—lots of taxes—to fund public transportation. We should use the trams."

"But, Dad, if our taxes pay for the trams, why do we have to buy *stripennkaarten*?"

"Darius, do you want to ride the tram or do you want to walk?"

"I'll ride."

"Then shut up and vote."

The vote was not even close (four to one), but since Nazy was the "one," the issue was not settled. Fortunately a tram arrived and we decided to continue the discussion sitting down.

At least we thought we'd be sitting down, but we hadn't counted on everyone else in the city being on tram nine. I had thought everyone else in the city was at the *kermis*. The trip was enlightening.

"Dad, what do you think about entomological meaning of Greek mythology?" Darius inquired.

"Speak English, Darius, not Dutch."

"Okay, then, what's the capitol of Mongolia?"

My thought patterns were interrupted by a scream of anguish from Mitra. "My wallet! My wallet! My wallet is gone. Oh, no! Mommy just gave it to me. It's gone."

Melika was quick to offer comfort and a commonsense approach to the problem. "Where did you leave it?"

"It was in my purse. It's gone. Gone! GONE! *GONE!*"

Ever the mercenary, Melika asked the next question. "Was there any money in it?"

"I had it in my purse with twenty-five guilders, and Ulan Batar is the stupid capitol of Mongolia, Darius. Oh, damn."

We never discovered what happened to Mitra's wallet. Either she was the victim of a pickpocket, or her wallet had bounced out of her purse in a fierce bumper-car collision. Insult was piled on top of injury when Mitra noticed that her collection of carousel tokens remained unscathed in her purse.

We arrived at Scheveningen at about ten p.m. The sun was just beginning to set and the sky was still bright, but the fireworks were over.

The family was disgusted. Darius summed up the situation. "This is sick, Dad. We left the *kermis* for this? I feel like throwing up."

I was ready. "See? You didn't really miss the Vomit Machine. You feel the same way you would have if you'd gone on that ride." Darius was not amused.

We're not sure why the fireworks went off during daylight. There are two opinions: (1) The Dutch like to listen to fireworks; and (2) The Dutch Bureau of Fireworks Displays, a part of the Royal Dutch Ministry of Popular Diversions, granted a license for fireworks beginning at nine-thirty. I prefer the latter explanation.

The children's feelings were assuaged when we suggested a visit to the trampoline center. It had been an up-and-down day. Once the children had finished and collected their shoes, we walked to the ice cream shop. It was closed.

The family trammed home in silence. (Except for Darius, who thought the whole day was stupid. He wanted to know what I thought of the proposed NATO agreement on biological warfare in eastern Europe.)

When we got home, everyone morosely sat around, cursing fate. Sensing the overall boredom, Nazy zipped into the kitchen to prepare a surprise dessert. Shortly after, a cheery "Let's eat!" reverberated through the house.

Mitra grabbed a copy of *The Iliad* (original Greek), Melika headed upstairs for a deck of cards, and Darius tripped over his stamp collection and began to examine his chess awards.

Nazy's cry of "Let's go" is one of the two most common but scary sentences in the day-to-day life of The Martin Family. The other sentence begins, "What would you think of living in..." Of course, when you have children, there are lots of scary things—like (gasp!) third-grade homework.

When we moved to the Netherlands, we considered sending the children to Dutch schools. However, the Dutch schooling system is, like the language, very complex. Children are streamed very early, and we had missed the streaming. We elected to enroll them in the American School of The Hague (ASH). The school had three separate buildings in The Hague, and naturally we had a child in each one. ASH was moved to the town of Wassenaar a few years after we arrived.

ASH provided American-style education in an international environment. The school had students from about forty different countries, including Kuwait and Iraq—a situation that proved somewhat awkward during the 1991 Gulf War.

WHAT DID YOU LEARN IN SCHOOL TODAY?

Arriving home, I walked into the kitchen and saw Melika with a large bag of giant marshmallows.

"Melika! What are you doing with those marshmallows? We're going to have supper soon. Don't you have any homework?"

"I'm doink homeverk," she said, cramming another marshmallow into her mouth.

"What did you say?"

"Klpkfm!" (Quite articulate for a third grader.)

"Klpkfm? Are you practicing your Dutch?"

The telephone rang. Mitra, who had dashed to pick it up, called out to Nazy. "It's Melika's teacher, Mrs. Bunch. She wants to talk to Mom."

Nazy, ever ebullient, grabbed the phone. They talked briefly about Melika's homework and then, without realizing what she was saying, Nazy said, "Thanks a bunch for calling, Mrs. Bunch."

A bit embarrassed by her faux pas, she was able to explain the situation to me. Melika's class was studying the problems of the disabled, and tonight her assignment was to understand people with speech impediments. She was simulating someone whose tongue was stuck to the roof of their mouth.

Now I could offer encouragement to Melika, who was still struggling with the marshmallows. "That's an interesting assignment, Melika. Would you like to make the simulation a bit more realistic? Why don't I get a bottle of Super Glue?"

"Klpkfm qrtsw dddwwrt!"

"Does that mean, 'Yes, thank you'?"

Melika tried to spit a soggy marshmallow into my hand, but I quickly moved and the marshmallow fell on the floor. There were simultaneous responses from both her mother and me. I said, "Melika! Why did you do that?"

Her mother said, "Dan! Why didn't *you* catch it?"

I asked Darius to pick it up.

"Pick it up? Yuck! It's a soggy, gooey, messy marshmallow with germs. I might vomit if I touch it."

"Yeah, Darius, I might vomit if I have to keep looking at it."

"It's Melika's homework. She should pick it up."

"He does have a point, Melika. Do you want to pick it up?"

"You made me thpit it out, Daddy, you thould pick it up."

Grabbing a paper towel and bowing to the inevitable, I asked Melika how many marshmallows she still had in her mouth.

DANIEL PAUL MARTIN

She was still blustering. "I've got four marthmellowths. Thith homework ith impossible—my mouth ith too little to hold five humonguth marthmellowths."

"Why not try mini marshmallows?" Darius asked.

Melika spit out the remaining marshmallows. "They don't have mini marshmallows in the Konmar, Darius. We have to use the three-centimeter marshmallows."

Darius was ready for her simplistic response. "Come on, three centimeters doesn't matter—nobody knows how big a centimeter is, anyway. Maybe we can ask Lauren to bring some mini marshmallows with her when she comes from America."

"Darius! We have to do the assignment tomorrow. And I need a bigger mouth."

Seeing that the conversation was getting out of hand, I jumped in. "Melika, if they wanted someone with a big mouth, they'd have given the assignment to Darius."

Dodging a marshmallow, I dashed upstairs to change clothes. While the assignment was interesting, it was beginning to cause messy problems at home.

I walked into the bathroom with Melika at my tail. "Try going to the bathroom with your eyes closed, Daddy, that's what we had to do in school today."

"With my eyes closed? That's ridiculous!"

"Oh, come on, just try it."

Sighing, I closed my eyes and walked from the bathroom to the bedroom—where I was met by Melika. "Did you try it, Dad?"

"Yes, Melika, I did. Now my feet are all wet, the bathroom is a mess, and I need a new pair of socks."

"That's what happened to the boys in school, too. Sorry, Daddy."

The next day, I asked Melika how she did with the marshmallow talking.

"It was great. Since I had a small mouth, I only had to use four marshmallows."

"Could people understand you when you talked?"

"I don't know, but Jill said it sounded like Dutch. Tonight you have to tape my hands together and then I have to wrap a birthday present."

"But nobody has a birthday tonight."

"Oh, Daddy! You don't understand anything. Just tape my fingers together and get the wrapping paper."

"Only if you'll promise to untape them while you're eating."

Mrs. Bunch's assignments, while unconventional, were thought-provoking. Melika was enjoying herself and beginning to appreciate the problems of the disabled. Besides, at least it wasn't a science fair project—the inevitable baking soda and vinegar volcano.

After dinner, the children tried variations of the tape theme. Mitra attempted to write an essay with a pencil stuck in her mouth, Darius got a new high score in Crystal Quest using his feet to control the mouse, and Melika figured out a way to wrap birthday presents using tape stuck to her nose. My suggestion—to put it in a colorful box instead—fell on deaf ears. Well, not exactly deaf ears, but more like ears stuffed with cotton. Melika was studying ahead.

The assignments carried on in this vein for the remainder of the week. We "listened" to *The Phantom of the Opera* with our hands and watched TV while it was mis-tuned between channels. That really didn't matter—it was just BBC1 with a retrospective on New Guinea cannibals. We tied our legs together and tried to climb the stairs.

On Saturday morning, Melika declared that the assignment was finished. Unfortunately, there was a cloud on the horizon: Mrs. Bunch had announced a science fair competition.

At the office, we finally selected a supplier for the system that would replace the telex. The bids were far cheaper than we anticipated. I planned to save a lot of money. Luckily, Cormac was still around to offer sage advice.

"Get the biggest machine you can."

"But, Cormac, we don't need the biggest machine," I replied.

"You've got budget, you'll need the machine. It will be very difficult to upgrade later."

We bought the biggest machine we could find. And two years later, when we were running out of capacity, it was very difficult to find money to upgrade. If we had bought only what we needed, we'd have had a bad problem very early in the effort.

We weren't out of the woods, however. In spite of months of meetings, consensus remained elusive. I was very annoyed when I met with senior management.

"Your company is completed screwed up," I said. "You're lucky that people need gasoline, because if this consensus process is moving at all, it's moving at a geological pace. There's a guy in Aberdeen who just bought a new telex system. He'll never agree to an e-mail solution, and you tell me we can't make him agree. It's hopeless."

The response was unexpected. "You're right, Dan, we can't make him agree...but we can transfer him. Let's make him IC manager in Gabon."

Although there was light at the end of the job tunnel, there were a few challenges at home. In fact, it was just...

THE WORST DAY OF MY LIFE

We were headed for the ballet. More specifically, The Martin Family was going to the Circus Theatre to see *Romeo and Juliet* performed by the Bolshoi, and we would look go-oo-oo-d.

Melika was most particular. She spent long hours scanning her wardrobe. As the youngest Martin, Miss Melika had an awesome number of potential outfits. She had her old clothes (they didn't fit anymore but were "favorites"), new clothes (they didn't fit yet but looked "sooo good"), and current clothes (they fit, but were "yucky").

While Melika's lengthy wardrobe examination did not resolve the problem, it did create genuine bedroom clutter. She had tried on selections from each of her three clothes categories. The selection process came to the typical end, with Nazy and Melika attempting to achieve European-style consensus, but Melika kept changing her mind. After an afternoon of discussion, negotiation, and ultimatum, agreement was finally reached. Totally exasperated by the mountain of tried-on clothes in Melika's bedroom, Nazy began to make her own selection.

A few hours and several "Let's gos" later, we were almost ready for departure. Melika refused to respond to the authoritative ringing of the bell, so I went upstairs to get her. She was sitting on her bed in a nightgown.

"I'm not going, Daddy." (This was the setup.)

"Why not?" (I walked blindly forward, ignoring years of parental experience.)

"That dress is uncomfortable. I can't wear it."

"Then wear something else." (The trap is sprung.)

"But Mommy said I had to…" (Uh-oh!)

"On the other hand, Melika, I like the uncomfortable one." (Can I pull it out of the fire?)

"Oh, Daddy. Then I'm not going." (Now what?)

"Okay, turn off the lights at nine-thirty when you go to bed. We'll be home about midnight." (Now *I'm* doing the setup.)

I started down the stairs, loudly announcing to the family that Melika wasn't going to come.

"Oh, all right, Daddy. But it's uncomfortable. I'll be miserable the whole night." (Victory!)

At the Circus Theatre, we purchased the Dutch program. Browsing through it, Darius was worried. "This is in Dutch, Dad. They didn't even have an English one. Are we going to be able to understand the show?"

"Understand the show?"

"Yeah. Is it in Dutch or English?"

"Of course you'll understand it, Darius. It's a ballet. It's the story of Romeo and Juliet."

"Who?"

"It's like *West Side Story*."

The lights were dimmed and the curtain fell. At the end of the first act, it was clear that not everyone in The Martin Family was familiar with the story. Melika ("Well, I don't get it.") was most confused. Mitra, who did get it, was just disgusted ("I'm not sitting next to Melika in the next act. She keeps asking me what's going on. It's just…just…childish."). Darius wanted to know if "Riff was the guy with a red shirt and black tights." Nazy, the only truly cultured parent, was busily explaining the story. Meanwhile, I had discovered that I remembered the Jets and Sharks much better than the Montagues and Capulets.

The story became clearer and the dancing got better in the second act. The family departed at about midnight on Sunday. Melika and Darius promptly fell asleep, and neither could be aroused when we pulled up in front of Badhuis. Nazy and Mitra continued their cultural discussion and headed into the house. I carried Melika up the stairs—in fact, *way up* the narrow and very steep stairs—and deposited her in bed. She was so exhausted that I decided to just pull off her shoes and the uncomfortable dress and let her sleep.

I went back downstairs to get Darius. I couldn't carry him up. And he had awoken—with questions.

"Did you like the ballet, Dad? I think the guy with the red socks was the best. I bet that guy who played Romeo defects. Why did ballet stars *always* defect, Dad? Where is Timbuktu? Who do you like best—Shakespeare or Bernstein?"

Notice that there were lots of questions and few answers. Darius generally doesn't stop talking long enough to give you a chance to answer.

Once upstairs, I tucked Darius in and strolled over to tuck in the girls, tripping over a large pile of clothes as I entered their room. Mitra was asleep, and Melika was putting on pajamas. The pile of clothes I had tripped over had been tried on and discarded. Our little girl, the one who had been too tired to walk up the stairs, had somehow collected enough energy to change pajamas. I waved good night.

The next morning arrived much too soon. I stirtred the children out of bed. After telling me that the capitol of Burkina Faso was Ouagadogou, Darius pulled the covers over his head and refused to move.

I walked toward the girls' room boldly. The various heaps of clothes, primarily pajamas, reminded me of the mountainous landscape of upper New England. I turned on the light, climbed to the summit of a nearby knoll. and cheerfully invited them to get up.

I maneuvered back down the stairs, got dressed, and assured Nazy I would get the children to the tram. Well aware of my ability in this area, Nazy was certain we'd be on time. She was less sanguine about whether we'd have what we were supposed to have when we got there.

"Don't let Darius leave without his stuff, Dan."

"What stuff?"

"He has to bring his tram pass, locker key, lunch, poster, homework, backpack, permission slip, soccer shoes, PE clothes, bassoon, bassoon

---

DANIEL PAUL MARTIN

music, school pictures, twenty-five guilders, and social studies report. He needs money for bassoon reeds."

"I shouldn't have any trouble remembering that, Nazy."

"Make sure he's wearing his coat—and his socks."

I was about to answer when Melika stormed into the bedroom, wailing. Leaving this catastrophe in Nazy's hands, I dashed off toward the kitchen.

"This is going to be the worst day of my whole life!"

"What's the matter, Melika?"

I could barely hear the background disaster as I descended the staircase. "I've tried everything, Mommy. My hair just won't stay. It's the worst day of my life!"

Nazy resolved the problem. Melika was fortunate that she didn't ask me for aid. I'd have gotten her hair to stay, but I would have used nails and staples.

After a quick breakfast, we began the pre-launch countdown.

"Got your lunch, Darius?"

"Check."

"Backpack?"

"Yep."

"Soccer shoes?"

"*Yes!*"

"Locker key?"

"*Okay, Dad.*"

"PE clothes?"

Sitting on the floor stuffing items into his backpack, Darius was clearly getting annoyed.

"Did Mom tell you to do this to me? You don't have to keep asking things. I *know* what I'm doing."

"PE clothes, Darius?"

"Dad!!"

"Okay, we'll do it the easy way. Get your tram pass, permission key, lunch slip, school pictures, soccer report, bassoon shoes, ship music, and coat."

"Right. Mitra! Have you seen my red PE shirt?"

I glanced at my watch and began the process of actually leaving the house. We were delayed by Melika's shoes—more specifically, by Melika's shoelaces. There were four of them—two sets for each shoe. Each was a different color, and each was at least a meter too long. In order to avoid tripping and falling on her butt, Melika had to tie each lace several times. We waited. We fumed. Darius suggested tying them around her neck. Then we ran and just (barely) caught tram number seven.

At Centraal Station, Darius didn't have his bassoon. He wasn't happy, and neither was I.

"She'll kill me Dad. This is going to be the worst day of my whole life. Can't you bring it to me? Can you write a letter and tell her I'm sick? Do I have to go? Why didn't *you* remind me?"

Undaunted, I shepherded them toward the bus. I was just waving goodbye when I noticed a momentary look of panic on Mitra's face. "Ah," I thought, "I wonder what Mitra the Unflappable has forgotten."

"Eh, Daddy, could you call Mommy when you get to work and ask her to fax my French homework to the school?"

"Fax your homework?"

"Well this is an emergency. And would you remind her to pick up my Halloween costume on Fredrick Hendricklaan?"

I waved them off, noting that Darius looked a bit like a condemned criminal about to enter death row.

When I got to the office, I called Nazy and informed her of Mitra's requests, then gathered my courage.

"And, uh, Nazy, ah, it seems that Darius forgot his bassoon."

"He forgot his bassoon? Didn't you check before he left?"

"Well, I did try."

"So now you want me to drive to Wassenaar with the bassoon."

"It sounded like he'd be in real trouble."

"Dan. I have to go to the PWC board meeting, I've got a lunch with Truuska, and I'm supposed to write to the band about the Black Gold Gala Ball. I'm on the volunteer schedule for Mauritshuis. I don't have time to drive to Wassenaar."

"Sorry?"

"Real sorry, Dan. Real sorry."

I hung up the phone. It immediately rang.

"Dan Martin." (In Europe, it's polite to answer the telephone by announcing your name.)

"It's Nazy. Look at your feet."

"My feet?"

"Your feet, Dan. Your feet."

"Why?"

"Just look."

I pushed back my chair and took a downward glance. It wasn't a pretty picture: one black shoe and one brown shoe.

"I see what you mean, dear."

"Asking you to make sure Darius doesn't forget something is like asking King Kong if he likes to make model airplanes. I'll bring your shoes over on my way to Wassenaar. This is really going to be the worst day of my life."

I thought things couldn't go any farther downhill. I was already trapped in Death Valley at the bottom of the Dead Sea. But I was wrong. A departmental reorganization, a new deadline, a reduced budget, and more requirements resulted from an unscheduled review meeting. It was the worst day of my life. I was really looking forward to a relaxing evening at home.

I arrived home late but determined to be cheerful. Mitra, dour and sour, met me at the door.

"Don't say it looks good, Daddy. I know it looks like crap."

"Hello, Mitra. Did you have a good day?"

"It's really revolting."

"Hi, Nazy. What's revolting?"

"I picked up Mitra's costume and she's not happy with it."

"Why isn't she happy?"

"We took it to the seamstress on Fredrick Hendricklaan and asked for a hoop skirt."

"Yeah, so…"

"I would have gathered the material on both sides, but she…"

"What's wrong with it?"

"She cut the material into a circle and then cut a hole out for the waist."

"Seems like a reasonable way to make a skirt."

"She wasted a lot of material."

"Who cares? Didn't the cloth come from the box that was shipped here by mistake? Remember? The box that should have gone to Goodwill?"

"That's not the point."

"What is the point?"

Mitra, disgusted, set me clear. "It looks like crap, Daddy."

"Crap? Why? It *is* a hoop skirt."

"The seamstress cut the cloth into a circle."

"Of course. Hoops are round. What's wrong with that?"

"It's too short, Daddy. It looks like crap. This was the worst day of my life."

"I see," I said. "And how did *your* day go, Nazy?"

"It wasn't the best day I've ever had. In fact, I think it was the…"

Darius chose the bassoon because it looked cool. It is a very interesting instrument that generates a low bass sound akin to the rumble made by an earthquake. When Darius began to "play" the bassoon, George, our pet cockatiel, began to flutter. The cat dashed for cover. Seismic rumblings were picked up at the European Earthquake Centre outside Madrid. The subatomic particle accelerator at the CERN laboratory in Geneva was misaligned.

Fortunately for Martin family sanity, Darius didn't like to practice and frequently left his bassoon at school.

In fact, it only appeared to be the worst day of my life. Early in our sojourn in Holland, attempting to be Dutch, I rode my American bicycle through the streets of The Hague. Unfortunately, the thin racing tires on it fit (exactly) into the tram track groves, and I crashed and broke my wrist. Friends at the office presented me with a set of training wheels. About three months later, a few short weeks after my cast was removed—a fluke, but nevertheless—a repeat occurred and I broke the same wrist again. The doctors were understanding.

"I don't think we'll need another X-ray, we've got plenty of pictures of your wrist."

The Dutch doctors weren't inclined to use anesthesia. I was placed on a gurney and my arm was attached to a pulley. Every fifteen minutes, a nurse came in and added a few kilos to the pulley. I thought they were setting my wrist, but then the doctor arrived, grabbed my arm, and twisted my wrist into place. (Actually, almost into place.) When I asked for a painkiller, they gave me some Panadol (which turned out to be Tylenol.)

When I returned to the office, Shell reexamined my employment contract. I was precluded from using any transport with fewer than four (full-sized) wheels. Unfortunately, I had a meeting in London. I called my colleague Mike to reschedule. He, too, was understanding.

"Well, Dan, if it were the first_time you'd broken your wrist, we could accommodate you. But you've made a habit of this."

At home, Mitra was concerned with more mundane things. She had a grand plan for grocery shopping. You might not think grocery shopping is worthy of a grand plan, but you haven't been to the Konmar. Besides…

IT'LL BE FUN, DADDY

Mitra was insistent. "Come on, Daddy. It will be a lot of fun. I *personally* guarantee it."

I was sure it wouldn't be fun. Grocery shopping is not fun! Grocery and clothes shopping, in fact, top my shun list. Mitra would have to be more than insistent: She would have to be persuasive, persistent, and perfidious. I did not want to go grocery shopping. My wrist hurt.

Family adjustment to the move had been speedy—Europe is the cradle of western civilization. (Although I admit that there were times when we fully understood why our ancestors fled the cradle.) Sophisticated, refined grocery stores are not part of the accumulated western heritage. Population density may be the problem: The entire country accumulates in grocery store aisles during their limited open hours. I don't like crowds, I don't like buying groceries, and I don't like being bullied by a teenager.

I was adamant. "Mitra, asking me to take part in a grocery expedition is like asking the Dalai Lama to break dance. It's like asking the English football team to win the World Cup. It's like stirring hot coffee with uncooked spaghetti."

"Okay, you don't have to come. I'm just trying to put my education to use. It's the division of labor concept that I learned about in history. Just like Henry Ford and the Model T."

"Henry Ford and the Model T? That wasn't division of labor, it was an assembly line."

"Yeah, well. Division of labor was first. It's what makes America great. It's planning, it's great family adventure, and it gets the shopping done in thirty minutes. And it'll be fun."

"Fun? Like a root canal?"

"Well, if you really want to let the family down…"

"Since I don't *have* to come, I guess I'll just have to steel myself to missing all that 'fun.' I think I can live with the loss."

"Maybe you didn't understand the plan, Daddy. I've made five lists. You know, things like fruits and vegetables, breads, and meats. When we get to the Konmar, each person is going to grab a cart and take a list. The first one finished seizes a place in the checkout line. The lists are scientifically designed and computerized. We'll be able to do this every single week."

"Every week, eh? I can't tell you how happy that makes me, Mitra."

"And scientific! I've divided the store into quadrants and adjusted the lists to match the physical capabilities of family. Melika gets to pick stuff by the low shelves, Darius…"

I interrupted. "I would have thought *you* would concentrate on the short shelves, Mitra."

"Very funny. Darius gets the nonfood items, Mommy gets the fruits and vegetables. All together I've created five lists."

"If Mom has fruits and vegetables, she will be the last one finished. Besides, don't you think it would work with *four* lists?"

"Four lists would make it twenty-five percent less efficient. If you want to stay home, I suppose…"

Nazy, who had been listening to the conversation, interrupted. "If he doesn't want to eat next week, then he can stay home today."

It is the mark of a great leader to recognize and graciously accept rare but inevitable defeat in interpersonal struggles. I gallantly agreed to take part in the adventure.

Mitra printed out the lists and the diagram of the Konmar. My helpful suggestions ("Why not do it next Tuesday morning?"[6]) were ignored. Darius and Melika were corralled into the escapade by making it appear to be an impossible mission. "Your task, should you accept it, Agent 007, is to locate the following twenty-three items at the Konmar. When finished, you should eat this secret list."

---

6 . *I would be in London by then.*

So with feelings ranging from high adventure to deep desolation, we departed for the weekly trek to the Konmar. My negotiations about membership in The Martin Family Expeditionary Force (MFEF) had delayed our exit. The MFEF would be entering the Konmar at the dreaded busy time.

In fact, our arrival occurred a bit after the busy time. Mitra's calculations had omitted the time required to locate and maneuver into a parking spot. As we dashed through the rain into the pandemonium of the Konmar, Mitra shouted encouragement. "We'll be done in half an hour. The first one finished gets to buy the flowers. And don't forget to claim a space in the checkout line."

We might have made half an hour if it hadn't taken twenty-three minutes to find five shopping carts. This part of the plan required substantial improvement. As it was, each family member devised a unique strategy. Darius and Melika concentrated on little old ladies. Darius offered to help one empty her cart, and Melika waited until one turned her back. Nazy, a Konmar veteran, simply waited at the car loading lane. Displaying amazing luck, Mitra was handed a cart by a patron who was dazzled by her sequin hat. I ventured to the far corner of the parking lot in an almost futile search for a discarded cart.

As soon as we pushed our way into the store, each member was on his or her own. There were a few minor problems. The *licht bruin brood* (light brown bread) and the *zes granen brood* (six-grain bread) were sold out; we'd be eating sandwiches made of rice crackers for the next several days. Somebody selected a brand of toilet paper significantly more abrasive than our usual. The salad oil was the consistency of the heating oil we had used in New England, and no one had volunteered to eat hard-boiled *quail* eggs for breakfast.

Nevertheless, it is true that our passage through the store was significantly faster than normal. Even checkout was rather quick. Mitra finished first and claimed a space in the queue. The MFEF wasn't queue-popular. Every time a family member dumped a completely loaded basket into the waiting cart, we heard grumbling, moaning, and shouting from Dutch locals in line behind us. We hit the checkout counter just before the threats started.

We were unpacking the car when I realized how badly I'd been bamboozled. "Mitra, why was it so important for us to get this shopping done so quickly?" I asked.

"That's simple. Now we have time to go to centrum. We need to get some clothes."

Nazy overheard. "That's right. And you have a coupon from the cleaners for a pair of pants, so you have to come, too."

In preparation for the CMD authorization of my project, there was a preliminary meeting in London. Consensus was the purported objective. The meeting began with a lengthy litany of "challenges" (problems were not permitted). At lunch, the head of the Central Office service group in London, Mike, asked me how I thought things were going.

"About normal. We'll meet, we'll prepare minutes, people will object, we'll make a recommendation, the CMD will…"

"Let's try a different approach, Dan."

When the meeting resumed, Mike directed that I prepare minutes for review at the end of the session. Jan, who had worked on the telex for twenty years, was representing telex operations in The Hague. He asked about our recommendation, and Mike jumped.

"Recommendation? They didn't ask us for a recommendation. They asked us for a decision."

The cast on my broken wrist crashed to the table. "A decision, Mike? An actual decision?"

Movement was quick. By the time Jan's boss, Roel, had arrived from The Hague, the minutes had been agreed upon and the decision had been made. Dates for telex retirement had been determined.

"Thanks, Mike," I said. "I'm looking forward to working with you on this project."

"Actually," Roel said, "Mike has taken a new position. He won't be working with you."

"That explains why he was willing to make a decision," I thought.

The CMD endorsed the decision and the project finally began in earnest. My contract was extended again. (Well, not actually extended. An extension would have made me permanent

STUMBLING THROUGH THE TULIPS

staff—a situation that would make it impossible for me to be fired. Accordingly, I was given a new two-year contract with a different Shell company.)

The family was pleased with these events, but Darius had other concerns—specifically, the loss of rain forests in Brazil. His letter to the president of Brazil has gone unanswered, but he was still plugging away.

RAIN FOREST REDUCTION

Darius was puzzled. Typically, he wasn't speechless. "What's this, Dad?"

"It's your allowance," I replied.

"But it's in an envelope."

"That's right. I've provided your first regular monthly pay slip. It details your gross pay as well as various deductions."

"Deductions?"

"Just read the pay slip, Darius. Your mother and I are going out for a walk. We'll talk to you when we get back."

As Darius began to rip open the envelope, I dashed downstairs and grabbed Nazy. "Let's go, dear, we've got to get out of here for a few minutes to let him calm down. We don't have much time. I only used five embedded envelopes, a roll of cellophane tape, and a tube of Super Glue."

The door slammed shut behind us just as an ear-piercing screech wafted down from Darius's room.

Nazy and I had decided that Darius needed an introduction to the world of personal finance. In particular, we thought it would be nice if he could last an entire day with his allowance in his pocket. We felt that Darius suffered from a surplus of thoughtfulness and a dearth of common sense. The situation was difficult—the common sense we wanted to inject would probably mean he wouldn't be buying us flowers as often.

Our approach to financial training began with the monthly allowance. This month we had kept a journal of Darius's overdrafts. Typically, he had spent each allowance the day he received it. Predictably, he borrowed money from me, Nazy, Mitra, Melika, his friends, his teachers, the neighbors, the tram driver, the principal, and the queen. We had deducted these additional expenditures from the allowance of this month. We weren't completely accurate—that would have required presentation of an invoice. In our case, deductions exactly matched income.

After a moderately long walk, Nazy and I returned home. Darius was in a complete tizzy. He had nailed a formal petition to our bedroom door and demanded a family meeting.

He was in luck. Nazy had just been elected president of the Petroleum Wives Club. She had a gavel and a grasp of Robert's Rules—which she used to call us to order.

"The chair recognizes Darius."

"Daddy put a bunch of reductions in my allowance and I didn't get any money. I move we throw Daddy out of the family—right after he pays a fine for annoying me."

This was a bit too much for me. "They're not *re*ductions, Darius, they're called *de*ductions. And we used them because you must learn to manage your money."

"Oh, yeah? My allowance is reduced. isn't it?"

"No, your allowance is unchanged. The deductions are subtracted from your unchanged allowance."

"The amount of money I get is reduced, isn't it? Besides, how can I learn to manage my money if your stupid reductions don't let me have any?"

I grabbed Nazy's gavel. I wanted to use it on Darius's head.

"That's out of order, Dan," Nazy said, seizing control of both the conversation and the gavel. "Besides, Darius," she continued, "it wasn't just Daddy who decided on the reductions. We decided together."

"It's *de*ductions, Nazy," I interjected.

"Deductions, reductions—what's the difference? The bottom line is…"

"Zero, Mom. That's what the bottom line is. Zero!"

"That's enough!" I shouted.

"It's not enough Dad. That's why we're having this meeting."

"Nazy! I need the gavel!"

The discussion continued. Darius wasn't mollified, but all further comment on allowances was ruled out of order. I moved for quick adjournment, but Melika wanted to bring a new item to the floor.

She was direct. "Can we adopt a whale, Daddy?"

"A whale? We don't even have a swimming pool."

"Oh, Daddy! We adopt it. For Earth Day."

"Earth Day? What's that?"

"Earth Day is our opportunity to redress the devastation we've rained upon the planet."

Darius, who had been sitting around looking glum, piped up. "It's not *re*dress, Melika, it's *de*dress."

"Melika, *I* have not rained devastation upon the planet," I said. "I'm a pretty nice fellow. I don't even drop gum wrappers on the streets."

"People ruin nature, Daddy."

"People are part of nature. What do people do to ruin it?"

"They build dams and mess up rivers."

"Beavers build dams, too."

"I don't care about beavers, I just want to adopt a whale. Or buy an acre of rain forest."

"Rain forest?"

"Can we buy an acre?"

"Well, that's an interesting proposition. I like rain forests. Where's the acre? Brazil?"

"I think so."

"Find out which rain forest and how much it costs. If it's Brazil, see if you can find an acre with good frontage on the South Atlantic Ocean. I'd like to get the land, chop down most of the trees, and build a house."

"Daddy!"

From this point on, the conversation drifted out of my control. We finally agreed that The Martin Family would subsidize an investment in planet Earth—to the tune of fifteen guilders per child. I thought we were finished, but Mitra noted that special lunch funds would also be required for Earth Day. Earth Day was also vegetarian day.

"Vegetarian day? What's wrong with good old-fashioned meat?"

"What do you mean? Have you tasted this Dutch beef?"

"Mitra!" Melika said. "We shouldn't eat any meat. Don't joke about it. Eating meat is not nice."

"Melika, what's good about eating plants?" I asked. "Do you know that bread is made of wheat kernels? Wheat kernels are seeds. Seeds are baby wheat plants. When you eat a slice of bread, you're eating wheat fetuses. Now *that's* really cruel."

The meeting would have descended into complete disorder if time had permitted. Instead, Nazy used the gavel to execute a quick adjournment.

The allowance pay slip had absolutely no effect on Darius's spending habits. Fortunately for him, a friend gave him a few guilders for his birthday, which occurred just before Earth Day. This, coupled with our fifteen-guilder donation, gave him almost enough for an entire acre of rain forest. He needed the *whole* acre because he didn't want any of his friends to have *their* name on *his* acre. He supplemented his money with a small loan from Melika, but he still wasn't happy.

"She's charging money for lending me money, Dad. It's not fair."

"It is fair. It's called interest. Let me explain how it works with a mortgage."

I explained the standard thirty-year mortgage to Darius, adjustable rates included. He wasn't amused.

"That's sick. And I still don't think it's fair. Will you talk to Melika for me?"

I began the discussion with Melika by asking about the interest rate.

"For Darius it's 50 percent, Daddy."

"Fifty percent? Isn't that a bit steep?"

"Steep? Have you looked at his balance sheet? Have you looked at his assets-to-liabilities ratio? I'm taking a big risk. If he gets his allowance when I'm not here, it'll all be gone before I can collect. He's a problem client."

I agreed to pay off Melika with the proviso that I make another deduction in Darius's allowance. Once again, he wasn't happy with the monthly payment of zero.

"Dad, I can't wait until I get outta here and get a job."

"Why's that?"

"I just want *all* my money. With a job they'll just give me my whole salary, none of these stupid deduction things."

"Darius, my boy, you've got a lot to learn. Let's start with the IRS."

It wasn't kind to talk to Darius about the IRS—a subject that is at least rated "R" and more likely "X." Now he was having nightmares.

At Shell, the project was picking up steam and I was beginning to travel outside of Europe. The trips were grueling. In Japan, every single minute was planned, including a late dinner. Suffering from jet lag, I slumped onto a pillow and arranged myself in front of a low table. I didn't recognize any food, but I was determined to be polite. I grabbed a piece of something with my chopsticks and swallowed. (I was going to be polite, but that didn't mean things had to spend extraordinary amounts of time on my taste buds.) My co-worker, Henk, who traveling with me, was more urbane.

"How do you eat this?" Henk asked our colleague, Tanaka-san.

"Well," said Tanaka-san, "you pick it up with your chopsticks, you dip it in this sauce, that sauce, and finally this sauce."

"Ah," I said. "Does that bring out the flavor?"

"No, it kills the microbes. If you don't use the sauce, you'll have terrible problems this evening."

"Oh...I think I'll have another." I hoped the overall combination would work in my stomach.

It could have been worse. A colleague, from Malaysia asked about the dessert.

"Did you like it?"

"It wasn't as sweet as I like. What was it?"

"Toad spit."

"What?"

"Toad spit."

"Thank God! I thought you said something else."

His friend was quick. "Toad spit. I'll never eat anything that came out of a frog's mouth. Pass the eggs."

CHAPTER 6
SEEING EUROPE

Note: This chapter is a little out of sequence with the rest of the book because I thought it would be a good idea to bundle the European trips together. The trips span almost five years and are in the order in which they occurred. As we settled in, my job activities picked up. I had been hired to manage the work of retiring the fifty-seven-year-old telex system used to handle Shell Group communication. I decided that an American approach would be best: Do something and worry about the details later. I had made several miscalculations. To start, I knew absolutely nothing about telex, but I didn't let lack of knowledge influence my decision to accept the assignment. (Perhaps I overstate the case. I had heard of telex—in a World War II movie.) Second, I had estimated it would take about six months to retire the system. I knew that Shell had a very extensive private telex system, but I didn't know the entire company revolved around the features and limitations of it.

Additionally, I had assumed that since I had been hired to manage retirement of the system, the company had made the decision to actually retire it. How naive! My first task was to "achieve consensus" on the objective. This happened because there is no Dutch verb that means "make a decision." The closest is *beslissen nomen*, which means "to take a decision." Taking a decision meant that everyone (and I mean everyone) had to agree. Thus there were lots and lots of meetings. (Note: Meeting is not *equal to action.) I traveled to London, Manchester, Paris, and Hamburg. I cajoled, prodded, pled, encouraged, listened, pushed, shoved, explained, described, argued, presented, and begged. The airport authority was about to name a departure lobby after me.*

The family, who hadn't been on a business trip, thought I was getting to see Europe while they were stuck in lowland backwater. Rumblings of mutiny ("We have to see something, Daddy") eventually resulted in an out-of-country visit. It was our bad luck to have a simultaneous out-of-body experience.

I'M FINE
(JUST LET ME LIE HERE)

Paris! The Martin Family had finally arrived. The winter break had broken, and our planned London trip had dissolved in the midst of a rearranged business meeting. As blasé Europeans, we couldn't spend the holiday in Holland. "Gad, Dad! That's boring to the max!"

The family chose the comfort of a first-class, family (traveling together) Eurorail pass. It didn't seem to matter that I, generally considered a family member, was traveling by an alternate route. As we now expected, even the simple purchase of a railway ticket was an "event." Everyone needed passport pictures, but the passports themselves, while necessary, weren't sufficient. The special ticket required an advance purchase, a preliminary reservation, and three liters of blood. We were lucky. Nazy found the fare that applied to American residents of Holland working at Shell with three children (blond), available only if one spouse is of Middle Eastern origin, with an overnight stay (on Saturday). In fact, she even got the four-guilder discount because one child (the youngest) had a birthday en route.

In spite of all of our careful preparation and (I say modestly) because I wasn't with them, The Martin Family managed to get on the wrong train. The Paris trip began in potential disaster as the family departed by express for Rotterdam. The mistake was quickly noted when Nazy discovered that the compartment she'd reserved didn't exist. Fortunately, there is only one track between The Hague and Rotterdam. Even more fortunately, the Paris train left after the one containing The Martin Family and it also stopped in Rotterdam. A brisk stroll with four tons of baggage for the three-day trip resulted in eventual embarkment onto the correct train.

The EuroRail train to Paris was wonderful. The meal service was delightful, and everyone was "whelmed"—especially Darius, who got his passport stamped.

Meanwhile, back in Manchester, I had taken the opportunity to "see the city" and could confidently report that there was nothing to see. The shops, even on the late shopping night, closed at five-thirty (rather than the normal five o'clock). The taxi that would return me to my hotel arrived at the Weeber Store on Market Street. Unfortunately, there are two Weeber stores on Market Street, about a mile apart from one another. The night was cold, the wait was long, the rain was sleet, the departure was delayed, and the family was waiting. And Paris, adventure, and excitement were in store.

Following my late British Air flight, the family reconvened in the Paris apartment of Nazy's cousin. A cacophony of languages—French, Farsi, English, and Dutch—brought a feeling of continental sophistication. It's not clear that anyone understood anyone else. After proper oohing and ahhing over Nazy's cousin's new baby, we departed for the luxury of the LeClerc Hotel, which has the Parisian ambience associated with starving artists.

The next morning dawned bright, but not much brighter than our room in the LeClerc. A blinking Hotel sign had brought the luster of daylight into our sleeping quarters. No one was well-rested, but everyone wanted to see Paris.

And we were off. We ventured in dual cars driven by experienced Parisian drivers, each of whom continuously kept one hand on the horn. Driving rules were simple: He who hesitates is lost. We bullied our way through the streets and saw the sights when we were able to pry our hands away from our eyes.

The high point? The Eiffel Tower: 1,050 feet of Gallic grandeur. From the tower, you can see all of Paris. The crowds were heavy and the queue disorganized. The French don't line up neatly like the British. We squished our way onto the elevator and made it to the second level. From here, Darius "needed" two francs to use the telescope. I didn't understand. The whole point was to get up high so we could see everything, but Darius rented telescope time to get a close look at where we had started.

Another queue later, our bedraggled crew conquered the summit. Another two francs and we were looking back at the bottom. The view was spectacular. Even the weather was cooperating, but Nazy's tummy didn't feel good.

The trip down began with a bullet elevator ride to level two—a seven-hundred-foot descent in twenty seconds. Nazy's tummy really didn't feel good. We bunched up (again) for the final plunge to terra firma. Just as our portion of the line began the final surge for the elevator, Nazy called out, "Dan, I don't feel good."

"Oh, sh…"

As Nazy's knees buckled, I knocked over a little old lady just in time to grab her before she hit the ground. I carried her to fresh air.

"Are you okay?" (I don't understand this question either. Of course she wasn't okay, but I always think if you ask, perhaps the answer will be yes.)

"I'm fine, I just want to lie here for a minute." That idea certainly made sense. Just lie down on the floor of the Eiffel Tower and watch tourists step over you.

The family, completely and confidently prepared for any emergency, was quietly entering a panicked state.

Darius: "Mommy, talk to me. Who broke her leg? Are you all right?"

Melika: "Is Mommy okay, Daddy? Daddy, is Mommy okay? What happened?"

Mitra (who speaks French): "I don't know these people."

Lionel, our second cousin somewhat removed, only speaks French, and even he looked helpless.

Meanwhile, firmly in control of the situation, I was quietly responding to the developing crisis. "Nazy! Are you okay? No, you can't just lie here. What happened? She's all right, Darius. I don't know, Melika. Don't worry, Darius. Are you okay, Nazy? Mitra, can you understand what Lionel is saying? Yes, *you*, Mitra!"

A passerby offered some candy. "It's probably low blood pressure. A little sugar always helps."

The gendarmes arrived accompanied by six special officers from the local fire brigade. By then, of course, everything was okay. The sugar worked, Nazy was smiling again, and Lionel was dealing with French officialdom. (As usual in Europe, there were forms to be signed. They were in French. It hadn't occurred to the fire brigade that there might be non-French speaking visitors at the Eiffel Tower.)

The family's conversation continued in confusion. "No, Darius, fainting is not an emergency. No, Melika, when Lionel said '*Oui, oui,*' he did not mean Mommy had to go to the bathroom. Mitra, can you tell me what these people are saying? Nazy, *are you okay?*"

When we returned to the ground, everyone agreed that Nazy should rest. Accordingly, we spent the remainder of the afternoon touring

STUMBLING THROUGH THE TULIPS

Pompidou Centre, Notre Dame, the Moulin Rouge, the mayor's residence, Les Invalides, the Louvre, the Arc de Triomphe, the Champs-d'Élysées, Place de la Concorde, and the opera house.

Nazy was fine. I, on the other hand, fell asleep in the middle of a family Iranian dinner. Later that evening, while picking rice kernels out of my beard, I asked Nazy a simple question.

"So tell me, Nazy, are you okay?"

She was fine. She just wanted to lie there and sleep. Unfortunately, that was a sad choice. The bed at the LeClerc Hotel was about as appropriate for sleeping as the second level of the Eiffel Tower, and the LeClerc didn't even have the BBC.

I've mentioned "queue policy"—such as it is—in France. The situation in the UK is very different. I landed in Gatwick for a Shell meeting, but the train to Victoria Station was out of service because of an IRA threat at the Clapham Junction rail hub. Passengers were directed to "take a taxi." I was in the middle of a cavernous terminal building, looking for a taxi sign. Someone approached and asked:

"Pardon me. Are you the taxi queue?"

"Well, yes, I guess I am."

He got in line behind me. That wouldn't happen in France or the Netherlands.

In this book, Darius' interest in getting passport stamps is highlighted. In spite of his initial reluctance to move, he jumped at the opportunity to see Europe. His desire to see the world continues. He spent eighteen months working on his thesis in Iceland; celebrated completion of his education with a trip to Cambodia; scuba dived in Sri Lanka, Thailand, Jordan, and Egypt; and hiked in Romania and Ethiopia. His passport is impressive.

Nazy was fine, although we still shy away from tall sights and fast elevators. We had spent our first few months exploring Holland. We traveled to Utrecht to see the clock museum, the train museum, and Dom Kerk. ("Dom" means "stupid" in Dutch, and Darius, having seen this particular church every time we go to Utrecht, would tell me, "The stupid church was great the first few times." I think "dom" also means "dome.") We traveled to Amsterdam, Leiden, Lisse, Vollendam, Maakum, Maastricht. But it seems that...

WE NEVER GO ANYWHERE

Rebellion was in the air and Darius was leading the insurrection. "We never go anywhere! We never do anything! School is over and I'm bored. I want to go to Berlin. Tonight!"

I ignored years of parental experience and tried reason. "Darius, we've only been here half a year and we've already been to Belgium, Germany, and France. We've seen Amsterdam, Vollendam, The Hague, Leiden, Utrecht, and Maastricht. We're planning a long vacation to Italy during the summer. You have lived in three different countries from the Pacific to both sides of the Atlantic."

"Big whoop! If we were going on the vacation I planned, we'd be seeing eighteen countries in twenty-one days. My passport would be full of stamps. You picked a dumb trip to Italy. We're never going to get to Berlin before the whole country disappears. I'll never get an East German passport stamp."

"Darius! If we had gone on the trip you planned, we wouldn't even remember the places we visited. There are no hotel rooms in Berlin this weekend. We simply cannot go."

"Oh yeah? Have you read this brochure? It says you can go and sleep on the bus."

"I've read it. You leave on Friday night, arrive on Saturday morning, leave for home on Saturday night, and get back Sunday morning. That doesn't sound like a relaxing weekend to me."

"At least we'd do something. I'm bored."

"I'm bored too," Melika interjected. "School's out and there's nothing to do. We have to go someplace."

"Melika, school vacation just began. Two days ago you were in school. You can't be bored yet."

It didn't work. Everyone wanted to go somewhere. I was afraid Darius would convene a family meeting to propose an amendment to the family constitution. (He wanted the job of managing director.)

"What about Luxembourg? Would you like to spend the weekend there, Darius?"

"Luxembourg? They don't even have a border. Big whoop. Luxembourg isn't even a country."

"What do you mean, it's not a country? Of course it's a country. And it *does* have a border."

Reveling in his geographical expertise, Darius was ready. "It is not a country. It's a duchy."

I, too, was prepared. "It's a *grand* duchy. A truly *grand* duchy. And it does have a border."

"Will they stamp our passports?"

"I hope so, Darius."

"All right. But what's there?"

I was stumped. I knew that Luxembourg was stuck between Belgium, France, and Germany, and I knew it was little. I also knew it was a grand duchy, but I didn't know anything else. The children were mollified, though. Nazy said she would get a map to Luxembourg from the ANWB, the Dutch motor club. We'd drive down the next morning.

The ANWB estimated travel time to be five hours. The roads are the quality of the U.S. interstate highways. Our only complaint concerned the road signs, which were difficult to read. Though environmentally friendly (i.e., small), the signs had so many words that it was tricky to find the pertinent part. (At least that's what I said when I took the wrong turn to Ghent.) Nazy and I divided the task—I'd start reading from the left and she'd start from the right. It seemed fair—her native language, Persian, is read from right to left.

The drive itself was beautiful. Shortly after passing Brussels, we entered the Ardennes, which reminded us of the Vermont landscape. The children were reintroduced to vertical geography. The trip was somewhat marred when I missed both the Belgium and Luxembourg borders. No passport stamps. However, the total drive only took three hours. I like the 120 kph (75 mph) speed limits. (Especially since we, like everyone else, interpreted the limit liberally.)

Our sign-reading prowess broke down inside the city. I kept following the *Autres Directions* signs, thinking it meant tourist information. Mitra, our resident French expert, put me straight. We did eventually locate a hotel on the outskirts of the city of Luxembourg and took a taxi into the centrum. Luxembourg Belgian francs were the official currency in Luxembourg and we were confused by the cost of the taxi.

"Two-hundred francs, Dad? How much is that?" Darius asked.

In point of fact, Darius probably already knew the answer—he had a collection of foreign money and had memorized the exchange rates.

"I think it's about twelve guilders. You divide by ten and then divide by two and then add a little bit."

"Wait a minute. I think you cheated me when you sold me the hundred Belgian francs—you charged me seven guilders."

"That was two months ago. The exchange rates have changed. Besides, you had to pay a surcharge for an odd-lot purchase."

"Yeah, well, I think I got gypped. And what about the passport stamp?"

"Darius?"

"Yeah?"

"Are you hungry?"

The ancient parental ploy of subject changing appeared to work. Now we just had to find a place to eat. Mitra and I were adventurous and bought sausage from a street vendor. Nazy wanted salad ("It's healthy, not junk"). Darius and Melika wanted basics. We found a MacDonald's in the town square. Being European, we ate at an outdoor table.

We picked a good weekend to visit. The city was in the midst of its Italian festival and a troop of singers from Venice was regaling the crowd with ancient favorites like "O Sole Mio." We planned to polish off the food and plunge into the shopping district.

"What is Luxembourg famous for, Dan?" Nazy asked.

"Well, dear, it's the smallest real country in Europe."

"Hey, Dad, you said it was a grand duchy."

"Aren't you still hungry, Darius? Why don't you stuff that hamburger up your…"

"Dan! You did tell him that it was a duchy."

"He said it was *grand* duchy, Mom."

"Eat your hamburger, Darius."

The shopping expedition netted something uniquely Luxembourg—sneakers with Velcro fasteners. We also walked around the city to see the sights, including the cathedrals and ancient buildings. We decided to take a bus tour the next day to learn the names of the buildings we'd seen.

Luxembourg is a very beautiful city built around a spectacular landscape of hills and deep valleys. Our search for details would have to wait until the next morning. We ate at an outdoor café, picked up the bus back to the hotel, and spent the remainder of the evening watching the Dutch soccer team tie the English in the World Cup.

The sightseeing tour began inauspiciously. The driver spoke only German and Luxemburgish. Darius was disgusted. We drove to the city center, where we collected a real tour guide—who spoke English (sort of).

"Onyourrrleftseezeancientforrrtrresssoflumemburgdatingfrrromzetensecenturybuiltonthebanksofzerriverdeeeeepinzevalleys."

I asked Mitra, who was sitting next to me, for assistance. "Is that French?"

"No, Dad, I zink it's English."

"Yeah? Well, if it's English, it would probably help if he moved his lips while he was talking."

The family was saved by a group of Spanish tourists who asked the guide to speak more slowly. The end result wasn't much better.

"On ze left is ze cazedral fon ze lady ov Luxembourg."

Ever educationally minded, Nazy asked when it was built.

"Zat vas built a long, long time ago."

"In a galaxy far, far away," I whispered.

Nevertheless, we saw the cathedrals, the ancient city wall dating from the tenth century, the headquarters of Patton's Third Army, and the U.S. military cemetery from World War II. On the drive home (remembering to stop at the border to get a passport stamp), we admired the beauty of the Ardennes landscape.

Back in The Hague, we went to dinner at a Chinese restaurant in Scheveningen. We didn't drive home from the restaurant—the car wouldn't steer (but it did make a very bad noise).

"See, Darius," I said, "if we had gone to Berlin, we'd have been stuck in the middle of East Germany with a broken car."

"Just what I said, Dad. You never let us have any fun."

"Darius?"

"Yes?"

"Eat your egg roll."

So there you have our trip to Luxembourg, arranged on the spur of the moment by The Martin Family. Unfortunately, Darius was right—we didn't make it to Berlin before East Germany was gone—but we did eventually make it to Berlin. With this trip behind us, we were ready for a real summer vacation. In fact, the speed with which we adjusted to the vast amounts of European vacation time amazed me. (And made repatriation to a two-week vacation somewhat problematic.) Fortunately, our expatriate arrangement provided for home leave. We decided that Europe was home and took the "cash option."

Given the somewhat messy experiences that resulted from our amateur arrangements, we decided to seek professional assistance. Surely we would do better with a qualified travel agent. Our goals were simple: elegant Italian surroundings, an exciting visit, and reasonable expenses (the cash option was not infinite). Perhaps we shouldn't have picked Italy.

ROAMIN' WITH THE ROMANS

About to depart for The Martin Family Italian vacation, we were in the midst of the last-minute checklist:

"Passports?" ("Yes, dear!")
"Tickets?" ("Of course, dear.")
"Suitcases?" ("Naturally, love.")
"Sunglasses?" ("Certainly, honey bun.")
"Children?" ("Why?")
"Daddy! That's not nice."

We continued the checklist: No one had to go to the bathroom, everyone had a book for the airplane, the milkman had been canceled, the fax machine was turned on, and the lights were turned off. Nazy was sure nothing could go wrong.

"Wrong, Dan? What could go wrong? Did you remember money?"

Did I remember money? I had just paid for the all-inclusive trip. It would be a long time before I would be able to forget money. We were prepared for this trip: We were bringing guilders, dollars, lire, Eurocheques, and credit cards, but we knew we wouldn't need much money. Gus, our travel agent, had arranged everything. This was an *all-inclusive* vacation. We just needed a few lire for meals and trinkets.

The time had finally arrived and we were ready to go. Mitra called the taxi, and I sat in the sun room to enjoy a relaxing pipeful of tobacco. I was blowing rings when Mitra stomped in through the clouds of smoke.

"Daddy! You said you were going to stop smoking on this vacation!"

"No, Mitra, I said I wasn't going to buy tobacco in Italy. And I'm not. Besides, we're not on vacation until we're outside of Holland."

The doorbell interrupted Mitra's plaintive "Daaaddddyyy." The Martin Family was on its way.

Nazy and I reviewed our itinerary and plans on the Alitalia flight. Our first stop was Rome. I asked Nazy where we were staying.

"Gus has set us up in a superior, three-star hotel—the Hotel Portamaggiore. It's right next to an ancient ruin."

"Nazy, *everything* in Rome is right next to an ancient ruin," I said. "That's the charm."

The Alitalia DC-9 landed in H^3 (Hazy, Hot, Humid) weather in Rome. There wasn't a Jetway; we disembarked onto the tarmac and climbed into a crowded bus for transport to the terminal.

We cleared passport control and the baggage claim easily. Exiting international arrivals, we looked for the TourAlitalia office that was "next to the exit." When we couldn't find it, good military procedures were

STUMBLING THROUGH THE TULIPS

abandoned and our forces were divided. Nazy and the girls marched off to an Italian language lesson.

Darius and I ventured to the refreshment stand. We wanted to find out whether Italy qualified as "western." In particular, was Coca-Cola available? The friendly sight of the red-and-white Coke logo was a welcome and cheery reminder of the American way, but trying to buy a bottle was a strange experience.

In Italy, you pay first, get your receipt, and then get your item. If you're buying a Coke, this doesn't present a problem. However, if you don't know what you want to purchase, you're in big trouble. You have to fight your way through the masses of people brandishing receipts, examine the available food, make your decision, commit it and the price to memory, barge back through the crowd, push your way into the line to pay, and then plunge into the throngs by the sales counter. All of this presented no problems for me; I simply asked Darius to get a large Coke.

He returned with a small cup. "Darius, I asked for a large."

"This is the gianto size."

"Gianto?" I said, grasping the cup between my thumb and index finger. "Why is it empty?"

"Sorry, I drank some of it. I spilled the rest."

"That's all right, Darius. Get another one. How much did it cost?"

"Eight thousand lire. How much is that in real money?"

"I don't know. I'll try to figure it out. Here's a ten-thousand lire bill."[7]

Hoping Darius would be able to navigate through the crowd without spilling my drink, I began the mental exercise of converting eight thousand lire to guilders. I started with the lire/guilder rate in the *Wall Street Journal*. It seemed simple—cross out two zeros, divide by five, subtract 10 percent, and round up to the nearest guilder. The answer came

---

7 . *Since the bill was the size of a piece of notebook paper, I should have realized there was a problem.*

out absurdly high. I decided to convert to U.S. dollars and then convert those to guilders. That was simple—cross out three zeros, subtract 12 percent, double the result, and round down to the nearest five guilders. This answer also came out absurdly high.

Undaunted, I opened my briefcase, pulled out my calculator, and decided on elegance. I'd convert lire to Greek drachmas (multiply by the population of Rome and divide by the volume of the Parthenon in cubits). Then I'd convert the drachmas into Polish zlotys. The zlotys can be exchanged for a Yugoslavian dinar at par. The dinar is worth eighteen million rubles on the black market. Then…

Computation was no help. My calculator flashed "Error" just before the battery died. With pen and paper, I sadly confirmed my first impression. I grabbed my pipe, lit it, and sat down to wait for Darius and the ladies. Everyone arrived at the same time.

"Daddy!" Mitra shouted. "You said you wouldn't smoke in Italy."

"I said I wouldn't *buy* tobacco in Italy," I replied calmly. "I brought this tobacco with me."

"Oh yeah, how many pouches of tobacco did you bring?"

"Nazy, "did you find TourAlitalia?" I said, craftily changing both the subject and the conversational partner,

Nazy had found TourAlitalia: it was closed. More fortunately, she had also discovered that we were supposed to be met by TourItaly, and their offices were next to the international arrivals hall. TourItaly, having given up on us, was calling in a replacement driver. We faced a short wait. Nazy wanted a cup of coffee, so I sent Darius (armed with another ten thousand lire) back into the crowds.

He returned with three coins and a thimble.

"Save the coins, Darius. I'm sure we'll see a fountain," I said, finishing my monetary calculations. I grabbed Nazy's arm. "Nazy," I exclaimed, "that 'cuplet' of coffee cost eight dollars and twenty-five cents. It's about sixteen guilders."

STUMBLING THROUGH THE TULIPS

"Yeah? Then why'd you grab my arm and make me spill it on the floor?"

"We just spent thirty dollars for a deciliter of Coke and thimble of coffee."

"You're wrong. It wasn't coffee in the thimble. What is a deciliter?"

TourItaly interrupted with news that our "deluxe motor coach" was ready. The weary family paraded to the minibus. Darius located the brochure for the Hotel Portamaggiore.

"Dad? What's a three-star, superior, second-class hotel?"

"*Second*-class, Darius?" I said with a sinking feeling.

Check-in at the Portamaggiore was smooth, but we had a little trouble distinguishing the ancient ruins of Rome from the modern ruins of our hotel. Our rooms were on the sixth floor. After a delay of several minutes, the elevator that arrived was too small to simultaneously hold a person and a suitcase. Melika and Darius ran up the stairs to intercept the suitcases, and Nazy and Mitra decided to wait for the next elevator. I walked up the stairs anticipating the thrill of seeing our rooms in the eternal city.

Melika, Darius, and I carried the suitcases to the children's room. It was neither elegant nor air-conditioned.

"What does 'three stars' mean, Daddy?" Melika asked.

"Well, the hotel gets one star if it is located in the solar system. It gets its second star by being on planet Earth. Since the 'star-system' is only used in Europe, it gets the third star for being on the continent."

Just then, Mitra and Nazy arrived. Mitra's quick mind completed her hotel evaluation: "Yuck!"

Nazy was more practical. "What does our room look like?"

"I don't know. I've been afraid to unlock the door."

Because I don't want to frighten readers, I won't go into details about our room. Suffice it to say that nothing, including the dust, had changed in that room since it was used as a hideout by Brutus after he killed Julius Caesar.

We dropped off our suitcases and left for dinner. It was a good idea. Unfortunately, no one knew where the restaurants were. Naturally, the family had different ideas about what to eat. Darius wanted to find Chinese food, Melika preferred fish, Nazy wanted something healthy, I craved a Big Mac, and Mitra, for some stupid reason, wanted to look for an Italian restaurant.

After a family consultation, we arrived at the conclusion that it would be easiest to find an Italian restaurant. Completely unfettered by the fact that this was my first trip to Rome, I sauntered off, leading the family in the general direction of the *centero*.

We quickly discovered that the Portamaggiore was not in the best part of the city. We were walking through a shopping district that specialized in wedding dresses. (Would you buy your wedding gown from Discounto Angelo?) After what seemed like hours of walking, I agreed that Nazy's idea of asking for directions deserved a chance.

Nazy found a really nice Italian restaurant on the other side of the Tiber. We ate outside in a vine-covered courtyard, and were serenaded by strolling minstrels. The food was good, the ambience was charming, and the music was fun. The only sour note was the worrisome thought in the back of our minds: The family would have to return to the Portamaggiore.

The hotel, which had looked bleak in the daylight, was positively dismal at night. We climbed the gloomy staircase (the lift didn't after eight o'clock) and entered the barren, desolate wasteland of a dungeon-like sleeping compartment.

The children, feeling a bit sticky, wanted to take showers before bed. Melika noticed the first problem.

"Dad, there's no shower curtain. And where are the towels?"

"There's not supposed to be a shower curtain. And these are the towels," I said, picking up a white cloth.

"Those are towels? I thought they were pillowcases," Melika replied as she turned on the shower.

A few disadvantages of the shower-curtainless bathroom were quickly discovered. The shower sprayed directly onto the wall. From there, it dripped onto the toilet paper, ended up on the floor, and bubbled toward a drain that didn't. It flooded out of the bathroom and onto the soggy carpet of the sleeping chamber.

The flood didn't bother Melika. Her problem was the towels. The work of a towel is rather simple. These towels, which had the consistency of waxed paper, failed to absorb water. Surveying the impending crisis, Nazy and I tiptoed away.

The sad thing was that the children had the good room. We, too, had to suffer through shower indignity. Our shower didn't spray on the wall. In fact, it didn't spray anywhere, it just dribbled out of the spout. Nazy wasn't happy and asked me to call the front desk to complain. I wasn't happy when I realized that talking with the front desk meant walking down six flights of stairs.

Nazy was patiently waiting when I made it back to the room. "Well, what did they say about the water pressure?"

"The aqueduct is clogged. They'll fix it in the twenty-third century."

We dropped into, then through, the bed. The H^3 weather continued. Because the room was stiflingly hot, I opened the window—and let in the noise of the city.

It wasn't ordinary city noise—traffic and a few random sirens—this was Rome, the infernal city. The Rome Sanitation Department was having a Dumpster-emptying contest outside our window. If we closed the window, room temperatures climbed and we stuck to the bed. If we opened it, noise levels climbed and induced a dangerous vibration in the walls.

Following the sleepless night, a bedraggled Martin Family arrived in the lobby of the Portamaggiore for the continental breakfast. I ended up in the kitchen after making wrong turn, and saw the staff making "fresh-squeezed" orange juice: They were squeezing red-and-yellow food coloring into small glasses of water.

I caught up with the family in the hotel dining room. The continental breakfast was part of the advertised "living archeological experience." The Italian breakfast rolls, recovered from the ruins of Pompeii, were hermetically sealed in volcanic ash. The coffee had been mopped up from the floor of Rome's Leonardo da Vinci Airport, rushed into the city, and poured into paper cups. The whole affair was served by surly and smelly staff.

While Nazy met Alessandra, our tour guide, to arrange the day's activity, I walked to the newsstand, bought an *International Herald Tribune*, and lit my pipe. I was just about to enjoy myself when Mitra materialized. "I threw away the other pouches of tobacco, Daddy. I hope you enjoy the last pipe in Italy."

"Thank you, Mitra. I love you, too."

At this point, Nazy showed up with significantly fewer Eurocheques. The all-inclusive tours had been arranged, but we hadn't paid for them—until now. Everyone was a bit down, so we decided to get a fruit snack before the Panorama tour began.

Half an hour and fifty-three thousand lire later, we were sitting in the motor coach.

"Nazy, it cost us one hundred guilders for those three bowls of fruit. That's fifty dollars. It's absurd. The strawberries weren't even red."

"Oh, come on, Dan, it just *seems* like you're spending a lot. Lire are worthless. Besides, it was your fault. You let them put out the linen napkins."

"Well how was I to know that the cloth napkins changed the cover charge from fifteen hundred lire to five thousand lire? Forget it. Let's try to enjoy ourselves. Have you seen my pipe tobacco?"

"Mitra and I threw it out."

"Threw it out?"

"You said you weren't going to smoke in Italy."

"I said I wasn't going to *buy tobacco* in Italy. I won't buy any tobacco."

"Don't you think bringing twelve pouches of tobacco was cheating a little?"

Pretending to pout, I plopped down in a seat next to Darius. "They think they've got me, Darius, but I've got news for them. I hid a pack of Borkum Riff in my sock after I got dressed this morning. We'll show them, won't we?"

"But, Dad," Darius began. "I filled that pouch with cat food."

I quietly dumped the cat food into Darius's lap. "*Et tu*, Darius? You traitor!"

There was a look of panic in his eyes. "It's not good for you."

"Darius, just shut up," I muttered, cutting up one thousand lire bank notes and stuffing them into my pipe. This was going to be a long vacation.

And this was only the beginning. We had just made it through the first night. We had Florence, Venice, and five more exciting nights at the Portamaggiore. Darius's plan of twenty-one countries in eighteen days was beginning to look good. At least we would have been able to sleep on the bus. It's not to say that we didn't like Italy. The people were nice, the country was exciting, and it was educational. We saw paintings, sculpture, and ruins, and counted twenty-nine different kinds of military or police uniforms. The Italians weren't the problem. It was the Aussies that made us weep.

DROP ANOTHER SHRIMP ON THE BARBIE

Proving that sheer, complete, total exhaustion could outweigh noise, heat, and humidity, Nazy and I were actually asleep in Rome. But this was the Hotel Portamaggiore; the staff wouldn't permit the guests to rest. There was a knock at the door, then a shout through the keyhole.

"Diza tourismo isa come. You an yo familo musa coma downa!"

"Is this the wake-up call?"

"You musa coma downa now!"

"Dank u, uh, gracias, merci…yeah. Just a minute."

I wasn't alert. I rousted Nazy awake and banged on the children's door.

Our first days in Rome hadn't gone smoothly, but we were determined to have a good time. We had to because we were stuck in Italy with nonrefundable tickets.

Alessandra, our guide, was nervously pacing the aisle of the tour bus. We were late, and there were several stops to go. The good news was that we didn't have time to stop for the continental breakfast. The family plopped down in the second and third rows, behind an Australian couple. The bus collected tourists at several more hotels, drove on, and parked at Circus Maximus.

Darius wanted to know what happened at Circus Maximus.

"Well, they had chariot races and fights between lions and Christians. Things like that," I explained.

"Lions and Christians? Who won?"

"Who won? Who do you think?"

"Wow. And real chariot races?"

"Precisely, real chariot races. They kept the horses at the Hotel Portamaggiore. We're staying in the same room where the centurions kept their horses."

Circus Maximus looked like Centraal Station at rush hour. There were hundreds of buses, thousands of tourists. and plenty of confusion. Everyone switched buses at the Circus. Sorted by tour selection and native language, we joined the English/Japanese group, and took seats behind the same dour-looking Australians.

Melika sat next to me and asked about our plans for the day.

"In the morning we're going on a panorama tour of Rome, then we go to Vatican City to see St. Peter's Basilica. We're on our own for lunch, then we'll see the Sistine Chapel."

"What's a panorama tour, Daddy?"

"That's when they drive us by all the important things in the city and explain about them."

"Big whoop! And why do we have to go to the sizzling chapel?"

"Big whoop, Melika? That's a really childish thing to say. And it's the *Sistine* Chapel, not the sizzling chapel. Don't you like the city?"

"Everything's broken. We went to that museum that had the broken foot statue. All the columns are just standing there, hooked to nothing, and most of the old buildings have even fallen down. They really need to repair this place. And I called it the sizzling chapel because it's really hot here. Why didn't someone think about air conditioning?"

Melika was not really interested in the panorama tour. The first stop was the Coliseum, which, as Melika pointed out, was falling apart. For this stop, we got to get out and walk around. We posed for a family photo and started back to the bus.

When we got there, someone was sitting in our seats. Mitra, Darius, and Melika picked alternate chairs. I selected a vacant seat in the front row that had been occupied by one of the Australian tourists. I reached in my pocket for my pipe. but because of sabotage, I was forced to chew rather than smoke. The Australian interrupted my reverie.

"Hay, mate. That's me blooming chair. Get out!"

"Big whoop, pea brain!"

Melika inserted herself in the conversation. "Big whoop, Daddy? That's a childish thing to say."

The Australian wasn't listening. "Get yer blooming arse off me chair."

"You know what, cretin? You're acting like a…" I paused for a minute to get control of myself. Just because he wanted to act like a jerk didn't mean I had to lower myself, but I had to get the last word. "Ya know, mate. I'd like to stick *you* on the barbie."

The children had seen the situation developing and were determined to get revenge. When Alessandra returned, Mitra asked (loud enough to be heard in Australia), "Alessandra, do you have to sit in the same seats for every part of the tour?"

"Most people do, but it's not really necessary."

"So if someone made a big fuss about his seat, he'd be acting like a selfish jerk, eh?"

Meanwhile, Darius was reading his tour guide and discovered that you can't get into St. Peter's Basilica if you're wearing shorts. Our next stop was St. Peter's; our Australian was wearing shorts.

"Alessandra," Darius asked, "can you get into St. Peter's if you're wearing shorts? Say, shorts like that guy over there?" Darius had forgotten that he was wearing shorts, too.

"*You* can get in, Darius—you're a kid. But *you*, sir," she said, looking at the Australian, "won't be allowed inside."

Pleased with himself, Darius proclaimed news in his announcer's voice. "Oh gosh! He can't get in! A ten-thousand-mile trip and he can't get into the church."

When we got to Vatican City, we had a few moments before the Basilica tour began. Darius talked his siblings into a crusade for a passport stamp. I wasn't sure the Vatican "did" stamps.

Mitra took over and herded the group into an official-looking building, where she showed her passport and asked for stamps. She came out with five thousand fewer lire, but she would be able to mail her postcards.

I bought the customary four-dollar Coke. It was an incredibly warm day of thirty-eight degrees Celsius (about ninety-nine degrees Fahrenheit). Even the Pope had left for a vacation. We collected with our group at the door to St. Peter's. The Australian had bought a pair of sweatpants—and he was sweating.

"Look at that guy from Australia, Dad," Darius bellowed, "I bet he's really hot."

"You know, I bet he feels like he's on a barbecue."

We left Rome in ruins, but it was not our fault. We continued on to Florence and Venice, where the hotels were a marked improvement. We learned to adjust to the high prices, although we never did it happily. We saw so many statues, paintings, and fountains that it all blended together in a cultural and educational mishmash. We became experts at avoiding the infamous Italian taxi supplemento (supplement).

Some of the educational benefits may have been lost on the children. They still wanted to go to a good museum—where "the statues aren't broken." Nazy got to make a few Gucci purchases, but unfortunately, Gucci items cost more in Italy than they did in Holland. When we returned to Amsterdam, we were amazed at how much Dutch we understood. Our time in Italy—where few speak English—had even made us wish for the BBC. BBC1, appropriately, was showing a special documentary the evening we returned: Arc Welding: A Welch Institution. A few things about the BBC had begun to concern me: first, I watched the arc welding special; second, I didn't quite hear the accents anymore.

After our summer vacation, we really began to feel like residents, not visitors, in Holland. Things weren't moving at the office and Darius, seeing me in a weakened condition, pressed for a new passport stamp. Denmark was the plan. But we're The Martin Family—we went to Berlin instead.

DON'T FENCE ME IN

Tension was high. A small blob of sweat dropped from my nose onto the table. I was sitting in the isolation booth working on my Dutch lab project for my teacher, Attila the Nun. My shirt was soaked, my head was pounding, and my answers were invariably late. The task seemed easy enough. I'd listen to a present tense Dutch sentence and convert into the past or the past perfect.

In reality, the problem had proved to be more complex. I wasn't at my mental peak—it's hard to sleep well when you're having nightmares about conjugating separable Dutch verbs. But Sister Saddam, the lab monitor, didn't care. It was crunch time and I had to deliver. I heard exercise seventy-six through the earphones.

"*Het regent veel in de herfst.*"

"It rains a lot in autumn," I thought. "At least the Dutch and I agree on something. Now, where sits the work word? Good grief, I'm thinking English with Dutch grammar. Oh yeah, the verb is *regenen*—to rain. Is it regular? Yep. Is it regular with the 'd' ending or regular with the 't' ending? I believe it's 'd'-regular. *Het regent*, that's third-person singular. They want the perfectum. Is that simple past or…?"

"*Het heeft veel in de herfst geregend.*" I could hear the answer reverberating in my earphone microseconds before I opened my mouth. I was really annoyed.

DANIEL PAUL MARTIN

"This is the most stupid lab I've ever done!" I shouted into the microphone.

"Mr. Martin," came the quiet voice of Sister Saddam, "we shouldn't get discouraged, should we?"

I looked up through the glass panel of the isolation booth and saw Sister Saddam smiling at me.

"I didn't know you could listen in on our lab work, Sister."

"Clearly, there's a *lot* you don't know. Would you like a special meeting with my colleague, Sister Genghis?"

And on that cheery note, I returned to the lab exercise.

"*Het ijs smelt door de zon.*"

Later that evening, I made my customary emergency call home. I usually asked Nazy simple grammatical questions such as, "What's a reflexive pronoun?" or "Does every adverb end in 'ly'?" I also got a daily update on the family status. Melika was sick—a situation that threatened our planned trip to Denmark. Moreover, the children wanted to be in The Hague for Easter and Nazy's birthday. Besides, the weather was cold and rainy. We couldn't go to Denmark.

While we couldn't go to Denmark, it also proved impossible to "not go anywhere." We faced a major rebellion from our male offspring, so we agreed to an unplanned excursion through Europe.

Given that we didn't have as much time for the mini vacation as we expected, our first task was to locate an exciting destination. We had been in Holland for several months and were seasoned western Europeans, so finding an exciting destination wasn't easy. Any place in Holland would be boring. We'd done Brussels, Brugges, Cologne, Düsseldorf, and Luxembourg. Copenhagen was too far. Paris was too French. There wasn't anything west of The Hague except the North Sea and it was cold and wet. We turned east and selected the first major city that appeared on our map—Berlin.

STUMBLING THROUGH THE TULIPS

Naturally, I told the children about the idea before I checked on the driving distances. Not that it would have made much difference: I still don't know a kilometer from a clamshell. Besides, everyone kept telling us that Europe was small. Berlin, as we soon discovered, was far to the east of old West Germany. It's even in the eastern half of old East Germany.

The day before we left, Darius examined his maps and discovered that Berlin is quite close to the Polish border. I knew we were in trouble. Germany? That was close! But Poland sounded very, very far away!

Unfazed, unprepared, and unencumbered with a plan, we departed late on a Thursday afternoon. We didn't make it to Berlin the first night. It is possible to zip along on the (speed-limitless) autobahn, but much to our dismay, the autobahn had several gaps, and the detours had speed limits, lines, and traffic lights. Not only did we fail to get to Berlin, we didn't even make it to "old" East Germany. We made it to Hannover. (The Germans insisted on missppellinng the namme.)

In America, we would have stopped at a roadside Travelodge. Europeans would have made reservations at a quaint inn in the countryside. Unfortunately, we were Americans in Europe. There was no Travelodge and we had no reservations. It wasn't easy finding a hotel in Hannover during the Easter holiday week. Nevertheless, we were safely (and expensively) installed in an airport Holiday Inn well before two a.m.

Our disgustingly late arrival in Hannover, coupled with Martin family tradition, made an early morning departure rather unlikely, and the huge all-you-could-eat breakfast buffet made an early departure improbable. If I told you we left early, you'd find that unbelievable. I tried to leave early, but as the Dutch say, *kan niet*!

In a refrain we were to hear frequently over the next few days, Nazy wanted us to "relax and enjoy ourselves." I was flabbergasted—Nazy appeared to be enjoying a buffet that didn't have a salad.

Darius and I were politely waiting for the girls to finish. We wanted to get to Berlin before dark. Inauspiciously, he had time to examine his European pocket atlas.

"Hey, Dad, look at this—the Polish border is only eighty kilometers from Berlin. Do you think we could stop in for a passport stamp on the way back?"

"It's only eighty kilometers, but it's eighty kilometers the exact wrong way," I replied.

"At least he didn't say *no*," Darius thought to himself.

We made it to Berlin by early afternoon. We even found a hotel in the *zentrum* (center) where we dumped our belongings and took off to see the city. Characteristically American, we headed for East Berlin by double-decker bus. We disembarked at the Brandenburg Gate and walked across to Unter den Linden, the main drag on the other side.

The children were devastated—they had all wanted a piece of the Berlin Wall, but it was gone. It was even hard to see where it had been. Fortunately, many former communists had become capitalistic entrepreneurs. Pieces of the wall (and old DDR military uniforms, Russian rubles, East German money, Russian army officers' hats, etc.) were for sale everywhere. We selected a wall splinter with a colorful chip of spray paint and an official certificate of authenticity, and took off on a stroll down Unter den Linden.

As far as I could tell, the two halves of the city were completely integrated. The buses, the *u-bahn* (subway), the *s-bahn* (elevated trains), and all the roads passed straight over what had been the border. The East German side looked bleak, but the old buildings on Unter den Linden, which were palaces, museums, and theatres built in the 1800s, were actually quite impressive. The *s-bahn* station at Alexanderplatz (East Berlin) had a decidedly somber and unmaintained look, but in the *zentrum*, it looked like one city.

We walked and walked and walked and walked past the Reichstag (the historical seat of German parliament) and back into West Berlin. Then we walked down the main shopping strip, casing the joint for the next day, and found the authentic German restaurant recommended by our neighbor, Patricia. Almost everyone enjoyed a real German meal of sausage, sauerkraut, and horseradish sauce. (Melika had spaghetti.) Following this culinary delight, we headed for the Kermis (a traveling amusement park), where we enjoyed the bumper cars, Ferris wheel, and the Cyclone and Wilde Maus coasters.

It had been a long and tiring day. Back at the hotel, Nazy was tiredly tucking in Darius, who saw an opportunity. He whipped out his map of Europe and observed again that the Polish border was only eighty kilometers away.

"Wouldn't it be great to just zip over to Poland and get another passport stamp? Dad didn't say we couldn't. Can we, Mom? Can we?"

"How far is it, Darius?"

"It's not far at all! You'll really like it! Thanks!"

We started off the next day with the breakfast buffet. Nazy's Berlin map was marked with Ka De We, the second largest store in the world, and off we went. Darius and I patiently watched Nazy and the girls meander through the store.

It was rather interesting. An entire floor and staff of five hundred were devoted to food. (You want pickled hippopotamus tongue? They've got it. Grated Burmese anteater lips? Check! Honey-dipped spider claws? Aisle eight. Dunkin' Donuts? Well, *almost* everything.) We also examined 49,231 different nutcrackers and 12,911 types of Berlin beer steins.

Later, we hit Europa Center and the zoo. At about five-thirty, we began our trip back home to The Hague (we couldn't stay in the hotel another night—it was booked), but we had one small problem. No one knew where the autobahn was. Berlin is a huge city about the size of the country of Luxembourg.

Unfazed, I began to retrace our route. Darius interrupted my quiet plan.

"But Dad, Mom said we could go to Poland."

"You agreed to that stupid idea, Nazy?" I wasn't amused.

"He said it was your idea."

We ended the beginning of the journey home (via Poland) in the middle of nowhere. More precisely, in nowhere somewhere near southeast Berlin, where parts of the Berlin Wall were still standing. It was amazing. There were two parallel walls with about fifty meters of completely vacant land between them. The wall blocking the street was demolished, but the rest of it still stood on both sides of the road. It was an excellent opportunity to augment our wall collection. We walked along the vacant land to the famous wall and hacked out several chips, chunks, lumps, and nuggets. Many of our selections had colorful paint and all were guaranteed authentic: We had chopped them out with our own hands. Darius and Mitra even carried a massive boulder halfway to the car. (I carried it the rest of the way.)

We were in a residential section of Berlin, where there was a major difference between the two sides. In old West Berlin, the street was full of nice, middle-class homes. The eastern side was bleak: The road had potholes and the buildings were falling apart. Even the highway signs were dreary-looking. Reflective paint hadn't been used in the East.

Eventually we found the ill-paved, bumpy, narrow autobahn and made our way toward Poland. All we wanted was a passport stamp. Five miles from the border, the road split: cars and other.

"Other" was for trucks—there were about three miles of trucks waiting to clear Polish customs. (Poland wasn't communist, but was very bureaucratic.)

At the border, on the German side, we saw what appeared to be a huge passport control station. We zipped right across the Oder River into Poland and met the Polish border patrol. We might have had a chance if the border police spoke English (or Persian or Dutch). We might have gotten a stamp if we spoke German or Polish. It might have been better if we hadn't said something like, "We're not staying, all we want is a passport stamp." We might have checked about visa requirements. There were a lot of "might haves."

The sad story? We could enter and get a passport stamp provided we purchased visas—at 365 deutsche marks—cash only. We didn't have 365 deutsche marks. And they wouldn't take Eurocheques. They turned us away, but without the exit papers required to enter Germany.

I wondered if we'd have trouble getting back. Nazy wasn't worried. "Come on, Dan, don't worry. We're Americans living in Holland."

"That's right, dear," I retorted. "Americans living in Holland wanting to enter Germany because they've been ejected from Poland. No problem."

I was right, it was no problem. An army officer at the river saw our American passports and waved us through as "diplomats."

Meanwhile, Darius was about to have a cow. We had gone all this way for nothing.

"Don't worry, Darius," I said. "You're in Poland as soon as you cross the river. You can mark it off your list. Besides, we'll get a stamp at that huge German station on the other side of the Oder."

I wasn't quite right. The single army officer at the river was German border control. The massive edifice that we had seen earlier was a huge Shell gas station.

Darius was really ticked. No passport stamp, peasant parents (without DM365), and all requests (and demands) that we turn around were ignored.

By now, of course, it was late and dark, and we wouldn't be able to make it back to The Hague. There wasn't a room to be had in Berlin. We ended up in Hannover at the airport Holiday Inn. The drive was long, the East German roads were bad, the autobahn wasn't smooth, and the thoroughfare wasn't well lit. And the "divided highway" wasn't.

There were hundreds of Trabant cars the size of matchboxes s-l-o-w-l-y heading west. Trabants are very dangerous. They only go about fifty miles an hour and their taillights are powered by drained AAA batteries. It's easy to drive right over them.

The consensus the next day was that the vacation had been a bit hectic. It didn't matter; the kids could relax at school and I could relax during the final week of Dutch lessons with the Nuns. Nazy had lots of WC (Women's Club) meetings.

Melika contacted a barrister to begin incorporation for her new company: The Berlin Wall by Mail.

"Look at this, Darius," I said at breakfast, "the newspaper says that Polish visas won't be required anymore."

"Thanks, Dad. By the way, did you hear what Mom said?"

"No."

"Well, she told Patricia about the place where we saw the wall."

"So?"

"Patricia told Mom that they haven't taken the wall down because they haven't removed all the land mines."

"Land mines?"

"Yeah, land mines. We could have gotten our heads blown off while we were chopping the wall down."

"Hey, Daddy!" Melika interrupted. "Doesn't that make my pieces more valuable? I bet I can raise my prices."

The lessons of Italy (and Luxembourg, Berlin, and France) convinced me that The Martin Family had a lot to learn. However, we had been in Holland for almost eighteen months. And, while people were different in many ways, they are the same in even more ways. While I wished that language was one of the many ways we were similar, I knew we had learned a lot. After the debacle of our hotel choice in Rome, we rented a casa from a friend in Spain. The Costa del Sol beckoned, and we were ready.

CASA CONFUSION

Mitra and I were at the *supermercado* (supermarket) in Mijas, Spain, picking up breakfast and dinner. We had already made one amazing discovery: Honey Nut Cheerios. Mitra was ecstatic.

"This is really a civilized place, Daddy. Honey Nut Cheerios—the definitive mark of civilization."

Too stunned to respond, I was examining the box. It was Honey Nut LOOPs. I knew it was a recent Spanish introduction because the box included instructions about how to eat cereal. The pictures were simple: Pour into a bowl and add milk.

We started toward the meat counter with a bounce in our step. Then Mitra dramatically confronted me with her major concern.

"This has been a really boring vacation."

"Boring, Mitra? Boring?"

"Nothing has gone wrong. What can we tell our friends? They expect disaster. We can't disappoint them."

"Perhaps we've become debonair and experienced European travelers."

"Maybe we've become boring American tourists. We didn't even stay at a quaint European hotel in Madrid. We stayed at a Holiday Inn."

"That's true. It wasn't at all like the Portamaggiore in Rome. We had a shower curtain, air conditioning, and an edible breakfast. We could tell the difference between toilet paper and wax paper. Boring or smart?"

"We need excitement."

"What about Lisbon? The cab drivers always overcharged us."

"The same thing happened in New York."

"But in Lisbon, they charged us three times more than they should have."

"So you lost one dollar and five cents. Big deal!"

"One dollar and five cents? How did you arrive at that amount?" I was getting excited. We had left Portugal a week ago and were still working on conversion tables between Dutch guilders and Portuguese escudos. Perhaps Mitra had made progress.

"I multiplied escudos by pi. I did an integer divide and discarded the remainder, then I took the numbers to the right of the decimal point and divided by three. I multiplied my two partial results and took the natural log of the rightmost four digits. Then..."

I seized control of the situation by sending her to look for a whole chicken, then thought back over the vacation. Was there anything to write about?

What about Toledo?

The roads were narrow and steep. I was driving while Nazy navigated. Naturally, we were lost. The car's left and right mirrors were scraping buildings simultaneously. The road, such as it was, had evaporated in the heat. The car was at the edge of a cliff on a steep downward incline and I couldn't find reverse on the manual transmission. Darius was being helpful.

"Does this rental car have front-wheel drive, Dad?" Darius asked.

"Yes it does," I replied as I carefully let up the clutch. The car rolled forward again. I really had to find reverse gear.

"What about the brakes? Do we have brakes in the front and the back?"

"Yes, we do." The car rolled a few inches closer to the brink.

"So if the front wheels fall over the edge, we can't back up, but we can use the brakes to balance on the cliff. Right?"

"Darius, just shut up until I get us out of the mess that your *mother* has navigated us into."

My unfortunate outburst provoked an immediate response from Nazy. Darius continued mumbling to the peanut gallery in the backseat. Ignoring the cacophony surrounding me, I set the hand brake and used both hands in a violent attempt to jostle the gearshift into reverse. Darius continued his soliloquy.

"Spaceman Dan wrestles with the controls of his starship but they won't respond. Is this the end of the road for The Martin Family?"

Toledo was out—I'd look dumb. Perhaps there was material in Madrid. Ah, yes, the cable car ride to Caso de Campo.

"But Mom, my guidebook says we'll love the cable cars," Darius said. "We'll end up in the Caso de Campo Park, where they have an artificial lake, a zoo, and an amusement park."

"Darius, it's a hundred degrees in the shade," Nazy retorted. "And nobody wants to walk to the cable car."

"You never let us do anything. We're going to be the only family in history that visits Madrid but doesn't ride the cable car. You're ruining my whole vacation. The book said we had to ride the cable car. How can I face my friends if they find out that we came all the way to Madrid and didn't ride the cable car because it was 'a hundred in the shade'? I just…"

I wanted to join the conversation, but the humidity was so high that my beard was plastered to the side of my face. I just didn't have the energy to open my mouth. Predictably, we ended up on the cable car. It dropped us off in the middle of the Caso de Campo—several kilometers from the zoo and the amusement park. It looked as if the artificial lake was within walking distance.

The Martin Family completed a successful trek across uncharted territory. Melika was disgusted when we finally arrived at the artificial lake.

"But, Daddy, it's real water."

"Of course it's real water. You need water to have a lake."

"But they said it was an *artificial lake*. I thought they'd have plastic water."

Back at the (thankfully) air-conditioned hotel, I located Darius' travel book and read the section on the cable car.

"Children will love the ride," it read. "Parents should be aware that the cable car discharges passengers in the middle of the park—several kilometers from any point of interest."

"Darius!" I shouted, too late.

Back at the *supermercado*, Mitra returned with the chicken in a plain brown bag. "Well, have you thought of anything exciting that's happened?" she asked.

"Actually, there's nothing I'd like to write about."

"What about Gibraltar?"

Gibraltar! My mind slipped back to our exciting visit to the rock of myths.

"Look at that huge line," Nazy expounded. "We'll be waiting forever."

"Actually, the natives call that a queue—this is a British colony. And I, for one, won't wait forever."

Melika, who had been dozing in the back seat, looked up and noticed the long queue of cars in front of us. "Who had the idea of going to Gibraltar, Darius?" she shouted.

I glanced in the rearview mirror. Mitra had a look of panic on her face and was grappling with Darius for control of the guidebook. "Let me have that book, Darius. Daddy, the safety of the family is at stake. Who knows what he's gotten us into this time? Make him give me the book."

Just then I noticed a Spanish guy walking up the row between the immobile cars, placing parking receipts under windshield wipers. He walked up to our car and stuffed a white piece of paper under the right wiper blade.

"Two thousand pesetas," he said, holding out his hand.

"Look, Mom, he's wearing a pink Benetton shirt." Mitra whispered.

"What do we get for two thousand?" Nazy asked.

"Parking in Gibraltar."

"Maybe we'll just walk. This is a long line."

"Walking impossible, *señora*. Too far."

"Just give him two thousand and let's get out of here!" The cars in front were moving and the cars behind were breaking in line.

I reached into my wallet and handed Nazy a five-thousand peseta bill. (I didn't have anything smaller.) She handed it to our friend. "How long can we park with this ticket?" she asked.

"Oh…one day, two days, all week!" he shouted, then started running. We didn't see him again. Nazy complained to a nearby citizen.

"Ah, *banditos*," he said.

"We're the victim of highway robbery, Dan."

"Not really," I replied. "This road is not a highway."

Gibraltar stories were out! I'd really look dumb—and gullible—if anyone were to read about our experience there.

Back in Mijas, Mitra and I finished the *supermercado* shopping and returned to the rental house for breakfast and an early departure to the Mediterranean Sea.

Nazy (as usual) was navigating. "Take the Campino exit after Calahonda. Turn right."

I was listening to her instructions, but I was also attempting to drive on a Spanish highway, or *autovia*, as they're called. It wasn't easy. The *autovia* was used by anything that moved, including not only cars, trucks, and motorcycles, but also buses (which stopped to pick up and discharge passengers), mopeds, tractors, and bicycles.[8] There was no breakdown lane. I didn't know if I was doing a good job, but at least I looked like a Spanish driver with one hand on the steering wheel and the other on the horn.

Finally we saw the Campino exit, and I dutifully turned right. The road quickly deteriorated and slowly petered out. Nazy thought that we were in middle of nowhere, but that gives the impresson that we were centrally located. It was too narrow for me to execute a U-turn, so I decided to back up. This decision proved to be a dreadful mistake.

The unpaved road was more than a match for our Renault's suspension. The children's heads were bouncing off the roof. After a markedly severe jolt, the car stopped moving.

Nazy was calm. "You've completely ruined the car, Dan! What's the matter with you? Why didn't you turn left? Why did *you* decide to back up?"

Sighing, I got out of the car and discovered the problem. The right front tire had fallen through a defective manhole cover and was spinning freely. The car's bumper was touching the road and the sewer was emitting noxious fumes. Nazy was shifting blame.

"I saw that sewer, Dan! I knew you were going to do something stupid like that! Why were you backing up?"

"If you saw the defective sewer, why didn't you tell me?"

The children chose sides (none chose mine). "What are we going to do now, Daddy? Boy, what a mess *you* got us into."

---

8 . *Once, we encountered a motorized wheelchair on the motorway (at least it was in the slow lane).*

While I didn't have any ideas about how to extract the car, it was crystal clear that I had to at least act as though I had a solution in mind. Accordingly, I opened the trunk and took out the jack. It wouldn't fit under the front bumper, so I put it toward the middle of the car and jacked. It lifted the middle of the car, but there was no parting of the way for the front tire and the sewer.

I was scratching my head (and beginning to get worried) when a Spanish mailman rode up on his motorcycle. He surveyed the situation, and while he didn't speak English, we were able discern the general thrust of his thoughts.

"Ohh, ughg, blech," he said—accurately. He continued, *"Mama, mama, mama!"*

And then he sprang into action. He dashed into a nearby ravine and returned with a giant cement block. He placed it under the middle of the car—the part I had jacked up—and moved the jack forward, then lifted the front tire and pushed the car out of the manhole. He covered the manhole with the cement block and remounted his motorcycle with a cheerful "Adios!" He was so quick with a solution that I concluded that this was a normal problem.

Chastened, we found the beach and settled in to enjoy the sun. Miles of pristine sandy beach and azure sea were only marred by acres of bare flesh. This visit showed us why God invented clothes. The highlight was a very large, mostly naked, woman whose lumbering trek toward the sea was captured on the University of Seville's seismograph. The tsunami generated when she splashed about caused significant devastation of North African coastal regions.

We returned home tanned, looking forward to a cool shower and a home-cooked meal. Mercilessly pushing the children out of the way, I established control of the bathroom and triumphantly turned on the water. I waited for the Spanish mechanisms to respond.

"There is no water." I announced the minor problem to the rest of the family.

"Did you hear that, Mom?" Darius shouted. "He knocked me down and pushed me out of the bathroom and then used up all the water. Can you believe it?"

"That's right, Dan," Nazy said, following the trend by siding with Darius "You've really been dumb today. First you drop the car into a sewer and now you use up the hot water."

"I didn't drop the car into the sewer," I said, trying to extricate myself from the situation. "A defective manhole cover broke while I was backing up. And I didn't use up the hot water. We don't have *any* water."

"Daddy used up all the water?" Melika jumped in.

I recognized a losing situation and (re)dressed to walk to our neighbor's house. Maurice was unflustered.

"No water? Let me see." He tried his garden spigot, but to no avail. "Yep, you're right. No water. They're always doing this to us."

"Always doing this?"

"Yep, I've lived here for eighteen years. They never tell us when they're going to turn off the water. Some people just can't get used to the situation."

"Well, we're flexible, Maurice. How long is it usually out?"

"Last week we didn't have water for five days."

"Five days? Five *days*!"

"Usually it's only out for a day or two. You can use pool water to flush the toilets and buy drinking water from the town."

"Thanks."

I was glum as I walked back to the house. Nazy was waiting with a sullen expression. The "whole chicken" Mitra had selected from the *supermercado* was on the kitchen counter.

"Do you see anything strange about this chicken, Dan?" she slyly began.

STUMBLING THROUGH THE TULIPS

"Strange, dear?"

"Yeah. Notice the cute little feet. The smiling and cheerful head. The feathers at the joints. There's not one thing right about this chicken."

"Well, at least Mitra picked a dead one."

"Maybe it died in our refrigerator. And don't blame Mitra. You were in charge of shopping."

"But I'm not a food expert."

"Never mind, I can still fix dinner. What about the water? You won't believe some of the stuff inside this chicken. We need to wash it out."

"Water, eh?" I grabbed a bucket. "Maurice said something about the swimming pool and chickens…and roads and…" It seemed clear that I would become good friends with the bucket. (At least it wouldn't blame me for anything.)

> *There was a pattern. In France, they spoke French and had a different word for everything. They did just to screw us up. The trend was repeated in Spain and Germany. We decided we should visit a place that shared our common tongue, but then someone noticed the language was called English rather than American.*

BLOODY HULL

The request had been ignored, delayed, deferred, neglected, and overlooked too long. The Martin Family wanted to see London. I had been visiting London at least twice a month, and viewed a pleasure trip to the UK as an oxymoron. It didn't matter: I had been set up by two Shell colleagues. Jim Cone had *flakked* the Lensbury Club, and Mike Eden had *touted* the West End. The children had a winter holiday, and we had a trip to take.

Things began to go awry when I booked the room at the *posh* Lensbury club that Shell provides for visiting executives and their families. It never occurred to me to ask if the room had a *loo*. Things continued in this vein when I decided to leave the ferry arrangements to Shell Travel Services. They booked an economy cabin in a *three-funnel* boat from Rotterdam's Europort to Hull in Great Britain. Unfortunately, there are no five-person cabins on the ferry, so they also booked a sleeping seat. My *chums* told me we would have to be *potty* to even consider such accommodations.

I should have contacted Darius, Mr. Map, but I neglected to locate our final destination of Hull until after the tickets arrived. I had plenty of problems just getting Shell to handle my (out-of-the-ordinary) request to bring the family. "*Sod it all*," I thought. "Just so long as we get to the UK." Besides, I was worried about other things. Important things. Would Nazy remember to pack my *mackintosh* and *Wellingtons*? (It rains a lot in

Great Britain.) What about my *braces*? (I'd need my formal *togs* for the theatre.) Would she remember the *crisps* and *crumpets* for the road? Would I drive clockwise or *anticlockwise* when I arrived at a *roundabout*?

The children prepared by reading *adverts* for the West End shows. They *memorised* the appropriate *tube* stops—*Leicester Square*, *Piccadilly Circus*, and *Covent Garden*. They were ready.

I left the office in plenty of time for an orderly departure, but it was not to be. In keeping with family practice, Nazy and I had a bit of a *row* about the importance of being on time. Naturally, Nazy got the silent last word when she left everyone sitting in the car *whilst* she made cranberry juice for Mary Lou, our housekeeper. I tried to calm the troubled multitudes huddled in the car by noting that "at least we won't have to drink it."

I was *gobsmacked* when we arrived at Europort just on time and had to listen to Nazy describe how I always rush everyone like a *gormless* fool. "If worrying and rushing caused weight loss, Dan, you'd drop *two stone* overnight." I really wanted to get on the boat and partake of a *wee dram* of whiskey.

The overnight trip to Hull was uneventful. The ferry was large, the ride was smooth, and the cabin was—well—small, but large enough to accommodate a sleeping bag. The good news was that no one had to spend a sleepless night in a sleeping chair. The bad news was that we could *all* spend a sleepless night in the cabin.

We arrived in Hull, in the (far) northeast of England, early on Thursday morning. Fortunately, we had checked the car before we left. The *accumulator* was functional, so we were able to drive directly off the boat. A short journey through Hull led us to a *dual carriageway* (the M62) and in *due course* we were on the M1 en route to Greater London, which was 250 miles away.

The M1 looked like a U.S. interstate highway, with three lanes (separated by a *central reservation*) in each direction. *Lorries* were restricted to the *nearside* lane (which was, of course, on the wrong side of the road). The *three-litre* engine under the *bonnet* of our Ford Taurus *Estate* ate up the miles. Since I couldn't find a speed limit sign, I was very happy not to be sighted by any members of the local *constabulary*. I think I was legal since everyone was going at least seventy-five mph. It was just as well—our Dutch *number plate* and left-hand drive marked us as tourists. We quickly discovered that at seventy-five mph, the Taurus not only ate miles, it drank *petrol*.

"*Bugger all*," I said as I dropped a several *quid* into the Shell Service Station account. We were three hours into our drive toward London, and it was a *ruddy* mess. We were all sick of the English countryside, and we hadn't even gotten to the M25—the London *Orbital*. A lengthy *tailback* was our first indication of approaching road construction. We were forced to drive on the *farside verge* for several miles.

This isn't to say we weren't educated. We noticed for example, the difference in Dutch, Belgian, and British road signs. Suppose you've just driven out of a tunnel. The authorities want to remind you to turn off your lights. In Belgium, you'll encounter a sign that says:

LICHTEN! (LIGHTS!)

In Holland, the same message will be given by the following sign:

Denk aan uw lichten (Think about your lights)

In France, it says something like:

Extinguish your luminance!

In the UK, you'll see this:

STUMBLING THROUGH THE TULIPS

> **Motorists are kindly reminded to extinguish their headlights upon exiting the tunnel as a courtesy to other motorists and in order to assure themselves that their *accumulator* will continue to be of service the next time they enter their vehicle in the morning en route to work or p…**

Quite so, *old chap*. It's best if you turn the lights off.

We were a *barmy* and tired group when we finally arrived at the Lensbury club. I dropped Nazy off at reception, parked the car, and unloaded the *boot*. It's hard to believe the next event: A distinct chill was emanating from a definitely steamed Nazy. She had discovered our *loo-less* rooms.

Actually, we ended up having a great time. A few *bob* got us tickets to *Cats* and *Starlight Express*—real cultural treats fully worthy of the country that brought us Shakespeare and Chaucer. (*Starlight Express* is a love story in which the protagonists are trains, and the actors spend the entire play on roller skates. *Cats* is a long-running but plotless musical.) The family saw all the important sights—Westminster Cathedral, St. Paul's, the Tower of London, Piccadilly Circus, the House of Parliament, Buckingham Palace, and Hyde Park. A favorite stop was the British Museum, where we saw the (Egyptian) Rosetta Stone and the (Greek) Elgin Marble. We mastered the *underground* and learned how to *queue*, and we saw *bobbies* and a few *twits* and *blokes* mouthing *tripe* at Speakers' Corner.

We arrived back in Holland by way of Zeebrugge, Belgium, on Sunday morning. The ride home was considerably more bouncy than the trip over. (It was a *ruddy mess*.) Everyone was glad we had most of Sunday to recover from our trip. Most surprisingly, we were all happy to be back in Holland, where we could understand the natives.

ENGLISH SIGNS

In the underground:

> **Obstructing the egress causes inconvenience for fellow passengers and can be dangerous.**

In a store:

> **Customers are reminded that this establishment expects payment before articles leave the shop.**

On the M25, the London Orbital:[9]

> **Carriageway renovation underway. Expect tailbacks and delays until April.**

(I didn't want to wait until April to come home.)

And on an elevator:

> **↑ Press to Ascend**

---

9. *The Orbital in London, the Ring in Rotterdam, the Periferique in Paris, the Loop in Houston, the Beltway in Washington, and the Perimeter Highway in Atlanta.*

At least these could be understood. Others were more obtuse:

> **No Naked Lights**

> **Warning: Hard Dog Patrols**

> **Absolutely no toading between midnight and 6:00 A.M.**

> **Caution: Adverse Camber Ahead**

We had to visit Denmark. My mother was Danish and Nazy had a school chum (the British idioms were still wearing off) there. Besides, we had planned to visit several times. Family pride demanded that we follow through at least once.

UDSALG!!

Darius was really excited: "You're not going to believe this, Dad. We can use pi to convert Danish kroner to Dutch guilders."

"You're right, I don't believe you. The sign says 314.159. That's not pi, is it?"

"But that's what you get for one hundred guilders, so for one guilder you get 3.14159 kroner."

"Oh, yeah? I want to see the *point* 14159 coin. It's probably got a hole in it, right?"

"Actually, Dad, Denmark does have coins with holes."

"Darius."

"Yes?"

"Go find your mother. *I'll* get the kroner."

Actually, I didn't get the kroner. I should have ordered in advance.

Darius—questions, comments, and suggestions included—had been deftly shifted into Nazy's court. He was worried about the hotel and wanted to make sure I hadn't selected it. He wanted to be certain it carried a five-star rating, and certification that it was in the centrum of *København* (Copenhagen). He wanted a written guarantee that we would get a Denmark passport stamp, and wanted to notarize parental promises that the Danish trip would not be postponed this time.

Trip preparations were proceeding normally. I had failed to accomplish my extensive task list (get foreign money). Nazy had obtained ferry reservations, packed family clothes, acquired and read books about Denmark, and subcontracted hotel arrangements to Darius. Mitra, in a burst of pre-school enthusiasm, had packed a collection of literature in order to get a head start for the coming school year. Melika had selected and neatly stowed a number of appropriate games for the car, two books for recreational reading, her own supply of Danish kroner, and her pillow. She thoughtfully prepared a departure checklist for Darius.

The actual departure was most abnormal. We departed by car—on schedule. This unexpected development portended a long wait at the ferry terminal in Puttgarden, Germany.

The drive through Holland and Germany was tiresome. The German landscape was boring, and the farming countryside, fertilized with purely natural ingredients was…smelly. The famed autobahns were (sigh) under construction.

We made a single comfort stop near Hamburg. Nazy, well trained in pay toilets in the Netherlands, grabbed a deutsche mark coin and marched to the restroom, which was under armed guard.

The fierce German toilet *poliezi* had taken up stations around the perimeter. A hefty officer, obviously a former East German border guard, interposed herself between Nazy and relief.

"*Frau! War gehst du?*" she proclaimed.

Nazy understood little German, but she did understand a demand for payment. She dropped her mark into a leather glove and continued her trek, but her determined march was interrupted.

"*Halt!*" shouted the officer. "*Hier!*"

The sentry's arm was extended and held toilet paper (two sheets). Nazy turned back. The guard coughed—and wiped her nose with Nazy's toilet paper. Nazy turned and continued toward the restroom. She had her own paper and didn't care about getting a fifty *pfennig* refund.

The resumed trip was marred by Mitra's questions about *Moby Dick*. My answers were short. ("Call *me* Ishmael.")

"Daddy," Mitra retorted, after she'd heard that for the fifth time, "why have you memorized the first line of *Moby Dick*?"

"Because. I *started* to read *Moby Dick* several times both at college and in high school. I finally gave up and bought CliffsNotes and the Classic Comix version. Then I watched the movie where Orson Welles played the title role. *Moby Dick*, my dear, is at the top of my boring literature list."

"Oh, come on. It can't be that bad. It's a classic."

"Take a deep whiff of the air outside," I said, rolling down the window. "That's a classic fertilizer. But it's also bullsh…"

"Dan!" Nazy shouted.

"What I mean to say," I continued, "is that not all classic literature smells like roses. Some stinks like…"

"When do we get to the ferry terminal, Dan?" Nazy was insistently changing the subject.

"Daddy, just listen to this and then try to make fun of American literature:

> Like one who after a night of drunken revelry hies to his bed, still reeling, but with conscience yet pricking him, as the plungings of the Roman race-horse but so much the more strike his steel tags into him; as one who in that miserable plight still turns and turns in giddy anguish, prying God for annihilation until the fit be passed; and at last amid the while of woe he feels, a deep stupor steals over him, as over the man who bleeds to death, for conscience is the wound, and there's naught to staunch it; so, after sore wrestlings in his berth, Jonah's prodigy of ponderous misery drags him drowning down to sleep.[10]

---

10. *My Microsoft Word grammar checker indicates that this sentence, a direct quote, is "too long."*

"Mitra, this ponderous misery is driving me crazy. That sentence has neither subject nor verb. It's a convoluted concatenation of sub-clauses, phrases, and out-of-fashion words. People cannot, given the homogenized educational structure prevalent in culture—dare I say advanced culture—which predominates (at the current historical juncture) national thought, pretend—nay, expect—to be comprehended (shunning rest, sleep, and attention span) if they prattle in endless sentences, which in normal discourse could serve as paragraphs, monographs, and, indeed, encyclopedic volumes. In short, that paragraph says nothing."

I need not have commented, because Mitra, in "giddy anguish," was "drowning down to sleep."

With quiet assured, we endured a wait for the boat and a direct drive to the hotel. I was overjoyed to discover that the children would get their own room. Mitra asked for connecting rooms. I requested that the children be boarded in Sweden. We compromised with connecting floors.

While Nazy tucked the children in, I converted twenty-five guilders to kroner to get one hundred and five kroner. "It's one hundred and five kroner," I thought, "heh, heh...*Darius* was wrong."

I couldn't keep quiet. I rushed up to our room to tell Nazy the wonderful news. "Darius was wrong, Nazy. Wrong! Wrong! *København* may turn out to be a bargain. It's 4.20 kroner to the guilder."

Nazy appeared distracted. "You know, I think that giant sign means 'Sale!' Don't you agree?" she said, pointing out the window.

I looked out into the Danish mist. Far, far away, on the front of a nondescript (and closed) department store, hung a sign: *"Udsalg."* "How do you know that means 'sale'?"

"Just think. We can get Royal Copenhagen. We can get amber. We *need* Scandinavian crystal. And, since you said kroner are a bargain, we can get lots of everything. Why not? It's a sale."

The next morning, I collected Darius and marched into the hotel lobby to convert more money—and to humiliate Darius, the author of the multiply-by-pi monetary conversion concept. He walked into my trap.

"Look at that, Dad. The sign says the conversion rate is 3.1416. Ya just multiply by pi."

"Well, let's just see." I confidently placed a one-hundred-guilder note on the counter. The clerk gave me 314 kroner, then apologized. "We don't have a .16 coin. But have you seen the five kroner coin? It's got a hole in it."

"See, Dad, I told you so! Ha! Ha! It's easy to read these conversion tables. Why can't you…"

"Darius! Aren't you hungry?"

"Well, yeah, I guess I am."

"Then go eat breakfast with your mother."

It turned out that the night clerk had mistaken my guilders for marks. Denmark wasn't going to be the bargain I'd anticipated.

Nazy's friend, Dikte, and her husband, Flemming, arrived shortly after breakfast. For this trip, we'd have competent local aid in seeing the sights. We drove toward the famous little mermaid.

Before we began sightseeing, I called a quick family huddle. "Remember, guys, don't waste your allowance. Just because we're in a foreign country doesn't mean we have to squander money. These coins are valuable even though they have holes. Don't just throw them away."

There was silence as the children considered my eloquent soliloquy. Darius broke the quiet. "Hey, Dad. Could I have a kroner to toss in that fountain?"

Nazy's friends recommended a boat trip on the canals. It was fun listening to their Danish—the spoken version of the language is devoid of consonants. Nazy wanted to confirm her understanding and asked Dikte what *udsalg* meant."

"*Udsalg?*" replied Dikte. "That doesn't mean anything."

"*Udsalg*, U-D-S-A-L-G, *udsalg*. I think it means 'sale.'"

"Ah, '*usåø*,' that means 'sale.'" (It's not easy to phoenetically write what she said. It appeared that only vowels are pronounced in colloquial Danish.)

Our ineptitude with the language really didn't matter; everyone spoke English. You do have to be a bit careful that you don't get seasick listening to the Danes do English. They've got a little bit of lilt.

We hopped on the boat. The English translation at the departure point grabbed my fancy:

> The boat departs at ten-thirty. Boats depart every half hour thereafter until the last boat leaves at four forty-five p.m.

See if you can figure out what that means.

Fleming was able to provide a commentary that nearly overwhelmed us. He knew about the founding of the København stock market; the history of King Christian IV, Denmark during World War II, and Denmark and the Vikings; and the construction dates (and reasons for building) each monument in the city. There we were, rocking to and fro, on a small boat on the canal, and there was Fleming, a history teacher, explaining in Danish-accented English:

> The stock exchange was built in 1742 during the Golden Era to handle shipments that arrived in the harbour.

I was getting seasick.

We could see colorful houses from the boat: Red, green, blue, and purple homes stood right next to each other. The shops were more traditional, but each one sported a giant yellow *udsalg* sign. Scanning the situation with the calm confidence of a professional, Nazy pulled down her goggles, checked her Eurocheque stash, and rocketed toward the porcelain district.

Bewildered, I knew I was reduced to damage control. How much distraction would be permissible? Looking at the cloud of dust in Nazy's wake, I struggled to catch up.

"Hey, Dikte," I shouted, "Nazy has always had trouble figuring out how to spell her name with the English alphabet. Do you think some of the Danish vowels might help?" ("After all," I thought, "Danes are certainly experts on vowel usage.")

"Could we write 'Nåzy' with the funny little circle?"

"Nope."

"How about 'Nøzÿ'?"

"That doesn't sound good, either."

"What about 'Næzzij'?"

Unamused, Nazy interrupted my questions. "Look, Dan, Royal København. We *need* Royal København."

"Royal Copenhagen sounds a bit excessive. Can't we look for 'common Copenhagen'? And how did you learn to use Danish letters like 'ø'?"

"Common Copenhagen? Why don't you go buy some postcards with Darius?"

"How 'bout this, Nâzy? Let's go totally European and use all the funny letters to spell your name. How would you pronounce something like 'Ñãîëÿ'?"

"Postcards, Dan. I think we need postcards."

The day continued in the shopping district. Nazÿ and the girls kept being directed to the next, better, more complete shop. Finally, following my advice, they had surveyed everything and had decided what they wanted and where they would purchase it. Unfortunately, they were in Denmark, where the stores close at five p.m.—exactly. Luckily, the selected store would be open the following day.

It was a disgruntled and tired family that returned to the boat pickup point. My feet hurt. Mitra, Melika, and Nazy hadn't bought anything, and Darius's search for a Danish Monopoly game had been unsuccessful. We decided to ride the boat back to the cathedral and, more importantly, the cars.

Unfortunately, no one was paying attention when the boat stopped at the cathedral the first time. The second time we were paying attention, but the boat didn't stop. We were on the day's last boat, and it returned—eventually —to the centrum, where we had boarded. We had a long walk ahead of us.

The amusement park Tivoli (the Danes pronounce it "Tioee." We pronounced all the letters.) was a wonderful experience. And, according to our hosts, we had a rare visit—it didn't rain. The children enjoyed the lights, the rides, and the pantomime, and the adults enjoyed the ballet, the acrobats, the fountains, and the flowers.

The visit continued in this vein. We saw the Viking Ship museum and a reenactment of a Viking raid. We had a gracious, delicious dinner with Dikte's family. We saw crown jewels, palaces, and red-garbed guards.

Finally, however, we had to return to Holland. Our car was on the large ferry. Darius pulled me aside.

"Dad, there are lots of different ferry boats. We may be on the wrong one. Just think, we could be going to Sweden. That'd be great material for one of your stories. And Sweden—another stamp in the world-traveling passport of Darius D. Martin."

"Well, if this ferry is going to Sweden, I want *you* to remember that *Mom* drove the car onto the boat."

> *I've commented on Danish pronunciation. In fact, there is European-wide challenge with Scandinavian words. The Norwegian word for "autumn" is "høst." Imagine the confusion in France, where trailing consonants (the "st") are not pronounced and the leading "h" is not pronounced. The only thing left is the vowel, but it is crossed out.*

As The Martin Family continued to see Europe, my job had me branching out. My coworker, Henk Reimers, and I embarked on a series of meetings in the EA (Far East) Region. In the beginning there were more questions than answers, so we had lots of time to consult local experts. I also visited Korea, Singapore, Manila, Japan, Australia, Malaysia, and Nigeria. Although KLM Airlines treated me like royalty (I was a Royal Wing Flyer), the frequent flyer accumulation process was somewhat slow. According to my calculations, I only needed two more round trips (business class) to Mars before I'd qualify for a weekend (Saturday night stay required) trip to Brussels.

Everyone told us we had to see Italy, Spain, and Greece. We'd done Italy and Spain (and Belgium, France, Luxembourg, Germany, Portugal, Denmark, and Great Britain). Melika wanted beaches. Darius wanted Russia (and Latvia, Estonia, Lithuania, Ukraine, Finland, Belarus, Turkmenistan, Turkey, Hungary, and Bulgaria). Melika wanted beaches, Nazy wanted "culture," and Mitra wanted to decide about colleges. Greece was an educational experience that had cultured beaches close to Turkey. There was the small matter of potential Greco-Turk hostilities as a result of an ongoing war over Cyprus, but we didn't worry about that. We didn't worry about anything because…

IT'S GREEK TO ME

We should have been more prepared because the omens weren't at all positive. When we consulted the Oracle at Delphi, we were told that if we went to Greece, "a great tradition would continue"—we didn't know this repetition of our normal holiday capers. Eric, the owner of Limetree & Hamilton, told us it was extremely cold when he went to Greece. Since Nazy is Eric's largest customer, and single-handedly provides 20 percent of his annual revenue, we thought he was a reliable source. (On the other hand, Nazy's absence for two weeks from his store would adversely affect his cash flow, so he did have reason to stretch the truth.)

Unfortunately, others reinforced his dire warnings. Brian Levin, a friend from Shell, said he would never return to Greece. On his trip, no flight left within twelve hours of the scheduled departure and his return to Amsterdam was delayed for thirty-six hours by striking Olympic Air pilots. (He only got out when passengers attacked the crew lounge and physically dragged the pilot to the airplane.) Cormac joined the group recommending caution by noting that the only place hotter than Athens in July was "*possibly* ground zero for a moderate to large thermonuclear explosion."

We were undaunted, unworried, and unprepared. Our introduction to Greece was via Olympic Airlines. We were greeted by the Schiphol airport departure monitors:

KL312 Madrid On Time	KL491 Lisboa On Time	KL412 Brussels On Time
KL415 London On Time	DL038 Atlanta On Time	BA812 London On Time
SQ084 Singapore On Time	BD092 Aberdeen On Time	CX007 Hong Kong On Time
LH405 Berlin On Time	TG123 Bangkok On Time	AC345 Montreal On Time
OL806 Athens SEE AGENT	AF222 Paris On Time	AI767 Nice On Time
HX444 Hamburg On Time	NL412 Utrecht On Time	SA003 Oslo On Time
SA808 Capetown On Time	KL205 Milan On Time	KL441 Rome On Time
UK989 Inverness On Time	KL404 Moscow On Time	KL202 Munich On Time
AE339 Dublin On Time	KL200 Cairo On Time	KL876 New York On Time
KL998 Manila On Time	KL996 Bombay On Time	KL994 Dacca On Time

Normally, I would have been upset. This time, however, I was philosophic. In spite of all the portents of doom, things were actually going rather well. For the first time in my married life, all members of the family had been in bed before two a.m. on the eve of a major trip. This was the first vacation we had ever embarked upon with more than three hours of sleep. Even Nazy's stories about friends who had suffered a two-day departure delay didn't bother me. We were going to have a good time. And at least Schiphol was air-conditioned.

Actually, our departure was delayed less than three hours. The sun hadn't even set on Athens before we arrived and picked up our rental car. Or, more specifically, we acquired a four-wheeled device that was presented to us as a "car." The good news? It got good mileage (so does a lawn mower). The bad news? The "car" wasn't designed for full-sized human beings. Worse, even Melika was too big to fit comfortably in the backseat. Getting The Martin Family and our luggage into the vehicle seemed about as likely as getting a quick decision from Shell. Luckily, the rental company supplied a shrink-wrapping device and a hydraulic press to assist in the entry process. We had seven days of "exciting exploration by auto" in our future. Mitra had been clever enough to bring audio cassettes appropriate to the trip, such as the soundtrack of the musical *Grease*.

Exploring ancient sites on the Peloponnesian Peninsula was the long-term objective. The more intermediate-term problem was finding our hotel in Athens. We quickly discovered that the Greeks have a different alphabet. How would you pronounce a street named "Μαιν Στρεετ"? (All the letters had points on them.) I wasn't worried, though; *Nazy* was navigating and when we got lost, I could blame her.

We made it to the hotel with only minor problems. Everyone (except possibly Melika) was looking forward to seeing the ancient ruins of the Acropolis. No one (except Melika) realized we would have to walk to the top of the Acropolis on a hot, hazy, muggy, dusty, polluted day. No one (Melika excepted) knew that the famous Sunday flea market would feature a collection of street urchins selling rusted torque wrenches. Fortunately, *Melika* had remembered to get the address of the local McDonald's. Unfortunately, I had forgotten to bring the Athens map with me on the Acropolis excursion.

The crowded bustle of a ruined capital city gave way the next morning as we embarked on our tour of ancient Greece. In our attempt to depart the central part of Athens, we made several scientific observations. For example, a nanosecond can be accurately defined as the maximum amount of time that exists between a traffic light turning green and the trailing motorist blowing his horn. (I did tell a passing taxi driver that in the United States, a surgical procedure to detach human limbs from automotive horns had been perfected.)

En route to Corinth, we also noticed that most buildings were under construction. It is important to understand the Greek concept of "under construction." It doesn't mean the building is vacant, and it *certainly* doesn't mean that construction work is actually taking place (we never saw *any* actual work). "Under construction" simply means that several girders are exposed, so that the upper floor is only a skeleton. Most importantly, it means the owner gets to pay a lower property tax. The upshot? *Everything* is "under construction" and nothing is actually finished.

This is not new to Greece. The temple of the Olympian Zeus, for example, was begun in 526 BC and completed in 125 AD. The Corinth Canal was begun in 423 BC and completed in 1893 AD. I'm actually convinced that the proud ruins of ancient Greece are misrepresented. For example, the guidebooks would have you believe that the Parthenon's roof was lost through centuries of war. The truth is rather more mundane: The Parthenon has actually been "under construction" since Pericles offered the architect a tax break in the fifth century BC. It really never (ever) had a roof.

But enough of philosophy. The cultural part of our trip was an adventure. Every day we were faced with the challenge of cramming all family members into the "car." It is clear that no one had made offerings to the Greek god of road construction (Asphaltus). The sand dunes in Scheveningen look more like a road than the National Highway on the Peloponnesian Peninsula (and there isn't a two-thousand-foot drop-off from the peak of the dunes). As if that wasn't enough, we were forced to share the "road" with native drivers who insisted on taking their half from my side. The problem was compounded because no one ever used brakes. (Once I was wedged into the driver's seat, it was too crowded for me to lift my foot off the accelerator and place it on the brake pedal.) My most frequent comment was, "Look at that jackass." In fact, the first time I saw a donkey walking up the road, I said, "Look at that jackass!" and the whole family thought I was commenting on another local driver.

We did see the sights, including ruins from the golden age of Agamemnom, the Crusades, the Most Serene Republic of Venice, and the Byzantine Empire; and (in the form of "roads") from twentieth-century Greece. Interestingly, no matter how old it was, it all looked equally ruined. (There was one notable exception. Olympia looked more than normally ruined. In fact, the grounds of ancient Olympia looked like a textbook example of glacially deposited debris.)

The cultural week ended with a return to Athens, where we bravely boarded an Olympic Airlines flight to the Isle of Rhodes for sun and fun on the beaches. We certainly got sun. The day we elected to visit the nearby island of Symi, it was forty-four degrees Celsius in the shade (that's roughly one hundred and eleven degrees Fahrenheit). It was so hot that when we ordered boiled fish, they were simply dipped in the Aegean Sea, which was already bubbling. The hotel air-conditioning system generated lots of noise but relatively little cool air. Luckily, every day wasn't as warm and there was usually a breeze off the sea. (I think that the hotel even refrigerated the swimming pool.)

Nazy and Mitra revel in shopping excursions. Melika noted that there were only four kinds of stores on the whole island: T-shirt stores, jewelry shops, newspaper stands, and leather shops. Shopping excursions became prolonged because Nazy is unable to pass any jewelry shop without walking in. The problem was compounded because Greek shopkeepers had been on training courses run by Singaporean experts. They grabbed us and dragged us into their shops and asked where we were from, touting family specials. They had "anything you want."

A sample exchange:

Shopkeeper: "We have everything. What do you want?"

Dan: "A taxi!"

Nazy was not only willing to listen, she was also willing to talk. The result was usually a good deal.

We had less than the usual problems with currency conversion. You simply drop two zeros and get guilders. (I'm not sure this is exactly correct, because then if you divide by two, you should get U.S. dollars. For a reason I don't quite understand, the process only *almost* works.)

While we were waiting in line at McDonald's, a couple of young fellows showed Darius a one-thousand drachma Greek banknote and asked how much it was worth. Darius immediately leaped into conversation.

"It's easy. Just move the decimal point two places to the left and divide by two to get U.S. dollars."

"Listen, kid," the guy responded, "we're American soldiers. Just tell us how much it's worth. Don't confuse us with a complicated formula."

All in all, the vacation was quite enjoyable. We saw the sights and we returned home tanned (but not burned) and rejuvenated. To my mind, however, the infrastructure in Greece was much closer to that of Malaysia than to Western Europe.

Back at the office, I was instructed to convert from a Mac computer to an IBM PC. As part of the change, I replaced the Macintosh operating system with Microsoft Windows. At the time, moving from Mac to Windows was like replacing an automatic washing machine with a river and a rock. On the other hand, Apple was in a tailspin; the board had just fired Steve Jobs.

> *Things were desperate at work—a new computer, missing consensus, and entrenched traditionalists threatened the project. We were into our fourth year in Europe and the lavender of Provence was calling The Martin Family.*

IT'S SO MUCH NICER IN NICE

Vacation! In France! One of Nazy's countless friends agreed to rent us a house for the last week of June. The home was in "the south of France," a phrase that has always caused confusion for me. Why is it called "the south of France"? It's possible to vacation in southern New England or south Florida. You can even go to the South Island of New Zealand. But you never go to south France or southern France—they call it "the south of France." This phrase makes no sense whatsoever. Algeria, Nigeria, Zambia, South Africa, and Antarctica are all south of France and we're surely not on holiday in any of those locations. In order to keep things clear, it is absolutely essential to include the definitive article (the) in your phraseology. Thus, south of France and "the south of France" are two completely different things, both of which are a bit long-winded for normal communication.

It turns out that "long-winded" is par for the course with the French language. When we were in Canada, where all products are legally required to have both French and English instructions, I noticed that the French versions took, on average, 38.73 percent more space. For example, in English you might say something like, "Where is the soap?" If you literally translate the same sentence into French, you get something like, "Where does the soap find itself?"

"Where does the soap find itself?!" More importantly, why does the soap care about finding itself? I have friends who are still trying to find themselves. They've disgorged a lot of money in the guise of "professional fees" trying to find themselves. I find it hard to believe that soap has similar problems. On the other hand, it is possible to imagine a conversation between a bar of soap and an analyst.

"Nobody cares for me, I am simply used to clean up the dirt of others."

"People's dirt?"

"Of course, people's dirt. I'm inherently clean. And once I'm used, I'm flung into a moldy, scum-filled corner...."

This isn't the only example of long-winded French. In English you might say that Nice is fifty-five miles away. In French you'd say that Nice finds itself four-twenty and ten kilometers distant. There are even examples of English expressions for which there is no possible translation. "On time" is an English phrase with no French equivalent.

The family was excited by the opportunity of a trip in the summer of 1993. Because Europe is small, we decided to drive to Provence. Melika, who agreed to join the family only after verifying that the house came with a swimming pool, was, as usual, the first to complete packing. (Also, as usual, she was the only family member who didn't forget something.)

For Mitra, the annual family vacation did not generate all-encompassing excitement because she was still mourning the passing of high school. Friends were departing and the seemingly endless series of parties were winding down. We weren't sure how to react to Mitra's situation.

In preparation for the vacation, Mitra joined her friends Rodney and Tom on a "busking" outing at Scheveningen beach. "Busking" is an English (British) word that means playing a musical instrument in a public place in the hope of obtaining donations. Rodney had his saxophone and Tom had the trombone. Mitra's job was to offer encouragement.

They played for a long time but were not able to sufficiently distract the beachgoers. Then Mitra observed a tourist shyly checking out the group. The young lady, clearly an American, was obviously enjoying the music. After a massive crescendo, the tourist finally made her move. She strode straight for the trombone case and then, at the last minute, and just as Rodney and Tom began to salivate in anticipation of actually receiving compensation, she verged toward Mitra.

"Where did you get those sandals?" she asked. "I've been admiring them for several minutes now."

At this point, Darius walked up and, with his ready grasp of human nature, determined that help was needed. Although he could have been most helpful by vocally shaming people into paying, he took a more direct approach and dropped a ten-pence coin into the trombone case. The ten pence, of course, can only be spent in the UK.

I wasn't very helpful in the pre-vacation preparations because I was trying to recover from my trip to Asia. In the middle of all of this, I received a formal thank you from the EEMA (European Electronic Mail Association) for agreeing to speak at the opening plenary session of their upcoming conference in Montreux, Switzerland. When I had agreed to speak, I wasn't sure I'd have a job the next year. I had been planning to use the conference as a way of meeting people and generating name recognition. Now I had a job, but I was also stuck. My talk was scheduled to occur exactly in the middle of our family vacation in southern France. I didn't have the option of skipping the conference. I also didn't have the option of skipping the vacation. I took the next best option: asking the family to join me in Montreux.

The attitudes were predictable. Darius was delighted by the opportunity to see another city. Mitra wondered if she could skip the trip to Switzerland (she wanted to stay in Nice with one of her friends). Nazy wanted to see the splendid shops of Geneva (which was near Montreaux) and Melika would be willing to come—provided that the hotel had a pool.

The family meetings finally ended and we readied ourselves for an early (Saturday) morning departure. (Mitra prepared by spending Friday afternoon, evening, and early Saturday morning with her friends.) As Melika carried her luggage to the car, she sagely predicted a delayed departure. Darius gathered his travel essentials—327 Airline flight schedules and his Nintendo. (Melika remembered the spare batteries.) Although an empty 747 would not have sufficient space for Mitra's essential items, Nazy was able to stuff, jam, wedge, squeeze, and cram a wardrobe adequate for a six-week trek from the Arctic Circle to the Tropic of Capricorn into a space only marginally larger than the Taurus.

This packing adventure took us through the late hours of Friday night and into the early hours of Saturday morning. Accordingly, when the alarm clock shattered our brief somnolent respite, I reacted by shattering it. (It wasn't intentional. I simply hurled it to the floor while attempting to drive the "alarm off" button into China.) The death cry of the clock was insufficiently loud to awake Nazy. Naturally, we did not get out of the house early.

"I told you so," Melika triumphantly announced when I dragged myself toward the shower. "I knew we'd be late."

"How long have you been awake?" (I was groggy, but not completely out of commission.)

"I've been up a few hours. I'm knocking Darius off the top ten high scorers for Pipe Dream." (Pipe Dream is a computer game.)

"Why didn't you wake us up?"

"If I'd done that, Mom would have been grumpy the whole way. It's a long drive—you wouldn't want that, would you?"

"It is a long drive, Melika, but I would have preferred to get up on time. I'm told it will take ten hours to get there."

"Ten hours? I bet it takes longer. Are you sure they have a pool?"

"She said ten hours. Ten hours it will be. We can drive very fast on the French highways and Europe is very small. They do have a pool."

"It will take much longer than ten hours, Dad. Do you want to bet?"

"We rented the house from Mom's friend, Melanie, and she said ten hours. Ten hours. Ten hours!"

Ten hours later we were at Dijon—somewhere in the middle of France. We hadn't been dawdling. Our average speed was one hundred and thirty-four kph (that's about eighty mph). I don't think we could have possibly gone any faster. (Melanie must teleport into Provence.)

Several hours later, we arrived at the correct motorway exit. Fourteen and a half hours on the road had gotten us within a few kilometers of the vacation house. We only had to traverse the unmarked, narrow, unlit, winding, dangerous countryside roads of the Côte d'Azur to get to the house.

"Thank God we're on vacation," I said as we meandered about in the dark. "At least we won't have to get up early tomorrow morning."

"Hey, Dad," Melika said. "Can we go swimming when we get to the house?"

"Swimming? Are you crazy? It's two in morning."

"That's not my fault. I told you it would take longer than ten hours."

The vacation was busy and enjoyable. We saw wine country, we saw lavender we went to Monaco, and we visited Nazy's relatives in Nice. We sniffed perfume and admired butterflies. And, in the middle of it all, we went to Switzerland.

It would have been smarter if I had just flown to Switzerland from Nice, but the family claimed they wanted to see Geneva and Montreux. The whole journey could have been easier if I hadn't gotten on the A57 instead of the A8. And I would have been more popular if I'd recognized my mistake before we got to Toulouse. (In my defense, I didn't realize there were *two* motorways. I knew we weren't going in the direction of Cannes, so I took the other choice[11]. The family was not impressed.)

---

11 *It was like you were driving to Boston. You were in New York and saw a sign that said "Washington". Aware that that was wrong, you chose "other" – which turned out to be Cleveland... and you didn't discover the problem until you hit the Ohio border.*

My talk at the conference went well. We had a bit of time to see Geneva—in the rain. Lake Geneva was really pretty; mountains climb directly from the shore. And in Geneva there is a huge fountain near the lake that shoots water about 150 feet into the air. Because the wind had picked up and water from the fountain was landing on office buildings' roofs several blocks from the lakefront, the fountain was turned off just after we arrived—just before we could take a photograph.

Darius was not happy that this vacation would not result in any new countries. Accordingly, he was determined to collect at least one passport stamp. He thought Switzerland would be the best choice. It and Monaco were the only non-European Union countries on our itinerary.

Border guards stopped us, but they weren't the passport-stamping patrol, they were selling *tax* stamps that permitted you to use the Swiss freeways. It wasn't really a sale; it was more like extortion. If you didn't have a Swiss number plate, you had to buy the stamp. While I was paying, Darius walked back to the customs shed. He was unsuccessful. The guards told him they could only stamp passports from countries that weren't in the United Nations.

The diversion to Switzerland took a couple of days in the middle of our trip, and we got to see the French and Swiss Alps on our drive. Geneva was extremely expensive. (Even Nazy was astonished at the prices.)

We were about to leave when Nazy decided she wanted to look at cuckoo clocks. Since we didn't know where such things might be found, she volunteered to ask for directions at a nearby store. The rest of us, thankful she was getting the directions, relaxed in a nearby park. Time passed and a sinking feeling came over the group.

Darius broke the silence. "What kind of a store did Mom go into, Dad?"

"I was just thinking about that. It's that store with the blue door. Can you check it out for me?"

A short time later, Darius (but not Nazy) was back. "Bad luck, Dad. It's a jewelry store."

"A jewelry store?"

"That's right. She's looking at jewelry. *Big* jewels, *heavy* gold. I think we should get her out of there."

Get Nazy out of a jewelry store? Why not try to repeal the law of gravity?

Girding for action, the family marched across the street and went (boldly) into the claws of death. Nazy was deep in conversation with the owner.

"That green necklace looks very nice," she said. "Is it Venetian crystal?"

"Actually, those are emeralds."

"Emeralds? I thought emeralds were a deeper green."

"Usually they are, but these are special Burmese emeralds that have a touch of blue," the shop owner explained. "Notice how each stone is perfectly matched with all the others. This piece is a steal at eighty thousand francs."

"It's a steal, all right," I thought. "The only way we'll ever get that necklace is if we steal it."

I steered Nazy toward the cuckoo clock store.

"We're in Switzerland, dear," I said. "We should get a cuckoo clock."

"Yeah, Dad," Darius interrupted. "They make 'em here. It's sure to be a bargain in Geneva."

I was excited to be (Burmese) emeraldless, but Darius' statement was too absurd to stand unanswered.

"*Nothing* is a bargain in Switzerland, Darius. It is *never* cheaper in Switzerland. This is a fundamental truth that you can take with you to your grave. It is not cheaper in Switzerland!"

"Maybe not, but they do have a good selection," Nazy replied. "And remember, we got stuff from all of our vacation stops. We bought Portuguese tiles. We got olive oil in Greece. We…"

"Yeah, and we bought a Gucci purse in Florence. Nevertheless, I think the family can survive without a cuckoo clock."

"Let's just look. What harm can it do to look?"

So…we looked. At first glance there was a magnificent selection. Singing cuckoo clocks of every description were mounted on the wall. It was a sight to behold. There were clocks of every size and shape.

After some (extended) discussion, Nazy and I decided upon a ceiling price, then eliminated all the clocks that exceeded our budget. There were two left.

The one we could see without a magnifying glass was plastic. It had a quartz movement and was assembled by fake clock experts in Singapore. The other one was *small*. Nazy and I discussed the situation.

"You're right, it is unique. I've never seen a cuckoo clock with an optional wrist strap. On the other hand, if that thing is defined as a cuckoo clock, then my straight razor is a Swiss Army knife."

In the end we decided not to buy a clock in Switzerland. Although she'd agreed with the decision, Nazy wasn't entirely happy.

A few weeks later at my office in The Hague, the backlog was enormous. Electronic files were overflowing, electronic mail was poking out under shuttered Windows, and action points were multiplying at a troubling rate. I had forwarded my telephone and had retreated behind the mounds of paper mail. Then my associate, Patricia, called with news of an urgent delivery. My speech at the conference had been voted best and I had been awarded a cuckoo clock. I brushed the mess off my desk and called Nazy.

Recognition dawned when the clock arrived. It was exactly the clock we had liked—the one that was not within the budget. Happiness was now reigning at Martin Manor.

You may notice that Melika likes swimming pools and beaches. Sometime after this holiday, she was invited to a vacation with a friend. She said that they spent all their time by the pool and…

"After about three days, Dad, I asked if there were any nearby ruins."

Following this vacation, Mitra and Nazy began to prepare for their trip to America. Mitra was deluged with mailings from Princeton. She had letters from her resident adviser, samples from the daily and weekly newspapers, information about computers, an announcement about her roommate, background about the health service, and forms, forms, forms to complete and return by mail. Together, Mitra and the CFU (core family unit) were excited and wary.

After she left, we had time for another holiday.

Showing clear corporate ineptitude, I suddenly realized in early 1994 that my project at Shell was gathering momentum and would actually end soon. Shocked by the unusual event, Shell didn't know what to do. (In fact, it was more than unusual. Not only was the project ending, it was ending early and under budget. It was unprecedented.)

I was feeling good about the project. My friend, Mike, was visiting the Badhuis from London.

"We finished on-time and within budget!" I explained proudly.

"Well, that was pretty stupid, wasn't it? Now your contract is up and you have to go home."

In short, our stay in the Netherlands was coming to an end. But there was so much more to see. The family—sans Mitra, who was attending Princeton—kept reminding me of all the places we hadn't seen. Pressure was building. And then...a school vacation. There was no choice. We had to go somewhere.

WALTZ TIME

It was an ominous week. Darius and Melika were lucky enough to be on holiday in the midst of the winter break. Naturally, this meant they would be bored before the first weekend expired. As expected, Nazy wanted to do something *exciting*, so we planned...uh... decided[12] to drive to Vienna.

Vienna is the capital of Austria, as Darius was quick to inform us. It lies about one thousand and sixty-nine kilometers (over seven hundred miles) from The Hague. Vienna had always been high on Nazy's list of places that *must* be seen. I have to admit that considering the long drive

---

12 . *Unlike the Dutch, we're better at "deciding" than "planning."*

ahead, I was less enthusiastic. Aware of Nazy's deep desire for the trip, I began the pre-departure negotiations cautiously.

"Vienna? Are you crazy? Austria isn't even a real country—they speak German and act Swiss. There's no reason to go."

Shaken by the clear logic of my statement, Nazy began sputtering. I thought I had scored, but in a major miscue, I had not noticed that Darius was in the room. He took up the gauntlet.

"It is so a *country*, Dad. The Austrian-Hungarian Empire was huge. The Hapsburgs ruled most of Europe for centuries. Vienna is a world-class city, and the capital of European culture."

"But Darius, I thought it was the capital of Austria," I replied sarcastically.

"He's right," Nazy said. "Vienna is home of the waltz. The Danube flows through it. Mozart lived there. It has beautiful palaces and is famous for crystal. We can't leave Europe without seeing Vienna. *It's not possible.*"

At this point, Melika, who had slipped into the room, deposited the coup de grâce. "I'm bored, Daddy."

We left for Vienna on Wednesday morning.[13]

A glance at a map of Europe made the trip look quite straightforward. The one thousand and sixty-nine kilometers to Vienna followed a straight-line (diagonal) path southeast. Admittedly, things became a bit more complex when we consulted a map that included the German autobahn system. Our planned path was not as direct as we'd hoped.

---

13 . Since we're also better at "deciding" than "departing," we left in the afternoon.

Planned Route

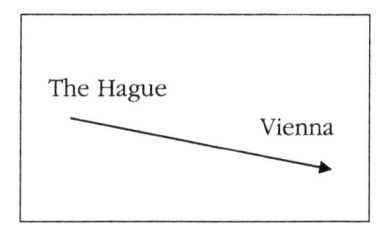

The Hague → Vienna

Actual Route

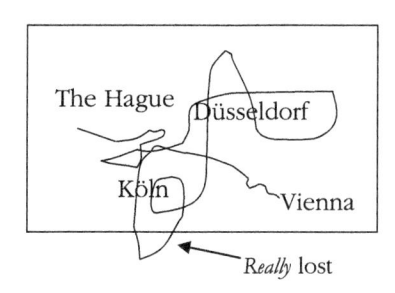

The Hague, Düsseldorf, Köln, Vienna ← *Really* lost

    The German autobahn features unlimited speeds and confusing signs. (They insist on utilizing German for all information indications.) There are at least fifty-seven different autobahns (expressways) between Köln and Düsseldorf, and we spent time on all of them. (We always get lost in that area and now avoid any city that contains an umlaut in the German spelling.) Accordingly, München and Nüremberg have been eliminated from Martin Family consideration.

    As you can imagine, the trip was quite long and very tiring. Alone among the participants, Melika was prepared. She'd packed three books, a deck of cards, a few car games, apples, cheese cubes, audio cassettes, crackers, cookies, and her customary little round ball.

    Even I have to admit that Vienna was nice. We went to see the Schoonsbrunn Palace, which had far more rooms (four thousand!) than our hotel. Nazy was thrilled by the elegance of the edifice and took great joy in reading about the history of the building. I tried to educate Darius and Melika. Surprisingly, Melika was quite willing to share her expertise in the field of architecture.

    "See those columns, Daddy?" she said. "Those are Doric columns."

    "I know. They were invented by a couple of dorks in the small English village of Dorking during the mid-twelfth century. The other columns—the ones with the little curly tops—are called ironic columns. That particular architecture helped shape western literature. Shakespeare wrote most of his plays in ironic pentameter, you'll recall."

STUMBLING THROUGH THE TULIPS

"Dad! That's absurd." Darius was exasperated. "Shakespeare wrote in *iambic pentameter*."

"Don't be a show-off, Darius. Just stand there. I will find a pentameter because I need to measure my feelings toward you."

"Why do you need a pentameter to measure your feelings toward me?"

"If you disagree with me again, I'm afraid my pent-up emotions will overflow. That's why I need a pent-ameter! Now, just listen as I continue to enlighten you on the culture of Vienna. This palace was the home of Mother Teresa."

Nazy interrupted, "That's Marie Theresa."

"Correct! She won a Nobel Prize by treating poor people in India. Her son, Prince Leopold, became emperor after she died. If you read the brochure, you'll see that this palace has a zoo on the grounds, which was established by Prince *Leo*pold to house the *leo*pards that he imported from *Leo*theso in Africa."

We didn't spend the whole trip seeing the cultural attractions of Vienna. We had a little time left over for shopping. Nazy stopped in an exclusive gem store in the heart of the city that featured museum-quality pieces handmade in Russia. They were beautiful—even I could see that. She asked lots of questions and got a personal explanation from the shopkeeper. She was particularly excited about a piece that cost two hundred and forty thousand Austrian shillings.[14]

In the meantime, Darius, Melika, and I played with the round bouncy ball outside the shop, which was on the fourth floor of a multi-story shopping mall that featured a delightful Viennese coffeehouse at the basement level. Unfortunately, the atrium in the center of the mall was open from the fourth floor all the way to the basement. Although I was the one who threw the ball, which took ever so long to descend from the fourth floor to the basement, it was *Melika* who failed to catch it.

---

14 . *Seems like a lot of zeros to me.*

After we were evacuated from the mall, we went to the flea market. No one was very excited—the market consisted primarily of food stalls. (We'd seen food in The Hague.) Nazy found a small shop (actually a table) that sold hand-painted Easter eggs from the Czech Republic. They weren't very expensive and she wanted all the facts.

"Are these eggs real?" she asked. "Is the paint waterproof? Can you tell me what kind of bird laid the eggs? Are they normal size for that species of fowl? How did they clean out the yolk and white? Are you sure they won't rot? How do you get these eggs across the border? I thought these thing were made in Russia—are these Czech eggs simply copies?"

The salesman must have been good because we bought a few special eggs. Cradling our purchase, we made our way to the U-bahn (subway). As we departed from our hotel, someone waved at Nazy and wished her a good day. It was the jewelry shop owner.

Because the drive home was so lengthy, we decided to stop in Nüremberg. (I'm aware that this broke our umlaut rule.) True to form, we had no planned hotel, so we simply cruised through the city. We discarded the first hotel we saw—the Schmuckhaus—for obvious reasons. Instead we selected the Hotel Martinim (for an equally obvious reason). The next morning we walked through the old town and took a tour of the citadel in the center of the city. With her mastery of German that was unsurpassed by the family, Nazy acquired the tickets for the only available tour—a German-language extravaganza.

"Is this an English tour?" she asked.

"Deutsche."

"No English?"

"Nein. Deutsche, Osterreich, Schweiz, and Prussian."

"Ik wil twee kindergarten en een Volkswagen, als u blief."[15]

---

15. *She meant to say, "Twee kinderkarten en twee vollwassen." (Of course that was Dutch rather than Deutsch.)*

Following the tour, we shunned the local McDonald's (it was abundantly clear that Nazy would not approve) and instead we went to a local eatery in the city square. Our culinary selection featured bratwurst—and only bratwurst. We all ordered a plate of *brockwörst*.[16] Nazy also ordered a German lager that was served in a stein capable of holding Lake Superior. Everything was tasty and enjoyable.

When it came time to pay, the waitress casually lifted the linen napkin off the breadbasket to count the number of dinner rolls we had eaten. Unfortunately, Melika had ripped the middle from each of the globular breadlets. The waitress returned with a calculator.

The drive home was uneventful. (We got totally lost somewhere in the Köln/Düsseldorf area.) The weather was absolutely perfect until we hit the Dutch border, where it began to rain. Amazingly, the thick fog, which also materialized at the border, lifted before the city limits of The Hague.

Nazy and I returned, by ourselves, to Vienna twenty years later. Nazy immediately found the 'delightful Viennese coffeeshop and the jewelry store. (The owner remembered her.) I had a similar experience. In my new job, I was responsible for all of the products my company sold to Deutsche Bank anywhere in the world. There was a small problem in Australia.

"We can't buy the product in Sydney," the customer claimed.

"Why not?"

"The pricing is not available in Australian dollars."

"They should be available in the local currency. How do we quote?"

"Austrian Shillings."

"The Austrian Shilling was replaced by the Euro five years ago."

---

16 . *As you can see, we don't even know how to spell it.*

"You see my problem."

Mitra didn't accompany us on this trip. Having graduated from the American School in The Hague, she was in the United States attending Princeton University. Accepted almost everywhere, Mitra had to make a choice. Decisions were not her forte. She dithered, delayed, fretted, and thought. We planned to visit the States to see the schools, but we couldn't schedule a trip. The only available week conflicted with the senior class trip to Crete. In the end, Mitra faxed her acceptance to Princeton at the last possible minute. Shell graciously allowed a parental escort for the first year of school. Nazy and Mitra flew home, visiting relatives and friends along the way. Princeton had arranged a special week of acclimation for international students. They introduced Mitra to shopping malls and fast-food restaurants, and reminded her that the money was all the same size and color.

Back at Princeton, it quickly became clear that we should have spent a bit more time explaining money to Mitra:

"How's your money situation, Mitra?" I asked.

"It's okay, Dad. But did you know that when you use the ATM card they take the money out of your checking account?"

"Of course."

"But it's not a check."

"Mitra! Where did you think that money was coming from?"

"I don't know, but it's not a check. Why should they take it from my checking account?"

In time, the academic year ended and Mitra returned for her last summer in The Hague. She was somewhat annoyed that she had missed Vienna. It "wasn't fair" for us to leave Europe without one final sling. The Iron Curtain had been dismantled (obviously associated with our arrival in Europe). There were new vistas and we had to go!

FLYING BUTTOCKS

School was over, Mitra was home from Princeton, Nazy was crystal-less, and Shell was confused. It was time for a holiday. Eastern Europe, able to survive fifty years of communist and fascist rule, was deemed resilient enough to host a Martin Family weekend. After careful consideration, we choose Prague, the capital of the Czech Republic. With the help of Holland International travel agency, Nazy arranged a suitable itinerary.

The travel agent told us we should be at the airport one hour before flight time. Scorning authority, we arrived twenty minutes before departure. KLM airport doesn't support preselected seating for passengers traveling peon class and living in Holland, but Nazy, desiring the nosmoking section, negotiated row twenty-one—only two rows into the smoking area. We were chagrined to discover that our F100 had exactly twenty-one rows of seats. Our row, the only one with nonreclining seats, also provided a great view of the engine—which was located six inches from the window and an equal distance from my starboard ear.

Upon leaving the Badhuis, Nazy had reminded everyone to visit the bathroom. In the resulting turmoil, she had failed to heed her own advice and dashed to the F100's WC just before the flight departed. Just as she locked the door, the captain announced imminent takeoff. Wearing an outfit that precluded normal bodily functions, Nazy knew she had to return to her seat and, in a frantic attempt to comply, threw open the lavatory door and crashed into the chief purser. Luckily, we were in an F100, so there wasn't room for the purser—who suffered only a mild concussion—to fall to the floor. Nazy stuffed her favorite belt into the seat pocket, apologizing profusely.

The flight was uneventful, and the meal not memorable. We arrived in Prague as scheduled. Once through passport control, we were amazed to see only two pieces of baggage—ours—ready for pick up. We were about to clear customs in record time when Nazy remembered that her belt—her "favorite" belt—had autonomously elected to remain on the aircraft. Frantic, she approached the nearest Bohemian official, who was happy to convert three hundred guilders into a random number of Czech crowns. I reluctantly gave up our coveted place in the customs clearing queue as the remaining luggage from KL261 began to arrive.

Nazy dashed around the spartan arrivals hall looking for someone who could speak English. The rest of us tried to figure out the currency conversion rate. Darius was the loudest.

"It's easy, Dad. It's about fifteen to one."
"So?"
"So you divide Czech crowns by ten and then by five."

"Ah….I don't think that will work. Perhaps we should divide by five and then by three."

"Whatever. But your way is very complicated."

"I don't know. We could also cross off the last zero, divide by two, and add the result to the number we got when we started."

"When we started?"

"Yeah, when we started. After we crossed off the zero the first time."

"The first time? I thought you said it was the last zero."

"We crossed off the last zero the first time."

"But, Dad, I've already forgotten what we had when we started."

Mitra joined the discussion. "It's really simple, guys. Each one hundred crowns is about seven guilders. So we just round to the nearest one hundred Crowns and multiply by seven."

"So eight hundred and seventy crowns would be…"

"Fifty-six guilders. Eight hundred and seventy is almost nine hundred and nine times seven is…"

"Sixty-three, Mitra. Sixty-three! It appears you slept through the arithmetic class at Princeton."

While we were discussing high finance, Nazy eventually found someone stupid enough to admit that they understood English. A supervisor was duly summoned and agreed to search the aircraft. (He didn't bother to tell Nazy that the aircraft had already departed.) Nazy was aware that there is no Czech word for speed, so she decided to make another attempt to visit the WC.

All the other passengers from KL261 had cleared customs. We waited.

Naturally, the supervisor returned just as Nazy located the lavatory. Tired of sitting on the floor, Melika rushed to alert her mom.

While this was happening, I spotted the only other passenger in the arrivals hall—a forlorn little old lady pulling a huge suitcase. She made the mistake of stopping to catch her breath directly in front of the door to the ladies' room. Nazy raced out at a speed unseen since the blitzkrieg and ran straight into this ragged refuge. The gray-haired victim was able to sustain a vertical position, but her suitcase landed in Afghanistan.

Two more flights arrived while Nazy carried out delicate diplomatic negotiations with CSA (the KLM representative in Prague). In the end, CSA agreed to accept a telephone inquiry about her delinquent belt.

We waited.

Eventually, we cleared customs and, following advice from KLM, shunned the taxi stand and marched directly to the limo counter. We had been assured a limo would be cheaper, safer, and more reliable than a taxi. Unfortunately, the only limo east of the Rhine was engaged. Imminent return was promised.

We waited.

"Dad, do you know anything about Prague?" Mitra asked.

"Absolutely nothing." (I had really prepared myself for this trip.)

"I guess we'll just have to *czech* it out, eh?"

We waited.

Nazy asked the limo clerk about the city, the communists, the weather, and, of course, the shops.

We waited. In fact, we waited far longer than we had flown. We really waited. We waited patiently (in the beginning) and impatiently in the middle (which lasted a *very long* time). We *czech*ed the taxis, but they wanted six hundred crowns. The guidebook, written in 1912, clearly stated that anything over three hundred and twenty crowns was thievery. We told the taxi drivers to forget it because the limo company had quoted us a rate of only three hundred and twenty crowns, a tidbit that outraged the drivers, who stormed into the terminal building to accost the limo clerk. I would have been upset, but I was surrounded by a score of potentially violent cabbies and the limo was still missing.

Nonplused, we waited in the decaying ambience of the Prague aerodrome.

Finally, as darkness began to fall, we gave up and grabbed a cab. Six hundred and seventy crowns later, we were in the Club Hotel Praha (four stars). The Club Hotel Praha was not centrally located, in spite of information to the contrary provided by our travel agent. In fact, it is the only hotel that, because of its "central" location, can serve both Budapest (which is in Hungary) and Prague.

Reserved rooms (a double and a triple) were waiting. The double room reminded me of a college dormitory: functional, basic, and cramped. I camped there, searching for CNN, while Nazy walked to the triple room to help settle the kids. Shortly thereafter, she called for assistance.

Imagine my shock as I entered the children's room—an opulent chamber furnished with museum-quality artwork and accoutrements. Melika was bouncing on the diving board suspended over the bath. Darius was nibbling the complimentary caviar, and Mitra was enjoying the fresh roses. It was clear that there had been a massive registration mistake.

"Isn't *our* room great, Dad?" (Darius was impressed.)

"Yes, *my* room is really magnificent," I replied.

"Your room? This is the *children's* suite—and how sweet it is!"

"The children's suite? I don't think so. The sign on the door says 'parental chambers only.'"

"How do you know that? You can't read Czech."

"But, my son, I'm writing the check, so I get to translate. And as for you staying in this room—well, you can just forget it."

"But…"

"You can just forget it."

Once the adults and children had settled in grand and pedestrian rooms (respectively), we took a trek into the center of Prague for a traditional Czech meal.

"So is this Hungarian goulash authentic Czech food?" Nazy asked the waiter.

While Nazy was making friends, Darius reminded us how it was crucial to obtain a Czech version of Monopoly.

"That's not possible, Darius," I observed. "This country has just left the communist era. There is no Monopoly. Forget Monopoly. Purchase the national game instead."

"The national game?"

"That's right: *czech*ers."

Abashed by Nazy's skill in selecting from the menu, Mitra handled her own order (dumplings) with considerable aplomb. The drink, however, was causing difficulty.

"Do you have water?"

"Yes, mineral water."

"No, I want plain water."

"Yes, mineral water."

"No. Plain water. No gas."

"Yes, mineral water."

"No gas?"

"Yes."

No. When the mineral water arrived, it had more minerals than a vitamin supplement. Harder than the Rock of Gibraltar, it contained (according to the label) sodium, potassium, magnesium, cadmium, zinc, aluminum, iron, lead, mercury, nitrates, lithium, potash, helium, argon, xenon, nitric acid, phosphoric acid, sulfuric acid, and several rare earth elements. It was gurgling as a result of radioactive decay, so it wasn't surprising that it contained bubbles. Mitra complained to the waiter.

"This *water* has gas."

"Yes, mineral water." (At least he was consistent.)

After a refreshing evening in the master suite (parents) and a passable night in the dorm (the children), we attacked Prague. We found the city beautiful. Because the previous government hadn't repaired or cleaned anything since World War II, the buildings had a quaint and ancient charm. Though dirty (Prague is one of Europe's most polluted cities), it was also elegant. We began our tour in the famous Prague Castle—a Renaissance palace and cathedral. Luckily, we had Darius along to provide commentary.

"Notice the flying buttress architecture, Dad. This permits narrow columns and huge windows. Each stained glass window tells a story. Most people couldn't read…"

"Of course not. No one reads Czech. It's too complicated."

"Right. Anyway, the stained-glass windows were the contemporary equivalent of books and the Internet. Isn't this architecture magnificent?"

"Magnificent? Can you imagine how much it cost to build this place? I bet you'd be outraged if your tax money was spent on a construction project like this."

"Don't be ridiculous. They didn't have taxes back then."

"Darius, my son, you have a lot to learn. They *always* have taxes."

"Perhaps, but this kind of project provided the only impetus for innovation in the Middle Ages. The flying buttress construction—the diagonal arches outside—holds up the walls and gives this place a light and airy look."

We walked out of the cathedral into a much more ancient medieval chapel, with Darius talking all the way.

"Look at this! Notice the small windows, the heavy columns, and the closed, dense look. Do you know why?"

"Yes," I answered. "The flying buttocks are sitting on their asses instead of being outside holding up the building."

From the Prague Castle, we walked to Charles Bridge. Myriads of products were offered by thousands of street vendors. Nazy took a fancy to a watercolor and even agreed to buy it. Aware that it was relatively early in the morning, I asked if she had bargained about the price. Stunned and abashed, Nazy marched back to the vendor, whom she had already paid.

"Would it be all right if I pay you less?" (Later, Nazy claimed she had assumed the vendor would be unfamiliar with basic capitalistic negotiation techniques.)

Over the next few days, we saw all the major sites—Wenceselas Square, the old city center, the Jewish district, and each of the three thousand, eight hundred and forty-three Bohemian crystal stores conveniently located near every landmark. Showing considerable resiliency, Nazy was in her element. The rest of us were stuck in the heat of an eastern European drought. Family conversations became clipped.

"Where's your mom?"

"She's at the *czech*-out counter."

"Where's Nazy now?"

"She's writing a Euro*czech*."

"What's Mommy doing?"

"She's looking at a crystal chess set."

"*Czech*mate."

We kept searching for "real" Czech food. The main course was simple—dumplings and goulash—but we continued to have problems on the fringes. One evening, having finished our meal, the waiter asked if we wanted dessert. Although we had already agreed that Darius and Melika would share a banana split, Darius (who is always hungry) immediately ordered his own personal ice cream. The waiter scribbled on his order pad. I corrected the confusion.

"One banana split," I said. Pointing at Darius, I added, "no ice cream."

"One banana split."

"That's right. *One.* And *no* ice cream."

"*Zonder slagroom,*" interjected Nazy, canceling (in Dutch) the whipped cream. (Dutch sounds closer to Czech than English.)

"One banana split?" replied the waiter. "And no ice cream?"

Noting he had still not erased Darius's order, I moved to control the situation. "That's right, no ice cream."

The banana split arrived—*zonder* (without) ice cream. When we complained to the waiter, he was ready.

"You ordered it without ice cream. I asked you three times."

We spent our final day in a seemingly impossible, frantic effort to part with our last few crowns. (Crowns cannot be reconverted into real money.) Darius, who was bored by crystal, kept suggesting—no, *demanding*—that we hide one bill of each denomination for his currency collection. (It's illegal to take money out of the country.)

"Don't worry, Darius," I told him. "It's impossible to spend all these crowns in the two hours before we leave."

In spite of Nazy's well-honed skills and valiant effort, we did have money left over when we arrived at the national aerodrome. The neo-modern (1939) building exuded the cozy charm of a decaying central city bus terminal, but this time we arrived early enough to enjoy the duty-free trowel and shovel shop. There was palpable excitement when Melika found a local mafioso with a canister of Pringles potato chips and cheese on offer. Pulling out my last five-hundred crown note, I outbid a starving German tourist. Melika and I dug into the Pringles. Some family members were not impressed. Having imagined the five hundred crowns for his currency collection, Darius was exceptionally annoyed. Nazy noted that Pringles are full of (bad) cholesterol. Even Mitra, picking at the cheese, was less than enthusiastic.

"What's the matter, Mitra? Think of all the goats that died to make that cheese."

"Goats?"

"It's feta cheese."

"It's Camembert cheese, Dad."

"Then think of all the bears that died to make that cheese."

And with that, we walked to the gate—a glass-enclosed cubicle that clearly demonstrated the greenhouse effect. Panting, we tried to hold our thirst in *czech* as we waited to return to a cool, wet, and friendly Holland.

EPILOGUE
AND WHAT DID THEY LEARN?

S o, five years in The Hague. We survived and we grew. We became continentally suave. We learned about ourselves and became more aware that there are always other ways to do things. Specific lessons:

Restaurant Etiquette
- Don't become nonplussed when the waiter asks if your drinking water should be served with gas. He's not trying to send you to the smelly section. It's simple: Do you want bubbles or don't you?
- You may have to share your quiet evening out sitting next to someone's slobbering dog. Think about getting a pet lion.
- If necessary, sing for your supper.

European Driving
- The streets, which are about as wide as a driveway in New England, not only support two-way traffic and parking on both sides, but are depicted in the city map with a heavy, thick, "major-thoroughfare" line.
- Bicycles always have the right of way—except when you're riding one. (There is one exception for everything. Drawbridges have the right of way over bicycles. So, in the unlikely event that you experience an upgrade in the roadway, back up.)

Foreign Language
- It is polite to ask the *bakker* for fresh bread that is *gesneden* (sliced). It is not polite to ask the same *bakker* for fresh bread that is *besneden* (circumcised). It is correct to ask for *aardbeien* (strawberries); the grocer is less amused when you ask for *aambeien* (hemorrhoids).
- The sauna placards in the Scheveningen public sauna do not read "men" and "women"—they read "women" and "mixed."
- Don't go to Holland if you want to learn a foreign language—the natives would much rather learn yours. If you really must learn a new language, you might try for an assignment in the United Kingdom.

European Corporations
European companies operate on the basis of "consensus"—everyone must agree to any plan before anything can be done. They don't *make* a decision, they *take* a decision.

Advertisements
- The HTM metro transit ad that says, "We're always on time—except sometimes there's an elephant in the way" or "We're always on time—except sometimes when we just can't do it." I just don't get it.
- I don't *want* to get the Shell ad with a picture of a bowl of prunes on the left side of the page and the following text on the right side: "Shell petrol works on your car like Mom's prunes work on your digestive system."

Organization and Bureaucracy
- The Americans are babes in the woods—Europe has been building governmental bureaucracy since the Middle Ages.

- There is a once-a-year reading of the electricity meter. It works like this: When you move in, electricity usage is monitored for two weeks. The results are used to compute projected monthly consumption, and you are sent bills each month based on this projection. As you pay the bills, you get the feeling that, well, you're paying the bills. At the end of a year, the meter is read again to determine the annual consumption. Then you are sent a final adjustment invoice. In our case, the initial two weeks occurred before the family arrived and while I was in London, so the projected use was very low. We got a *big* surprise after one year. In Cormac's case, it was even worse. He ignored the appointment for the annual reading (it was written in Dutch), so the final adjustment covered two years. Moreover, he had opted for the convenient payment method whereby the electric company simply took money from his bank account. The two-year underpayment was more than ten thousand guilders. Cormac was not happy.
- Telephone bills are not itemized, and you need a passport to pick up certified mail.
- If your sentence starts with "I need to" (or "I want to" or "Can I"), then the response will be "It's not possible." You know you're settled when you start your sentences with "Is it possible…"

SCHOOL SUPPLIES
- Twenty-three-hole notebook paper?

It was great, but it had to end. At the office, I had discovered that being project coordinator was nice—until the project ended. Like the project, my series of contracts ended. In a sure sign of impending turmoil, Shell had contracted with the global management company McKinsey & Company to study central office organization. Several events, including—embarrassingly—my project, had made it possible to significantly reduce central office staff—just when we wanted to stay. Thus there was both dismay and excitement as we planned our repatriation journey. Naturally, we decided to vacation en route.

LUVLY, LUV

Russia. Darius wanted to go to Russia because: "You said we'd go to Russia, Dad."

"That was when I thought we'd have a job guarantee for 1995, Darius. That was when I thought we could save money by using KLM frequent flyer points. That was when I thought that we'd be able to leverage Shell's repatriation policy. That was when…"

"Right. So now we just fly to America, abandoning Europe like a defeated army."

"We're going home, Darius. Home."

"Right, home. Like a misplaced…"

"Home. Like a normal family."

Darius was somewhat right. We had planned to visit St. Petersburg via Helsinki, and we had considered a grand tour of Scandinavia. But Shell's consulting guarantee was limited and the frequent flyer points, while available, had no effect on the stratospheric hotel costs in Russia or Finland. Absurdly, the only hotel "deals" available required a fully paid flight. It was cheaper to buy a package that included hotel and airfare than it was to fly free and book a hotel separately.

Contractually, Shell was obligated to business-class repatriation to Hanover, New Hampshire. Business-class stopover deals abounded, so I was sure I could work something out with the Shell Travel Division. I started the process by proposing a homeward journey via Finland.

"I'm sorry, Dr. Martin, that routing exceeds your travel allowance. Helsinki is not on the way."

"I know it's not on the way, I can see that from a map. Surely you professionals in the travel division can work something out. Remember, you're the people who routed me from Kuala Lumpur to Houston via Amsterdam."

"I'm sorry, Dr. Martin, but…"

"I know—'it's not possible.' Okay, how about this: We'll fly from Amsterdam to Helsinki tourist class, but from Helsinki to Boston business class."

"We could do that, but by traveling tourist class to Helsinki, you will have elected a tourist class return and you'll not only be uncomfortable, but we'll be forced to reduce your travel allowance to full-fare economy class…"

"Fine. How about this: Shell flies four people to America via Helsinki and I pay for one person." (I planned to use the frequent flyer miles.)

"We could do that. However, if you pay for one traveler, we'll reduce your travel allowance and you'll find that…"

"Okay! Finland is out. Where can we stop en route to America and stay within the travel allowance?"

"You could stop in London."

"London? London! Are you crazy? I've been to London sixty times in the last three years. I don't want to stop in London. I'm sure I'll think of something else."

It was clear that Finland wasn't going to be included in The Martin Family homeward routing. I considered Barcelona, Budapest, Bermuda, and Stockholm. All were rejected by Shell Travel. I finally confirmed Ireland—it was the only alternative other than London or (gasp!) Manchester.

I had been to Dublin, so it was decided that we would not only tour the capital, we would also rent a car and drive to the more idyllic and remote southwestern area. While the remainder of the family was busy with last-minute packing, I booked a modest hotel and an economy car for our first few days in Dublin.

Travel wasn't easy. Accustomed to traveling light,[17] we would have to cart our homeward bound suitcases with us. As we, our thirteen suitcases, and our eighteen carry-on items boarded an eighteen-wheeler that had been chartered for our journey to Schiphol Airport, I began to consider the efficacy of our Irish rental car arrangements.

In spite of *International Herald Tribune* warnings about work slowdowns on Aer Lingus, we arrived in Dublin without delay. Darius and I collected six baggage trolleys and joined the girls at the luggage reclaim belt. The Martin Family procession snaked its way through the terminal building to our rental car, but was immediately clear that no amount of packing virtuosity would make it possible to fit both the luggage and the family within the confines of the hired vehicle. Nazy, the girls, and a subset of the suitcases departed by taxi, leaving Darius and I to find the hotel on our own. Much to Nazy's surprise, we succeeded.

The family was extremely impressed with the Fitzpatrick Castle Hotel. Our first glance at the castle, The Martin Family suite, and the panoramic view of Dublin harbor made it clear that I'd made an error of enormous magnitude when I'd converted from Irish punt to Dutch guilders. The castle, hardly a modest hotel, was a *real* castle that had been converted to a hotel.

---

17 . In *The Martin Family* lexicon, "traveling light" means we don't have to charter a separate aircraft to handle the luggage.

We toured Dublin and were for the most part semi-impressed. Pretending to be natives, we took the DART[18] (according to the taxi driver, it was "*dart* cheap"). On the way into the city center, we passed a beach with a strange deficit: no water. After surveying the mudflats, Darius approached a local for additional information.

"What's wrong with your beach?"

"What do you mean?"

"There's no water. Where's the ocean?"

"I'm sure it's out there with the tide."

"Oh."

In town, Mitra liked the juggling shop, Darius found entertainment at a magic store, Melika was enamored by the funky hats, and Nazy found the sales enthralling—we saw lots of sweater shops. Whatever Nazy wanted was "luvly, just luvly." (Everyone was really nice even though they did insist on speaking with the funniest accents.)

With the exceptions of the wonderfully colorful Georgian doors and Trinity College, the city was, from a tourist's point of view, rather dull. We initially visited Trinity College to see the *Book of Kells*, an illuminated manuscript from the seventh century. (Nazy had been to a lecture on illuminated manuscripts.) Connoisseurs of medieval art would undoubtedly be impressed, but after queuing for forty-five minutes, I quickly classified the artifact as an old book that was hardly worth the wait. The exit passed through an ancient, impressive library that looked like the set of an Indiana Jones movie with old books from floor to ceiling. You could just imagine monks working there.

After our short stay in the castle, we set out for the naturally beautiful part of Ireland—the southwest. Because Nazy was with us, we naturally chose a (indirect) route through Waterford. and because there

---

18 . Dublin Area Rapid Transit

are five of us, we departed late. (We convinced staff at the castle to store our excess suitcases for the duration of our journey. They had an auxiliary baggage shed erected on our behalf.) Our journey was longer than expected given the narrow Irish roads, and as a result we arrived in Waterford somewhat later than we'd planned.

For Nazy, a tour of the Waterford Crystal Factory was going to be the highlight of the trip. Our late arrival put something of a damper on that plan. The desk clerk explained the situation.

"Yes, of course we have tours of the factory. In fact, you've *just* missed the last tour of the week."

"I've missed the last tour?" Nazy was *not* happy.

"That's right," the clerk replied with a happy smile, "and you've just *barely* missed it. The tour just left. You've *missed* it by the skin of your teeth. It was sooo close."

"Can I catch up with the tour?"

"Oh no! You've *missed* it. Just barely, but you've *missed* it. For sure you've *missed* it. The last tour of the week and you *missed* it by a hair. Of course a miss is as good as a mile."

Needless to say, Nazy wasn't in a happy mood as she sullenly marched through the display room. (No one thought it wise to remind her of her constant pleas that I slow down during the drive.) She viewed the offerings with disdain until she came upon a crystal lion, but unfortunately, the lion was out of stock (she had missed the last one "by an eyelash"). Moreover, since they didn't have the item in stock, Nazy couldn't avail herself of the free engraving. All in all, Waterford was a disappointment.

We decided to spend the night elsewhere and set off for Cork in County Cork. Like Nazy, I was interested in local craft and I knew that the specialty of the region—bulletin boards—would be cheaper than crystal. I was very disappointed to discover that no cork had ever been mined in County Cork. In fact, it didn't appear that there was very much of anything in County Cork.

We departed early the next morning for Blarney. The children were not familiar with the legend of the Blarney Stone, so I tried to explain.

"You see, Duncan O'Reilly, who owned Blarney Castle of the Magillicutty Mountains, was so good at sweet-talking the English king that it became…"

"Duncan O'Reilly? Are you sure, Dad?"

"Of course I'm sure, Darius. He's an ancestor of Cormac O'Reilly."

"What's sweet-talking?"

"The American translation is 'B.S.'"

"B.S.?"

"That's right. It's an especially useful skill to have when you're faced with an essay question."

"I'm already skilled at blarney."

"I'm well aware of that, Darius."

The drive from Cork to Blarney featured ever-narrowing roads. It didn't matter that I'd not quite mastered driving on the left because the roadway was only one car wide. We quickly discovered that the single lane in Ireland was treated as a dual carriage motorway, which was shared with oncoming traffic that was composed of motorcycles, cars, tractors, buses, horse-drawn carts, cows, sheep, bicycles, bulldozers, and wandering harpists. And, even though the Irish speak English (for the most part), we still had a bit of trouble understanding the meaning of the various traffic signs. Some were simple:

> **Danger!**
> **Acute Bend Ahead**

This means that the road has curves. It is totally useless information, because the road is *only* curves. Other signs were more problematic:

> **Danger!**
> **Loose Chippings**
> **Mind your windscreen.**

"What is a chipping, Dad?" Melika, was now interested in the surroundings, having finished her fourth Christopher Pike horror book.

"I'm not sure, but I think it refers to the cow droppings."

"Cow droppings?"

"That's right. Did you know that there's a cow-chip throwing contest in Houston?"

"No, I didn't. But now I know why we moved away from Houston. What's a windscreen?"

"It's like a sunscreen, but for wind."

"Oh."

Other signs were even more obscure:

> **Caution**
> **Heavy Plant Crossing**

"Okay, Dan, what's that one mean?" Nazy asked.

"I think it's self-explanatory. Watch out for sequoia trees crossing the highway."

We eventually made it to Blarney. The castle resembled the Fitzpatrick, our Dublin hotel. We climbed to the top and each of the children lay on their backs and leaned out over three stories of air to kiss a lipstick festooned stone. Nazy and I wisely demurred and took pictures of the children instead.

On the way back to the car, we were greeted by an itinerant bard who sold us a precanned poem wishing us good luck. It was clear that he had kissed the Blarney stone.

We left Blarney and headed toward the famous Ring of Kerry. We wanted to see Muckross House and the Ross Castle before settling in Dingle for the evening. Killarney and the surrounding environs were luvly. The drive to Dingle, on the far southwestern peninsula jutting into the Atlantic, was adventurous. The roads had deteriorated badly and resembled asphalt driveways. The view became ever more grand until the sun set just as we arrived in Dingle.

Naturally, we hadn't booked a hotel. Nazy found in her Fodor's book the largest and most impressive edifice in the center of Dingle. ("Center" should be taken rather lightly as Dingle is essentially a small line of large pubs.) There was no room for us at the inn (but the shepherds were watching their flocks by night). We had elected to visit Dingle the one weekend that the town hosted waterfront horse races. A hotel was not to be found. Nazy talked the hotel clerk into calling all the regional bed and breakfasts and found a sole vacancy in Dunquin—a mere twelve kilometers from Dingle. Nazy booked Clancy's B&B.

Family reactions were varied, especially when they found out how little it cost.

"I'm not sure about his place, Nazy," I began. "Clancy's costs one-hundredth as much as the castle."

"Yeah, Mom," Darius agreed. "It's bound to be a dump—an unsafe dump. Let's drive to Limerick."

Mitra was more phlegmatic. "I think you guys are overreacting. I'm sure it will be just luvly."

Melika came up with the next step. "I don't want to drive anywhere ever again." (Melika had been on the road too long.) "And I'm hungry—now!"

Everyone realized that the sinking feeling in the pit of their stomach was hunger. We surveyed the three restaurants with increasing desperation. A waiter helpfully explained that the first was fully booked for the entire weekend. We didn't even get to see a waiter at the second; they had a simple "Full" sign posted on the window. Realizing the gravity of our predicament, we sent Darius into the third—and final—establishment. To no one's surprise, he was able to negotiate a table. (It was, in fact, the final table: We were the last customers served that evening.)

Over dinner, Darius became increasingly agitated.

"Dad! I really think we should drive to Limerick. Clancy's B&B can't be safe."

"Of course it's safe. It's just a dump."

"Mom said it's next door to a youth hostel. I think we'll be robbed."

"You are a youth, Darius. So not all youths are robbers. Besides, it's just a dump. No one will rob us at Clancy's. No one expects the kind of people who stay at Clancy's to have anything worth robbing."

"This isn't making me feel better."

"I think you guys are overreacting. I'm sure it will be just luvly." Mitra, the official family optimist, tried to cheer us up.

"It will be a dump, Mitra. A roach-infested, dirty dump."

"But…" Darius began.

"A safe, roach-infested, dirty dump, Darius. Safe!"

And so following a good meal,[19] we departed for Dunquin. The instructions were simple. Leave Dingle on the main road, drive a few kilometers to Paddy O'Shea's Pub, turn right, follow the road to Tom Foley's Pub, take a left, and find Clancy's around the corner from Tim Kelly's Pub.

---

19 . *Darius was convinced it would be our last meal.*

We left the street lights in Dingle. The road, such as it was, became dark and narrow. Luckily, we could follow the dirt road—it was marked on the left by a three-foot stone wall and on the right by ten-foot swamp grass. It looked as though we were in the middle of nowhere. Darius was optimistic.

"It's not safe, Dad. I think we should turn around."

"Turn around? Here? We can't turn around, our wheels will get stuck in the bog or we'll smash the car on the rocks. Don't worry, we'll be safe. This family can weather a single night at a dump."

"I think you're overreacting. I'm sure it will be just luvly."

"Mitra, do you realize that's the four hundredth time you've said the same thing?"

Suddenly, out of the darkness, we heard singing and saw lights. It was Paddy O'Shea's. The darkness parted and we couldn't remember whether to turn right or left. We sent Darius and Mitra in to check.

Darius came back first. "Turn right. By the way, they say it's a dump."

We turned right onto a path beaten through the muck by a scraggly herd of flatulent sheep. I thought of stopping and mounting candles on each fender, but there wasn't room to get out of the car.

I wasn't sanguine about Clancy's, but wisely kept my concerns to myself.

"Nazy! Why didn't *you* think of reserving a real hotel in Dingle? Gad! Dingle! What a stupid place to visit. We're only here because the clerk in the Fitzpatrick Hotel told you it was pretty. I've never heard of Dingle. Dingle, indeed. What a stupid name! It's a dump. Here we are in the middle of a bog, in the middle of the night, surrounded by darkness blacker than the coal of Newcastle during a total eclipse of the sun driving on a road best suited for (small) salamanders en route to a B&B suitable for condemned prisoners."

"I think you're overreacting. I'm sure it will be just luvly."

"Mitra! Will you just…"

Like a desert mirage, Tom Foley's Pub appeared in the darkness. We sent Darius and Mitra in to find further directions. The way things were going, I expected we'd be told to park the car and take pack mules for the final plunge. Instead, Darius reported that we were in Dunquin, just two blocks from Tim Kelly's pub and the B&B.

Imagine our surprise when we pulled into a charming, clean home—Clancy's B&B. "See, Darius," I said, surveying the establishment, "I told you not to worry. This place is luvly. You were overreacting."

We woke up to a splendid view of the Atlantic, green fields, and a wonderful Irish breakfast. In fact, the ambience and friendliness of Clancy exceeded that of the Fitzpatrick Castle Hotel. It was a wonderful experience. Over the full breakfast, we heard a strange sound. Proud of herself for picking the venue, Nazy immediately identified the source.

"It's a shepherd singing to his birds."

"I think the birds are singing to the shepherd, Nazy. The shepherd is tending to his flock."

We took a leisurely drive back to Dingle, went to see the dolphin that freely roams the harbor, and then headed to Limerick for dinner. I was very disappointed to find out that limericks were not invented in Limerick.

> The Family of Martins was moving
> And packing was not very soothing
> We stuffed into boxes
> Our books about foxes
> While in fields the cows were still mooing.

We had lunch in Paddy Punch's pub, followed by an uneventful drive back to Dublin. In retrieving the luggage, Nazy was able to negotiate a super deal at the Fitzpatrick Castle. (It still cost much more than Clancy's.) The flight from Dublin was smooth, with a single stop in Shannon, just outside Limerick. Darius was happy to get a U.S. passport stamp (in Shannon) and we departed Europe for our return to the United States.

We had a luvly stay.

While we were on vacation in Ireland, Pokie the cat was parked in a kennel near Amsterdam's Schiphol Airport. We were flying Aer Lingus to Boston, and we had arranged a same-day arrival for Pokie via KLM. Both flights were on time. While Nazy collected our luggage, Melika and I went to cargo terminal to pick up Pokie. It didn't begin well..

"There was no cat on the KLM flight," the clerk informed me.

"But I have the papers."

"No cat!"

"Where is Pokie?" Melika shouted. "I told you we should bring her to Ireland."

"You heard the young lady," I said. "Where is our cat?"

"We do not have your cat. There was no cat on the KLM flight."

"Dad…" Melika wailed.

"Can you look around the warehouse? Our cat was on the KLM flight."

"Are you listening, buddy? We do not have any cats here."

The agent was almost shouting when we heard an even louder "meow!" from the some nearby cavern.

"No cat?" I asked.

"I'll take a look."

When the family (and Pokie) got to Hanover, Nazy realized she had left a scarf at Clancy's B&B. She telephoned the news to Ireland and Sean Clancy himself mailed the scarf to Hanover. The postage cost more than we spent during our time in Dunquin. We sent a gallon of maple syrup to Ireland.

Actually, I managed repatriation for The Martin Family the same way I coordinated my Shell project. It was a phased transition. The family moved back to New Hampshire in time for the beginning of the school year. The house, which had been rented to graduate business students for five years, was a far cry from the gigantic edifice on Badhuisweg. The yard, on the other hand, was vast and overgrown. (Graduate business students are not masters of the lawn mower.) We quickly realized that the belongings that had been so carefully (and expensively) stored for five years had been left in Hanover for a reason. They were junk. (Either our taste had changed during our sojourn, or we had acquired taste.) The house itself had undergone some decay. Later claiming amnesia, Nazy announced an absolute need for a minor renovation, thereby making it impossible to use two major rooms. Since we were another two rooms shy of the Badhuis estate and were faced with boxes from both Holland and New Hampshire, the Hanover hacienda (affectionately known as Bedlam Abode) was in some disarray.

It was a total chaotic mess. We had mismanaged our "emergency air shipment." This Shell repatriation feature was aimed at delivering the really important items the day of our arrival, but we'd used the special carton for everything we'd forgotten to pack. Our emergency shipment had the cat's scratching post, Darius's horseback riding boots, the asparagus cooker, and my cowboy hat.[20]

Luckily Shell was feeling guilty. I knew they didn't have much experience dealing with successful projects and played the sympathy card. Somehow it didn't seem right to just let me disappear. Accordingly, a consulting arrangement was agreed: I would spend two more months in The Hague—several thousand miles away from the construction, the boxes, and the mess. It didn't make me popular, but someone had to make the sacrifice.

---

20 . *Well, the cowboy hat was critical.*

I quickly asked Nazy to help me with some minor problems. She arranged a temporary apartment, a list of critical Dutch phone numbers, and an exercise and eating program. My first month back in The Hague went smoothly and, convinced that real progress had been made in New Hampshire, I was looking forward to a smooth and safe return. There was nothing to worry about—I was an expert, and I looked forward to seeing the family again.

Of course, nothing is completely easy. Our house in Hanover was stuffed with stuff. The front door was warped from five years of humidity. On the other hand, we were reintroduced to the stars. (It was dark in Hanover.)

The night before I was to return to Holland, the family went to Panda House for dinner. Afterward, we entered the dark house through the unlit living room—a room that was packed with unpacked boxes. It was a very dark room without an overhead light. I tried to shut the front door, but it was warpped and wouldn't close. Melika was concerned that the cat, which we couldn't see in the dark, would get out. It was a recipe for disaster. I held the doorframe while I searched for the switch for the outdoor light. Noticing that the door remained open, Melika launched herself toward it. With momentum last seen when the asteroid destroyed the dinosaurs, she hit the door. The resultant force accelerated the door to planetary escape velocity, just before slamming it against my finger.

"*Oh drat,*" *I said.* "*My gosh, that smarts.*"

I threw a towel around my finger and we jumped back in the car for a trip to the hospital. Darius was suitably helpful.

"*We can't go, Dad.*"

"*Why not?*" *I replied through gritted teeth.*

"*Don't we have to bring your finger? I think we left it on the ground somewhere.*"

Actually, I still had my finger. But it was broken. At least I hadn't done it on a bicycle.

REPATRIATION: EASY FOR EXPERTS

Returning to Hanover after my consulting gig was anything but smooth. It began in The Hague at five forty-five a.m. on the first Saturday in October. Since I'd rented the apartment through November, I decided to leave a few things in the ground-floor storage. Although I'd put most of my stuff away Friday evening, I had to stow a final suitcase, which was stuffed to the brim with my linens, towels, pillow (and anything else I'd overlooked) on Saturday.

I jumped in the lift and selected the ground floor. En route, I reached into my right pocket and extracted my keys. As I jockeyed the keys into position (so that I'd be ready to unlock the storage closet), the elevator arrived at its destination with a noticeable *jerk*. The keys slid through my fingers and plummeted toward the floor, which was rebounding from the arrival shock and therefore rushing upward at sonic velocity. The keys hit the floor and then, in a movement at variance with normal physical laws,[21] they *rolled* toward the edge of the elevator. At this point, quark reduction took effect and the keys shrank, becoming just large enough to slip through the gap between the elevator door and the elevator compartment. They fell to the bottom of the shaft. I was left keyless, shoeless and in my T-shirt.

Thrilled by the challenge, I tried the normal emergency responses. I tied two sheets together and made a hook from a clothes hanger. It didn't work. I looked around for a house phone. There wasn't one. I walked up the stairs to see if I had left the apartment door unlocked. I hadn't. I dashed back to the ground floor and reviewed the options. There weren't any.

I decided to see if there was a telephone in the outer lobby. I had to be careful, because the lobby door locked automatically. I arranged the towel to prevent the door from slamming shut, but was annoyed when I pushed (actually, slammed) the door open. It hit the doorjamb and

---

21. *The keys were neither round nor spherical.*

rebounded back with sufficient force to generate an artificial hurricane, the wind of which pushed the towel away from the door—just far enough away to let the lock engage. Now I was outside. It was cold and raining.

I walked to the nearby shopping district, located a public telephone, and dialed 06-11 (the Dutch equivalent of 911). National law makes the 06-11 telephone call free. However, I was in Holland.

> Free Call (n., Dutch): A telephone connection with nationwide emergency services 06-11. Deposit *een kwartje*, dial the number, and, upon completion of the call, your money will be returned.

In order to make the "free" telephone call, I had to have a *kwartje* (twenty-five Dutch cents). I checked my pockets and found two allergy tablets that had somehow survived several washing cycles, but I didn't find a *kwartje*.

I was beginning to get worried. I dashed around the shopping center and found activity at a nearby fruit stand. I explained the situation and asked if I could use the telephone to call the police.

"...and so, my keys are at the bottom of the elevator shaft and I've got a flight to America in an hour."

"Yes, I understand. That's a problem. I don't think we can do anything, but I'll alert the fire brigade. It will cost you some money."

"How much? Oh, fine, just send someone quickly. And thanks for the help."

I walked back to the apartment in the rain. The police and I arrived simultaneously. I explained the situation and they asked how I'd locked myself out. I tried to explain about quarks, the towel, and the artificial hurricane, but the police just started ringing all the doorbells in the building. Whenever someone answered, the police simply asked that they unlock the front door. (These were Dutch police and they were subtle: "Police! Open up!")

Needless to say, this generated a lot of activity. As my neighbors rushed down the stairs in their bathrobes, the fire department arrived in a long truck with lights blinking and sirens blasting. Ten firemen rushed into the building. The police described the problem, and after everyone stopped laughing, the fire brigade mounted an assault. They disabled the elevator, repelled down the shaft, recovered my keys, and presented me with an invoice and a fine (for calling the fire department when there wasn't a fire). I considered explaining that the police had called the fire brigade, but…

I rushed to my apartment, telephoned a taxi, and crammed into a shopping bag the fragile and breakable items that I'd planned to carefully pack. I rushed down the stairs. The taxi got me to Schiphol at seven twenty-four a.m.; my flight was at seven forty-five. I had just made it.

Unfortunately, I didn't have a direct flight. I had to change planes and airlines in London. I was returning through London because I had stopped in London on the way; I needed to attend the formal ceremony marking the end of my project. The ceremony was a disaster (my newest boss took credit for everything).

Aware that any connection, but especially an inter-airline, international connection, was risky, I had explored modifications in my itinerary. Unfortunately, my ticket had draconian change/modification covenants. I could modify my routing provided that I either: (1) buy an entirely new ticket; or (2) notify Northwest of an intention to change on the first Tuesday following the first new moon after the end of European summertime in leap years when Holland won the world beach volleyball championship. The first option was financially unpalatable; I didn't meet the qualifications for the second.

Accordingly, I expended substantial effort trying to get KLM to alert Northwest Airlines[22] of my status as an interplanetary, RoyalWing flying Dutchman. I wanted to use my excess mileage to upgrade my

---

22 . *A proud KLM travel partner.*

return flight. KLM was in the middle of a celebration marking seventy-five years of passenger service and marked the occasion by taking seventy-five days to respond to any request. I was booked in the back—the way back—of Northwest Flight 49 from London to Boston.

In spite of the massive delay in The Hague, I somehow made my flight out of Amsterdam. I thought things were looking up.

At London Gatwick, we boarded the flight exactly on time. And then... The captain had a message. I was concerned because the captain usually speaks only while the flight is airborne.

"We have a small, *tiny* electrical problem," he said. (His tone indicated that his problem was somewhat less than tiny.) "The engineers are going to replace a component downstairs, and we'll have to turn off the power in the airplane for about five minutes. I just wanted to alert you to the situation."

About twenty minutes later, the power returned, but the captain had another announcement.

"That didn't fix the fault. Our engineers are going to replace another component, and the power will be off again for a few minutes."

About an hour later, the power returned, but so did the pilot.

"Well, no luck. We have a circuit breaker here that won't stay closed. We're going to have to replace a third component. It's a simple procedure, but it takes about an hour. The electricity has to be off during the exchange, so the airplane will be very uncomfortable. Please deplane and wait in the gate area. You can leave your carry-on items. We'll be reboarding in about ninety minutes."

Northwest uses Gatwick's satellite terminal, a small and lonely outpost far from civilization. The single snack bar had a menu geared toward the random nibbling passenger. Through some unexplained chemical reaction, the temporary grounding of NW49 had stimulated the hunger genes of three hundred and seventy-six passengers—three hundred and seventy-five of whom queued in front of the single counter attendant.

I sat down to read my book, cleverly waiting until the crowd cleared. Proud of my patience, I marched to the counter as soon as it was open and asked for a tuna sandwich. They were sold out. I asked for a ham and cheese: ditto. I asked for a chicken salad. Sorry. I asked for a bag of potato crisps: not available. The only thing left was a freeze-dried kidney pie. Although I was hungry, I couldn't bring myself to buy it.

Northwest had been monitoring the situation. As I walked toward a seat, the airline announced that vouchers for a light lunch (£7) would be made available. Moreover, since the repair was taking longer than expected, passengers were directed to the main terminal. I was familiar with Gatwick and made it back to be the first on queue to get the vouchers. Unfortunately, the vouchers weren't ready: They were being printed. As the queue built behind me, I asked the agent where the vouchers could be spent. He indicated a small snack bar. I decided to spend my own money at a larger restaurant. As I was finishing lunch, I noticed the TV monitor. Our flight listing had changed from:

NW 049   Boston 11:45   16:45   Technical Delay

to:

NW049   Boston 11:45   xxxxx   See Agent

The agent sent me back out to the gate. I was informed that the flight had been canceled and that Northwest would put us up at the Hilton. Two guys next to me, noting that they only had carry-ons, told the attendant they'd just go into central London and would return to the Hilton later that evening. I telephoned home. Mitra, who should have been at Princeton, answered.

"Mitra? What are you doing in Hanover?"

"I just wanted to see you, Daddy. What's the situation?"

"The situation is bleak. My airplane has been canceled. We won't be leaving unt…"

"*Attention*, passengers awaiting the departure of NW49 to Boston. We can confirm that the electrical problem has been corrected. We can depart *immediately*. Please have your boarding passes ready. *Immediate* boarding through gate thirty-seven."

"...*now*. They're boarding now."

Almost everybody boarded. Two passengers were missing. Departure was delayed while someone from Northwest collected the missing passengers from the rail station. As the airplane backed away from the terminal, the lead flight attendant gave a decidedly nontraditional speech.

"Ladies and gentlemen, we are *finally* on our way. Please place your tray tables and..."

The trip from then on was uneventful. Upon arrival in Boston, I was directed to custom desk number six, where I was queued behind an Afghan family who didn't speak English. When I finally made it to the agent, I was surprised by his question.

"American citizen? What are you doing in this line? There's a rapid processing queue for Americans."

"It's been that kind of day."

Finally back in Hanover, I was stunned by the "progress: on the home construction front. It was the kitchen all over again. Nazy asked me to help with the renovation plans. I only had to move seven thousand, two hundred, and thirty-four boxes out of the living room so that work could begin.

Naturally, I began plans for a return to Holland and a massive garage sale. Gosh! It was great to be home.

There have been several complaints about the Dutch propensity for procedures in this opus. We finally learned to appreciate that characteristic.

Upon our return, we discovered that the movers had damaged several items. Negotiations with the insurers were fruitless. It seemed that I had overlooked some Dutch form when we were getting ready to move. I called Stefanie Verbeek, the HR representative.

"You didn't follow the procedure, Dan."

"I guess not. What do I do now?"

"Luckily, we have a procedure for repatriating Americans who forgot to file insurance papers."

"You're kidding."

"No, I'll fax it to you. And Dan?"

"Yes."

"It's written in English, so you should be able to handle it."

"Thanks."

THE MARTIN FAMILY IN 2010

It was clear that we returned to our home in Hanover, New Hampshire, a changed bunch. It was difficult to fit in and we all coped in different ways.

Melika: Quickly recovering from her first experience with the family car (she hit the stone wall adjacent to the garage), Melika was proud to be the cause of two speed bumpers installed between our home and the high school. (They were removed when she left for college.) After graduating from the University of California, Santa Barbara (with a course of studies that included a semester aboard a ship sailing around the world), she worked at a trendy restaurant in Montecito where she met several movie actors, including Carol Burnett, Michael Douglas, and John Cleese. She then went to law school in San Francisco, passed the bar (she celebrated at a party in Bali and with a hike to the top of Kilimanjaro). She is now a corporate lawyer in Santa Barbara.

Darius: After finishing high school, Darius got an undergraduate degree in economics from Syracuse University. Unimpressed with the weather in Syracuse, New York, he (also) enrolled at UC Santa Barbara. He embarked on an extended journey to "Ph.Dom," marked by a research stop in Iceland. (He arrived just as the Iceland economy cratered; the volcano occurred later. He claims it "was not my fault, Dad.") He is now an economics professor at the American University of Beirut. In the past few years he's traveled to Egypt, Jordan, Ethiopia, India, Pakistan, South Africa, Sri Lanka, and Cambodia. His mom wonders, "What's wrong with London, Berlin, or even Des Moines?"

Mitra: After completing a degree in comparative literature at Princeton, Mitra moved to New York. ("You know, Mitra, I've never seen a job posting like 'Desperately needed: comparative literaturist specializing in medieval French and Persian garden allegories,'" I told her.) She worked at a couple of brand marketing companies and rapidly rose through the ranks. But, while doing market research in Buenos Aries, she discovered the Tango, moved to Los Angeles, and, with her partner, Stefan, created Oxygen Tango (www.oxygentango.com), the best Tango school in the world. She and Stefan are based in California, but they teach and perform all over the world.

Nazy: Continuing her role as CFO (Chief Family Officer), but missing the international adventures she had come to enjoy, Nazy founded the International Women's Club (IWC) of the Upper Valley upon repatriation. The IWC is now a fixture in Hanover. Nazy also supervised a complex and complete renovation of the house while encouraging a troubled husband who didn't particularly enjoy commuting to Boston. She graciously accepted an award from a department store in The Hague that had named a floor after her. She continued (and continues) to be beautiful, smart, capable, and caring. She has her own website at www.paintingadventure.com.

Dan: The instant Melika entered college in California, I began an extensive search for a job in Europe. It took longer than hoped, but eventually I found a position in…

"Europe, Dan," the company said. "It's a European level job so you can live anywhere you want."

"Great. How about Rome?"

"Well, anywhere that the company is doing a lot of business. European headquarters are in Zurich."

"Hmm. What about Barcelona?"

"Barcelona is kinda on the edge. You can live anywhere you want. European headquarters are in Zurich."

"What about Zurich?"

"Great choice, Dan."

Nazy and I now live in Zurich, Switzerland. We still enjoy seeing the world, and especially enjoy getting together with all members of The Martin Family—an event that happens at least once a year. Our move to

Switzerland was not completely adventure-free. I am composing the Swiss sequel to *Stumbling Through the Tulips*. For details, visit www.seat26b.com.

The Martin Family 2010
Darius, Nazy, Mitra, Melika, Dan

CPSIA information can be obtained
at www.ICGtesting.com
Printed in the USA
LVOW04s2302200316
480013LV00023B/562/P